"Rock & Roll Music fosters rebellion, alcoholism, drug addiction, illicit sex, pornography, homosexuality, bestiality, everything you can think of that is wrong."
Jimmy Swaggart, TV evangelist

The Truth of Revolution, *Brother*

AN EXPLORATION OF PUNK PHILOSOPHY

Lisa Sofianos, Robin Ryde
& Charlie Waterhouse

Situation Press
LONDON

Published by Situation Press
www.situationpress.com

First edition published 2014
Second edition 2015

The moral right of the authors has been asserted
under the Copyright, Designs and Patents Act 1988

Copyright of the mss. texts, illustration and artwork
remains with the originators

Every effort has been made to obtain the necessary
permissions with reference to copyright material, both
illustrative and quoted. We apologise for any omissions in
this respect and will be pleased to make the appropriate
acknowledgements in any future edition

A CIP catalogue record for this book
is available from the British Library

ISBN 978-0-9930190-1-2

Typeset in Fournier MT, Plan Grotesque & Grot10

Designed and typeset by This Ain't Rock'n'Roll

Printed by The Printing House,
3rd Floor, 14 Hanover Street
London W1S 1YH

READ LOUD

Whistleblower

Dare to blow the whistle

Dare to speak your truth

Spill the beans — feel free to shout

Give it air — let it out

See through the blindfold

Speak out from behind the gag

Let's hear the voice that must be heard

Let a cat out from a bag

Yes dare to blow the whistle

Dare to speak your truth

Tell it like it really is

Let it be of use

If all of us together

Stop believing in the lies

We might still have a future

— That would be a surprise

See out beyond the blindfold

Speak out from behind the gag
Ignore the lies, propaganda and spin
Don't let the tricksters take you in
Politicians, bankers,
Gurus, priests and kings
With too much power and money
And far too many things
— Judge them not by their sermons
But watch for what they do
Is it one rule for them?
— Another one for you?
Let's dare to blow the whistle
Dare them to come clean
To join in with the rest of us
And do it quick and with no fuss
We gave them more than we ever got
They took it all - they took the lot
Do we owe them a living? NO, ABSOLUTELY NOT!!!

Vi Subversa

An introduction

It has been decades since the punk movement first reared its head. Books have been written, films have been made that record very well what happened. The images of the chaos surrounding the Sex Pistols on a boat on London's River Thames are forever etched in our memories. The life-affirming and at times surreal scenes of punk artists snarling and leaping around stages are part of our shared consciousness. History has been made, and it is because of this that we are even talking about punk.

But this project, and this book, is not about what happened then. It's not about the past. It is not really about the music or the art. It is about the ideas and the lived experience of punk as they relate to today. The past is important of course, and we perhaps can't understand our next move in the present without appreciating where we've come from, but nostalgia and romanticism are not becoming of punk – and this is not what you will read between these pages.

If punk was an explosion, then this is about what's happened after the dust settled. Or put in another way:

What the fuck was all that about?

To answer this question we wanted to speak to the influential figures of the scene. To ask them: "what can we learn from punk?"; "what are the enduring lessons?"; "what are the ideas, beliefs and philosophies from punk that might help us live more meaningful and rewarding lives?"

This led us to find the people you see between these pages. These were people with something of value to say. Many had used punk to go on an extraordinary journey; from the anarchist punk Jón Gnarr who found himself as the Mayor of Reykjavík to Gee Vaucher and Penny Rimbaud of Crass who have nurtured the 'living experiment' of Dial House for nearly four decades. From Steve Albini, member of Big Black and Shellac and sound engineer to the Pixies and Nirvana, who offers a radical reinterpretation of business, to punk agitator Gavin McInnes, the founder of *Vice* Magazine, that took anarchist ideas to a new level. And from Jello Biafra of Dead Kennedys who rages until this very day to radical feminist and anarchist Vi Subversa of the Poison Girls, who salutes the modern whistleblowers and offers reflections on the toughness of the punk stance. These are just a fraction of the people we have spoken to about punk and philosophy.

Our intent in this process has been simple – to capture these ideas, to share them, and to offer an account of what ties them together. These common philosophical themes, which include ideas of disruption, self-construction and a struggle against distractions, have been generated from the perspectives of the interviewees – following a grounded approach.

To the extent that we offer theories here, they come from, rather than being imposed on, the material. After all, we can probably all do without another round of punk revisionism.

So Much Generosity   This book is the product of hard work, genuine curiosity and a love for the genre of punk. But if there is one ingredient that explains it all, it is generosity.

The contributors to this book have all given their time, their ideas and their support to this endeavour. We have been fed, given beds for the night, driven around, cared for, welcomed into people's homes, and been given original artwork, poetry and prose to include in the book.

We have encountered genuine openness and honesty, and have seen our interviewees exhibit vulnerability and take risks in the ideas they've offered. And they have shared all this not so that they might then gain publicity for their next artistic project, nor out of vanity – but because they've wanted to understand and expand the thinking associated with the punk movement. We are profoundly grateful to the scores of contributors and supporters that have helped create this work. Thank you.

David King

David King was born in London in 1948, when there was still food rationing and children played in hazardous bomb sites. David described the scene at the time as one where "everyone wore dark blue, dark grey, or black." To avoid a job as a bank clerk, David went to art school where he met Penny Rimbaud and Gee Vaucher, later of Crass. For 10 years he worked as a graphic designer and art director spending some of his time living at Crass's Dial House.

He moved to New York in 1977 but not before he had created the iconic Crass symbol, which was designed as a front piece to Penny Rimbaud's work Reality Asylum. *In the late 70s David joined the band Arsenal while at the same time drawing illustrations for the Museum of Modern Art as well as creating graphics for many bands. He moved to San Francisco in the early 80s and recorded with the band Sleeping Dogs that then recorded with the Crass label. The band's sound has been described as "arty, dissonant, trudging, no wavey, quirky and angular" and likened to early Swans.*

Today, David still lives in San Francisco, working on a range of graphic design, photographic and film projects.

People in my generation wanted to escape the 50s; how dry it was, how there was still a post-war atmosphere that pervaded absolutely everything, and how our parents were the last Victorians (in the way they had been raised). We wanted to get away from that. We were thinking, what can we subtract? For example, if our parents are eating meat, OK we don't eat meat. If they have a car that they pull out every Sunday and wash, and go for a little drive then we won't have cars. I think a lot of it was reactive, but it ended up as a relatively gentle revolution. In many ways, at least in England, it was a polite revolution. It was about things that you could do for yourself. You could stop eating meat; you could grow your hair. Use the underground instead of buying a car. These are all things that you could just do on your own and you might get some flak. Someone might yell at you in the street because your hair was a foot longer than anyone else's. And by and large, I guess, it wasn't threatening ultimately. In America it was different because there were civil rights movements that had to do with racism and there were clear battles there and violent ones leading to death and destruction.

I think people who were teenagers in the 60s thought it was just going to continue in that somewhat benign way. In fact it seemed to get better day-by-day. It seemed to get more colourful. There seemed to be a few more opportunities for people to talk about the classless society where before people had only one option. If they were in the working class they would work in the factory, or some other minimum wage job, but they were starting to get jobs in design and advertising and photography and fashion. That was really a first and it seemed incredibly hopeful. But eventually it became clear that this wasn't cutting it; it wasn't changing the old guard, it wasn't changing the establishment. We were just being tolerated in many ways. Then when society lurched to the right, bringing with it mass unemployment and all the conflict with the unions; between the government and unions, it was obvious that we'd just been staring at the sky through leaves for years. As long as we sort of kept to ourselves, the government won't bother us. But when people started to say, "this isn't right, we don't like what's going on," that's when punk appears, out of that dissatisfaction. I think it came from dissatisfaction that things didn't keep going on an upward curve. There were advances made in the 60s that were not sustained into the 70s. It's a combination of disappointment and anger that lead to punk.

I left the UK in '77 just as Crass was forming and then I became involved in punk rock in New York, and then I moved to San Francisco to the scene here. From my perspective I got the best of both worlds. I mean I got to experience London in the 60s and then the beginning of the excitement of punk rock in London. Then to move to New York when it started to happen at the same time and then to San Francisco in the early 80s where there was a huge punk scene in San Francisco and Los Angeles.

Punk versus liberalism   I went to art school from '64–'67 with Penny and Gee from Crass. Between let's say '67 and '77 I was spending most of my weekends at Dial House. I really liked those early days then because it seemed like the possibilities were endless. As part of getting away from my own parents to a certain extent but there was a sort of openness I really liked. When the band was forming I wasn't sure if I wanted to go the direction they were going. I had a little trouble with the idea of telling people what to do. Because I would hate people telling me what to do and I felt that there was something a bit didactic lurking in that band and to a certain extent punk rock generally – although I could see how essential that was. Again, after the hippy era it had to go up several notches to try to make any difference but it was just my sort of personal discomfort with wanting to get up on stage and saying, you must do this or you must do that. I could see why people would do that or would want to do it and why, in fact, it could be effective but it was just on a very, very personal level that I wasn't sure that was what I wanted to do.

I was sort of uncomfortable seeing the harsher sides of punk. I'd been living out part of my life on a farm, this sort of somewhat detached, timeless existence, without all these urban references. Time seemed to last longer there than it did in London for example. I didn't care for the violence aspect. It was very early on when everyone at the house started dressing in black. I think I was one of the earlier people perhaps to do that because I thought it was kind of a graphic approach to dressing. I mean that's where it came from with me in a way. I thought if I get black pants and black jacket and black and white sneakers, that would look kind of cool.

I went to London's Brick Lane market one day, actually with Bron [*Eve Libertine*]. At that time this was just when the sort of the punk uniform was appearing and becoming understood. And the old guard who took the most objections to that were the rockers and the teddy boys. There would be gangs of teddy boys roaming certain parts of London looking for punks to beat up. It was the old sort of 'mods and rockers' thing back again. I mean you can just get beat up just because of what you're wearing. I saw this whole gang of teddy boys walk by and I thought, oh they look kind of cool too even though they were wearing mostly black. Then one of them turned around and he saw me, and gave me the whole up and down look and it registered in him that I was from a rival tribe and he yelled out: "PUNK!" Suddenly about 20 teddy boys are chasing me down the street. No one has said a word other than the word 'punk', which is kind of interesting. There were no insults that were traded really; it was we want to beat you to a pulp because you're wearing something that signifies something we don't care for. Luckily, Bron's then partner, Jim, was a schoolteacher and he somehow got between them and me and in his best sort of schoolteacher's manner, said, "Now boys, just take a moment here and think about this." I got away. I escaped [*laughs*]. That was another thing, speaking of the violence, how much I really wanted to dress in black if this is what it means every time I leave the house. I have to look at that whole thing. Then of course both sides embraced the violence fully, so the skinheads would beat up punks and punks, eventually, would band together and try to beat up skinheads. It was like the Cavaliers and Roundheads all over again.

A different kind of punk in the US   In the US there was none of that. In England, a lot of punk really came out of class differences and that really wasn't the case at all in New York. First of all New York is an island, it's a small town if you will. Punk there came out much earlier through other influences; from the 50s, like the beat poets, avant-garde film and out of literature. It came from a much more 'cultured' source than the UK. I mean New York is like a world capital of publishing to this day. It's a capital of old Europe if you will; with all the immigrants from the First and Second World War. There are lots of intellectual artists, filmmakers, you name it, they moved to New York, and a lot of the culture came from them indirectly. Any sort of new culture that had to do with words and pictures is going to come out right there. Even though there is Richard Hell singing about being a member of the blank generation, that's still quite an intelligent song. I suppose you could say the Ramones were the most simplistic and not perhaps from that educated tradition, but still there is an enormous irony in their work that indicates a great degree of intelligence — just the fact that they were sort of a concept band. They weren't brothers. I mean it wasn't like the Monkees but they were a construct and quite a thoughtful one.

The punk scene in the US was more inclusive, much more inclusive. In fact. I was involved in a group there called Pop Front, which formed in reaction to the gigs that were happening where the Specials, the ska band, would come from England and they would charge $10 a ticket, and at this time most bands in New York were playing for four or five bucks and somehow this seemed very extreme. It's hard to believe now perhaps but $10 was a big deal. So a bunch of us formed this collective, where we rented a performance space and we put on gigs and we would have a diversity of bands. We'd have a punk band, a reggae band, a poet and so on. So everyone was welcome. We kept the price at $3 or $4. That's one example but I would say it was very diverse and inclusive. And there was nobody to fight really. There weren't any other tribes.

There was one image that has always struck me and that's the kind of dancing that happened in England and in LA. In England where there is no room to mass dance you'll have the pogo where you are just going straight up and down trying to get more air than the person next to you. In LA there is a band called the Circle Jerks and their symbol was a little punk kid sort of doing this pinwheel dance, where all his arms and legs are flailing in a circle. That indicated to me that America is bigger than England. It's an odd place. You would never do that dance if you were in London. You'd just get flattened. There are huge differences in these different places to me.

Signifying rebellion   Regarding the Crass symbol, you can't get more powerful in Western society than a cross and a snake. I mean name something that's more culturally resonant. I think it's hard to find anything else and the only other thing you might mention would be the swastika and there were accusations that resided deliberately or not in the symbol. It immediately got people's attention. It was carefully wrought. I don't even really know at this point why I decided on two heads, but the moment I did it became this sort of spinning device. You know like, "You're feeling very sleepy" or "you're feeling very angry." [*laughs*]. It became like this very solid object. Nothing was trailing away in any direction; each component was separate and concise because it was designed to be used as stencil, and that gave it this solidity I think. It's easy to reproduce, it's easy to copy, and it's easy to make your own stencil, and put it on your clothes. It's easy to make a tattoo out of it. Someone in the recent film *The Art of Punk* says they weren't sure if they should like it. It seems like it's a little dangerous. Someone else asked me if it was a Celtic design and that never really occurred to me except that there were Celtic crosses in the landscape. I don't discount that.

An interesting thing of course is that it wasn't designed for the band [*Crass*] because the band didn't even exist at that point. It's become known as the Crass logo, but it was designed for Penny's piece of writing and he said that, in respect to the band, why shouldn't punk have its own powerful logos like the corporations do? I think that's sort of what happened to the peace symbol, you know it was designed for one specific thing. It was designed for an anti-nuclear movement and you know the origin of the design that comes from semaphore. The campaign for nuclear disarmament (CND) symbol and the circle peace symbol [*as it is known in America*] is formed from the two semaphore flags for 'N' and 'D'. There is a vertical, and then there is like two hands to the side that form the fork. It was a simple element of graphical design; then, when it came to America, where they barely know about CND; they just say it's a peace symbol. In that way something very specific has become something very generic. The peace symbol is a signifier now. If you put it on something everyone knows what you mean. The Crass symbol isn't detached from Crass but it has, at least in America, become a signifier for a certain kind of rebellion.

The power of social media to distract and disempower Think of the digital changes. My God how fast it's happened and how many diversions there are now. I mean you would have to have an incredible focus and amount of energy to strike off the number of diversions that exist today. I mean if people were active in the 60s, there was only one channel on TV and it was in black and white and there were a lot of other things you could be doing. There has been a manufactured society with Facebook and so-called social media that seems to promise change and human connection, but I'm not sure how much time that is taking up, and how active people are. It certainly does seem from this perspective of time that when things were grossly inequitable in society large groups of young people were in the streets in England and America, but certainly this is not the case now. Although there was a huge march before the outbreak of the Iraq war it didn't really do anything because they were already flying the ammunition over to the Middle East; they weren't going to stop at that point.

It does seem like George Orwell didn't know the half of it. And the most disturbing thing to me is how much people have volunteered to give away their personal lives. It's amazing the way that information is being gathered. If you, let's say, buy a couple of books on Amazon the next thing you know you're getting an email from Amazon saying, "If you liked this, you'll probably like this" – and they're absolutely right. It doesn't take them much information to triangulate, and you provided it yourself. You're building your own 'East German secret police files' on yourself everyday with more and more stuff. That's different. If you would have given someone a computer in 1976 and said "here fill in all your personal information" they would just throw it through a window, but now people are like "Oh yes and can I put my picture up their too?" That's the difference. I mean the digital landscape has made a huge change in that way I think.

A perpetual fight against injustice   My mother just passed recently and she was 95. I remember when I was speaking at her funeral that she had said to me many times, "I can't stand injustice", and I knew what she meant. She meant anything from the simplest kind of social interaction to larger scale societal effects. I think that I haven't necessarily lived up to that, but that's something I've tried to live by. To see what might be unjust and whether one can do anything about it. Again the moment you say these things out loud or you put them in cold print they can sound really arrogant, but with a little bit of kindness, it's a pretty great thing.

Dick Lucas

Dick Lucas was still a teenager when he joined anarcho-punks Subhumans in September 1980. He soon became known for his socially aware lyrics and musical style, which were far more ambitious than the usual punk fare, his lyrics often expressing outrage and defiance at a system that he considered to have let him down. An early recommendation from Flux of Pink Indians saw Subhumans sign to Spiderleg Records, with whom they released The Day The Country Died, *one of the defining LPs of the anarcho-punk era.*

With the breakup of Subhumans in the mid-1980s, Dick changed musical direction and formed Culture Shock, who mixed upbeat ska, reggae influences and punk politics, often appearing at free festivals. The band produced three albums, with Onwards & Upwards *being the pick of the bunch.*

Next, Dick formed Citizen Fish in 1990, a ska-punk group that embraced his philosophy that "anarchists and libertarians are free-flowing souls trapped by the rules of civilization" – a view echoed in the band's LP Free Souls in a Trapped Environment. *Following a 10-year hiatus, Citizen Fish reunited in 2011 to release the full-length album* Goods *on Alternative Tentacles. Dick continues to tour extensively with Citizen Fish, Culture Shock and Subhumans.*

Was progress made during punk? It depends on what you see as having worked or not worked. If you paint too big a picture of the problem from the start then it hasn't worked, but what has worked is the personal evolution of people's mindsets throughout the duration of punk rock, and the influence that it's had on a lot of people in the way they think. Or it has woken up what they already thought and put it into words, which is what I think mostly happens. I don't think people are blank slates, I think they've got it all in their heads from their own experiences, they perhaps just haven't seen it written down or sung about or read lyrics that gelled with what they were thinking, even if they didn't really know they were thinking that. I think that's why punk rock succeeded mostly, lyrically at least. It gelled with a lot of peoples' thoughts and they thought, "Wow! I'm not alone here. This is calling to me".

While I would say that I'm still angry, it is in a more thoughtful and considerate way – not in a 'going into a rage and spouting a lot of nonsense' way that doesn't make sense in the end. The things that make you angry in the first place become more defined in your head, as you get older. You know what they are, where they come from, how they work to a much greater extent. When you get angry at something when you're 18, you're flying at an unknown enemy. You are flying with a great amount of energy, vigour and anger and you are a ball of fire but it's kind of going in all directions. And that's what punk rock involved — being able to have the freedom to shout at something, and not be the only one doing it. On a mental level, when you're 50-something, it's probably not good for you to feel as angry as you did when you were 18 years old, because by this point that anger should have led to certain changes in your life or in your attitude that will make you feel happier and less involved with the things you don't like, such as the "system".

Living within the system taints your soul   We're stuck in the middle, aren't we really? Because we can't live without the system as it is at the moment. If you are going to drive a car you need to fill it up with gas. If you want to get most of your food, unless you've got the space to grow your own, you've got to buy it from someone else. We are all part of the whole capitalist system. We are born into it because of where we live. Working from the inside – I don't think that works. I think it really taints your own soul. You have to become part of the system to work within it and in becoming part of it you will be inescapably trapped and your ideas will not be able to come out and change the structure you are in, until you get to the top of the structure. But you can't get to the top of that structure to change it without denying everything you believe in to please the people who are currently higher up than you are in the hierarchy. So I don't think that can work.

Living completely outside the entirety of the system, which is the other extreme, is extremely difficult to do unless you have the luck to have all the cash and the land to live on and the support of other people who want to do exactly the same thing. And to an extent it can be done. But then you still have to pay the electric and the bills unless you are REALLY living on an island and you really can manage with the sun, the elements and catching fish. But dream on. That's the other end. Dream on about running the corporation in a way that makes it a really nice corporation to work for and/or living on the island self-sufficiently. These are very rare and dreamlike scenarios.

Follow a life based on your choices   Buy organic. Buy local. Do as much home teaching as you can. Read. Turn off the screens, except for a certain amount per day. Stimulate the mind not through so much visual stuff, but more audio stuff. It's very difficult, but do things where you think you've made a choice, like this is slightly wrong or this is slightly better. Major things like the food you eat. Why not go vegetarian? Hell, why not go vegan! Go as far as you can on your own personal level towards a better way of existence for the people that have suffered, or the animals that have suffered as a result of the way food is produced. That's one angle. Food is a very important thing that everyone's involved in. Products can be mass-produced using almost slave labour in Asia, Africa and South America. Try to avoid those; they may be cheap, but if you spend a bit more, you'll get something that will probably last longer and won't need replacing so fast and there's no suffering at the end of it. We've all got the internet; we can all find out this stuff. How do you get people to want to know, to chivvy them up… to want to feel more responsibility for what they do every day and take for granted. We take so much for granted.

Keeping people locked in front of the TV   When it comes to entertainment offered by the media, such as *The X Factor*, it's important to be aware of what's being fired at you. I mean watch this rubbish if you want to be marginally entertained, but realise that the stereotypes being shoved in your face non-stop ARE stereotypes. They are not true. It's people getting paid to invent that sort of fiction because it apparently keeps people entertained. It's distraction from the misery of actual life. It's distraction from the weather. It's a distraction from having a shitty, repetitive, underpaying job. I'm not surprised people go for it. After their meal, when people want to relax, you don't get the interesting and informative stuff, you don't get the documentaries, you get the soap operas, 'look at some people interacting with each other' stuff. People used to go out to the local pub every night and the fact is that people don't do that anymore. It wasn't banning smoking in pubs that stopped people doing this, they just managed to get more people in front of more screens more often.

How was your day at work?   I think that people do know about this stuff, but concluded a long time ago that there is nothing they can do about it and they have to go to work. They've got to pay the mortgage. They've got to raise the kids somehow. They're not lucky enough to be self-employed. While I don't agree with that position, I can understand that headspace. I would rather that everyone was self-employed or mutually co-operatively employed, or employed in jobs that were fulfilling and gave them something to talk about when they come home, "How was your day at work?" "It was fantastic, I did this, this and this." But I'm afraid that conversation probably doesn't happen much.

For people who give up trying to make changes because they feel that they are only doing it themselves and no-one else is doing it, well, that's a tragedy right there. If they can believe, true or not, that other people are doing it and they can keep doing it then more people will. It's important to communicate the ideas out there and receive new ones. Keep an open mind, although not too open otherwise people will rip you off and sell you lies… questioning everything and then relying on instinct.

Replacing government with communities   In terms of the responsibility to change what you can, there's no point relying on other people to do it. The whole nature of government is reliance. People rely on governments, people rely on councils and they rely on almost everybody else in order to make things easier for themselves. It's living 'the comfortable life.' But that comfort is at the expense of a massive amount of control. And if you run out of money one day, and suddenly lose the comfort of being able to pay the rent or feed your kids, or whatever, the fact that you didn't take responsibility to have some sort of option for that situation, means that you will be suffering on the wrong end of the rose-tinted glasses. And you will understand why there are people out there selling *The Big Issue*. If you are unlucky, it just all comes crashing down. So the sense of responsibility is there to give yourself some sort of back up. It's not about saving money for a rainy or panic-stricken day, it's about keeping a circle of friends and acquaintances. People who know how to do stuff, build stuff, help you out. People who have got the time to give you a lift. People who can listen well. Just good friends. It's about keeping friends together, keeping in touch with people and building a network of mutual, friendly support. It sounds an easy thing, and it probably is… but it can be vital.

Finding happiness   On the question of whether everybody has access to happiness, this is definitely not a 'no' answer, but a 'yes' answer is just too flippant. Little things make people happy and large things make other people happy. It's in degrees. A look in a kid's eyes can make you happy. So even people that are struggling completely can get that emotional bond. And that's a good version of happiness. I don't think that anyone is completely happy. But then I don't think that anyone should be. In a way, you have to balance happiness against sorrow and longing and other slightly negative emotions in order to appreciate the happiness when it comes along. People who live their lives on luxury yachts in the Mediterranean probably consider themselves to be completely happy, but I bet they're not. I bet they're bored shitless. Bastards! [*laughs*.]

Punk and philosophy

Punk was not conceived as a philosophy. It appeared to arrive suddenly and abruptly, like a car crash on the highway – full of noise, chaos, danger and energy. Punk was an anti-philosophy. It stood *against*. It snorted and snarled at everything in the vicinity. It raged against the system and it jeered at institutions, and the commonly held ideas that supported them.

And so we might wonder what place philosophy has in punk. It might appear in some ways to be too slow, or too ponderous for punk's immediacy. We might see philosophy as the domain of academia and people with letters after their names. We might view punk as something that was for 'us', and not for 'them'. They had their traditions and customs, and punk had its own, and they weren't going to get invited to the party – to our party. So the question might be, 'What would punk have to do with philosophy?'

It is exactly because punk stood outside of, and in opposition to, prevailing 'wisdom' that it found itself forging its own set of principles for living. And in doing so, it embraced important philosophical conundrums. The vacuum left by punk created the conditions for a set of alternatives, and a perspective that required a form of moral intent, however different from the preceding system. More than this, punk brought to life some profound philosophical ideas that largely remained parked on the pages of worthy tomes – locked between the bindings. It played with, and tested, these beliefs (usually not knowingly or self-consciously), and did so in ways that hadn't been done in quite the same way before.

Punk was an earthy and grubby movement rooted in action and practice, and in this way was entirely suited to the questions of 'How should we live in practice?' and 'What should we believe in?' This is what makes the punk ethos so different from the archetypal, purely cerebral pursuit of philosophy. But it was philosophical and experimental in nature.

So what are the features of the punk philosophy and how do they mirror other ideals found in the formal world of philosophy? We offer some thought here, but also make the point that punk was, and is, a diverse field. It simultaneously contains ideas that are consistent with, and supportive of, one another, while also housing perspectives that stand in opposition to one another. There is a tension within punk that has at times reached boiling point between differing factions, and this at least illustrates the deeper values and morals that are at stake in all of this. This was, and remains, a vibrant movement that for all its surface drama has a serious, and also playful contribution to make to questioning what matters most in life.

Punk and existentialism   An important way that punk brought to life a philosophical perspective is in relation to existentialism. Once again, very few punks would necessarily articulate it in these terms, and some would even prefer to distance themselves from it, but it is fascinating that there is such a close fit between an existential philosophy and aspects of the punk ethos.

The existential point of view, as articulated by people such as Albert Camus and Jean Paul Sartre, is captured in part by the proposition that 'existence precedes essence.' What this means is that there are no pre-existing determinants of what we are as humans, and what we should be. The existentialist perspective favours the notion of a *tabula rasa* (literally 'blank slate' in Latin) when considering human understanding. We do not arrive pre-shaped, pre-destined or pre-scripted; our thinking about the purpose of our lives and how we should live them is fully governed by our own choices and decisions.

"The future is there to be built. It's a blank canvas. It's a place to dream into. And anybody can make tomorrow." **Mark Stewart**

Of course this reaches beyond the point of our choices and our thinking, and concludes that action consistent with our thinking *must* then arise. If I believe it is wrong to eat meat, then I must not eat meat. If I believe that a war in the Gulf is wrong, I must take action. If I believe that I should be more authentic at work, then I must act on this. And our moral code, in this context is ours – and ours alone – to construct. It is not something that we should take from others. The way we conduct our interactions with people or our encounters with the world are based on the choices that we make to do this.

"I was liberated through existentialism... realising that you can create your own choice. You're no longer protected by a sort of moral framework. What the parent likes to believe is that they're offering not only agency but also a moral framework in which their agency can operate. These are the conditions yet we shouldn't worry too much about them because actually you're protected and you're safe; these are the parameters. They say this is God or this is the state; this is the village; this is the community. This is whatever you want. These are the things that will protect THIS particular way of thinking that WE'VE given you. Don't step outside it because you'll be in danger and it's true that you are in danger if you step outside."
Penny Rimbaud

We recognise this attitude repeatedly in the ideas offered by many punks. We also see more than a hint of the ideas of the German philosopher Friedrich Nietzsche in punk. In *Thus Spoke Zarathustra* Nietzsche proposed three central notions needed to transcend the human condition. In particular, he argued for a commitment to the destruction of old ideals and beliefs (in particular, the Christian faith and belief in God), an acceptance that we are alone and committed to creating our own ideals and beliefs, and finally, a determination to live in accordance with these self-authored ideals while resisting the temptation to return to the old ideals. In many ways the 'anti' stance associated with the punk movement (anti-state, anti-religion, anti-police, etc.) speaks to the first of Nietzsche's notions. This reflects the stripping away of pre-conditions, and imposed moral frameworks. The second two notions reflect an existential ambition, and the strict self-created discipline alongside it.

So there is a case for seeing punk as a manifestation, of sorts, of existentialism. It is captured best by the idea that many punks sought to determine and construct their own beliefs and moral framework, and importantly chose to take responsibility for what they caused in the world. Practically, this saw many people choosing to become vegetarian, for example, and in doing so they discarded the conventions they had inherited from their parents and society more broadly. Others found themselves travelling down different paths, but with a dual sense of freedom and personal responsibility, reflected in the existentialist philosophy.

Libertarianism, anarchism and punk   "Anarchism is freedom. But it's not freedom without responsibility. There is no freedom without responsibility because then it's chaos. And chaos is not anarchism." **Jón Gnarr**

With the notion of personal responsibility and freedom ringing in our ears, we also look to politics, which of course has a deeper set of motivations and philosophical foundations. The punk movement is a broad church in terms of its political philosophy, and while politically it has more often than not leant towards the left, it has typically elevated above most other aspirations the importance of freedom, self-determinism and the removal of rules.

There is no shortage of punk songs or slogans that illustrate this point, from the Clash's *Complete Control* to *Halloween* by Dead Kennedys to the concept song *From the Cradle to the Grave* by Subhumans. All articulate the importance of free thinking and the removal of external control whether manifest in the form of state intervention, for example, or appearing as social regulations. In this context we see a particular importance in punk of two related political philosophies, namely libertarianism and anarchism.

There are numerous tensions that arise in relation to seemingly small differences within, and between, these ideologies. For example, there is the question of the basic level of state provision and intervention with which anarchists or libertarians might be comfortable. This varies markedly in the punk community. And there is also the question of whether the ambition is to have good (or better) government or no government at all.

"My eldest daughter has been living in Congo and Rwanda for a great deal of time and she's involved with the law and international justice and she's dealing with women particularly who are rape victims in war. Everybody knows (I assume) the situation in the Congo of mass rapes, not just of women but of men and boys as well. A lot of those people who become soldiers were victims themselves as boys. The reason I'm saying this is because she's dealing with FAILED states. So here's me saying, 'We don't need the state, we don't need Big Daddy, we can get it together amongst ourselves' and she's saying, 'Yes, but I'm working in these places where the state has totally failed and it's a FUCKING MESS!' And so those anarchist/ libertarian ideas are really interesting, but still that can go both ways." **Steve Lake**

Another tension associated with a point along the libertarian spectrum relates, for example, to what is referred to as the political correctness (PC) agenda. Many libertarians would argue that PC impinges on notions of freedom and self-determinism, and is another form of socially regulated control.

"My agenda is freedom. I want to live in a world without tyranny, and I guess I got that from punk... I was always avoiding self-identifying as being an anarchist or something and just about a week ago I said, 'Fuck it, I'm a libertarian'... I like their ideals. Their ideals are that, 'this might be good or this might be bad, but I don't have to know because I'm not making a rule about it. Go ahead and do your thing, I'm not trying to force anything'. Whereas the modern American left says, 'If every single thing in the world does not perfectly represent a pie chart of the population then it's wrong and I have to fix it'. And so short, fat, bald, Jewish men have to be in the NBA doing their terrible shots and getting jumped over by giant black guys [*laughs*]. No, we don't need that. Some people are good at things. And the beauty of libertarians is that they say, 'Maybe they are, maybe they're not, maybe short, fat, Jewish bald guys would kill in the NBA. I'm not holding them back, go ahead chaps!'" **Gavin McInnes**

But all of these are practical manifestations of deeper philosophical aspirations relating to ideas of freedom and self-determinism that has always been a central component of punk, and it has always been a part of the experimentation that it has engaged in.

Zen and the art of punk   It might seem that the characteristically quiet, demur and composed image of a Zen Buddhist is not the most obvious philosophical reference point for punk, but it is hard not to acknowledge the connection between these two worlds. An anchoring concept for both might be the notion of looking within oneself for answers, and this is a strong theme in the thinking exhibited by the people interviewed for this book. But accompanying this we also repeatedly encountered other characteristics associated with Zen such as the importance of compassion, not being judgemental, of gratitude, of living in the moment, and of understanding happiness as arising from a full engagement with life.

"I don't believe in a life that's all happy, happy, happy. I think that as a concept it's false and you're taught to strive towards happiness as a child. There's as much melancholy in life as there is happiness... I think that what you strive for is a complete life with all of the emotions and feelings that belong to it... I'm striving to be honest and authentic and to be fair and not exploit anyone and to look on the world as it really is." **Tim Smith**

"I have this concept that you're on a road and you're driving up a cliff and you have the mountain on one side and the ocean on the other. The future is always at that point just around that corner and you'll never see it until it is the present. So you don't know what's there. It could be sunny skies; it could be an ice storm. The road could be out altogether. There could be a truck across it, you just don't know. All you know is what's right in front of you. So the most important thing to do is to take care of the vehicle and to pay attention. Be present. If you're driving along that road and you can see a boulder half a mile up shaking then you might think, 'Oh shit! That thing's going to tumble down and fall. I'd better think what I'm going to do about that.' Well, while you're looking at that, you've just driven off the road in front of you." **Ian MacKaye**

Of course, the Eastern philosophy of Zen goes well beyond the ideas presented here. But we also see punk borrowing (and not always intentionally) some of the disruptive tactics found in the Zen method. Whether we think of it as the master whacking a student around their head to sharpen their thinking, or the use of seemingly contradictory propositions found in Zen kōans, we find this too in punk.

"When we went forward with the Best Party we had strange slogans, like 'Adopt A Bum' and people said, 'Oh you're being negative. This is not very human of you.' But what has been done for the homeless? Not very much. So we say 'Adopt A Bum' and people start thinking about it and their responsibility in it." **Einar Örn Benediktsson**

At a still deeper level, we see in some instances, a willingness to connect the self-authoring concept behind existentialism with an attempt to bridge the notion of self and others found in Zen.

"Philosophy is a scientific attempt to heal the world through the intellect, through juggling of words to find the irrefutable, to find the great fire. Likewise, so is healing. In healing others, one is healing oneself, because you are others. There is no other. That, if you'd like, is the devastating existential responsibility and that's the process that I have become engaged in." **Penny Rimbaud**

An aversion to being constrained by ideology or philosophy We finish, as is so often the case with punk, with a provocation, or at least with a delightfully unresolved position. A common reaction by the people interviewed, in relation to the question of their philosophical beliefs, was one of discomfort or a distancing from the notion of punk philosophy.

"Regarding my beliefs or 'philosophy' I can't really cite any academic tradition or philosophy that I follow or adhere to, and I don't think I ever have." **Jello Biafra**

"Well, I never really studied any of these things like existentialism. I read some Zen stuff years and years ago, I had some early experiences with hippy stuff and drugs and that opened me up quite a lot and (of course) talking to people. But I've never really been a bookish person. I never seem to have the time. I didn't go to university and had to stop education when I was 15, to help my mum." **Vi Subversa**

"Talking about philosophical 'isms', I've never bought into that kind of thing. That sort of thing you can do at Dial House, but you can't really be Zen in the middle of Birmingham, can you?" **Steve Ignorant**

This apparent contradiction between the suggestion in this chapter of the de facto existence of punk philosophies, and the sense amongst some interviewees that such a thing does not exist, is not a problem or a source for concern, and this is for two reasons. First, at the heart of punk is a lived and enacted set of beliefs. The Do-It-Yourself principle, explored later, firmly demonstrates this by focussing on action over prevarication. This is illustrated well by the punk tradition of direct action as understood in its broadest terms:

"This whole thing of empowering people means you don't have to petition others to change things, you can actually do it and you do have the power to do it. It's the idea that you're not going to send polite letters to the Houses of Parliament begging your MPs to enact some law. We'll actually just go out and stop it ourselves. We do have the power to do that." **Deek Allen**

There is a directness and nimbleness in the punk tradition to the way in which people have moved rapidly from angst to action; a kind of philosophical shortcut, with learning, reflection and adaptation (of both method and ideas) following afterwards. Second, is the degree of aversion to attributing philosophical ideas to punk and the unwillingness to be defined by them. In this sense, punk seeks to avoid the limiting qualities of, and subsequent laziness associated with, ideology.

This attitude of constant challenge and determination to disrupt is another observed feature of the punk mindset.

Little Annie

Little Annie, often also known as Annie Anxiety, is a native New Yorker. In 1977, aged just 16, she was already fronting her own band, Annie and the Asexuals, at prestigious venues such as Max's Kansas City. A chance meeting in her neighbourhood with Steve Ignorant from Crass a year later resulted in her heading to the UK for a two-week visit. She ended up staying for more than a decade. First off, she recorded the ahead-of-its-time Barbed Wire Halo, collaboration with Crass drummer Penny Rimbaud for Crass Records. She was then offered the role of in-house vocalist for Adrian Sherwood's On-U Sound Records, and recorded three solo LPs during this period. She also collaborated with Wolfgang Press, Kid Congo Powers and Lee 'Scratch' Perry, Marc Almond, the Swans and many more besides.

Returning home to the States, Annie turned her attention to art and, as a self-taught painter, had her first solo gallery show in 2002. She has also written three volumes of prose, and has appeared in plays, theatre productions and films. Still based in the Chelsea area of Manhattan, in 2013 Annie and multi-talented Baby Dee released State of Grace, which Annie describes as covering "love, loss, leaving and the confusion of time."

I never really saw myself as a punk, and I don't know that the audiences did either. My thing was always soul and rhythms and musicals, but my behaviour, especially at the time, was punk. 'Street punk', well, that I definitely was. I was a delinquent; I didn't like being told what to do. My lifestyle was definitely about carving out my own way, but artistically punk was basically where I was allowed to be. It was a space where I was allowed to move. I didn't seek it out, it kind of found me. This was in New York.

I wasn't sure that I wanted to be a performer, but as a little kid I was always dancing and when I saw *West Side Story* I ran home and put on my mom's slip and lipstick and ran around being Maria. My first crush was Bernardo from the Sharks. I was always really wrapped up in film. Even now if there is a film or TV show I like, I just get totally fucking immersed. I want to devour it. But regarding myself, and coming from the neighbourhood I came from, I didn't know how you got famous. Maybe you got discovered like Lana Turner. So I left school when I was 14 years old and I was a delinquent and really crap at it because of my conscience. I felt guilty all the time, even when I really wasn't doing anything much. I just sucked at it. If I was shoplifting then I always got caught, I was really lame. So that wasn't a career option.

I was an underage go-go dancer at the time with a fake ID, because I had to eat. I would ride the subway, because I didn't have anywhere to go, with a feather boa and this big silver afro wig. I probably looked like Jodie Foster in *Taxi Driver*, y'know? I didn't realise what power you have at that age and it was probably good I didn't realise. And this junkie, Tommy, took me to Max's Kansas City. By then the punk scene was in New York. The New York Dolls were just starting out and Richard Hell was already around. And I got to see Suicide, with Alan Vega, and I was just so fucking blown away. I don't even know how we got upstairs, we must have snuck in, and Alan touched my head and it was like being anointed. I probably had my wig off, I remember that I was bald at the time, and he touched me and it was like being anointed. He laid his hands on me and I was healed. And I thought, I could fucking do this. This is something I could do.

It was so black and white where I grew up, just outside the Bronx, I was hungry for colour. I searched out pink dye and found a guy who would dye my hair pink and I would get a lot of attention just because of the way I looked. So I thought, I can do this. It was really that. It could have been that if he had taken me to a hospital then I could have ended up as a doctor, I don't know, but it was so alive, it was so not monotone.

Becoming avant-garde   We had an acapella band when I was a kid. We'd find a bunch of girls and sing harmonies and stuff. I wrote poetry also, although I didn't know it was poetry. And finally [*at Max's Kansas City*] I found a venue where I could see myself doing something. I didn't know what I could do, especially in those days. I couldn't sing but I could make noises. I could make noises like you ain't never heard before and that's how it became avant-garde. It was not because I knew what the avant-garde was; it was because I was limited to what I could do at the time. I would ride the subway and I would hear the train wheels going and I would be making up poetry or I would love the sound of my father's printing press. I just like whatever I like and it's always been like that. I'm a marketing nightmare and it took me a long time to realise that. Because they wanted to sell me, but they kept saying, "But we don't know how to sell you. We think you're great, we just don't know what to do with you." I used to think it was just a hand job, they're blowing smoke up my ass, but I see it now. Like when I have to do a 20-word bio for a gig I can see why I was so much trouble. I'm inspired by what I'm inspired by and then when I'm not inspired any more, then I'm not. So if I see a building that excites me then I'm going to paint buildings, or sing buildings or talk about buildings. I can't rein myself in, and that's probably a good thing, that's probably why I'm still working. But it didn't make life easy for me or anybody around me.

When I saw Suicide it was so out there, especially at the time. How could you describe it to anybody? It was totally about atmosphere. It was sexy, it was dangerous. It had that combination Marvin Gaye always talked about. It was God and sex at the same time, when he was talking about, "I've been sanctified" and Alan Vega has that. There's this guy wearing a Little Richard wig and Martin Rev with these glasses; you couldn't describe it and they just blew me away. And I thought everything could be like that and show business is such a great thing [*makes an expression like an ingénue*]. It hasn't all been like that y'know, though. I remember that my friend Tommy was a thief and he threw a handbag in my lap and said, "Run!" So I remember thinking, "I've got to lose Tommy the junkie, but I'm definitely coming back to this place."

What happened was that I wanted to go to Berlin, I don't know why, and had gotten arrested and couldn't leave the State of New York for a year while I was waiting for it to go to court. Everything got thrown out of court as a matter of fact and I ended up suing Grand Central Station. It was a wrongful arrest suit. In that time I met Steve from Crass. He had come over and I met Steve on my doorstep in the middle of the night. I had a dancing job and it was too hot to go to sleep so I was sitting on the doorstep. I saw this guy coming down the street with spiky hair, there weren't many of us and you knew everybody. And he had some band and they were called Clash, Crass, Crash or something. I couldn't even remember the name when I went to see them. So they said, "You can come to visit and you can stay with us if you like." And I took them up on it, and I stayed [*laughs loudly*].

Pen [*Rimbaud*] and I were writing. I was already performing in New York and I had done a bunch of stuff. Pen had seen my notebooks and he had found *Shaved Women* that I'd written and he asked, "Do you mind if we turn this into a song?" and I thought, "Go and knock yourself out" because it was really nothing, I was always scrawling. And it was he who came up with the idea of building rhythm tracks for me. Being there, especially with Penny, he had a vision for me that was great, because I didn't. I bounced around and I thought that I was a disco singer. I thought that I was making pop tunes and disco records, I really did. And of course those records are absolutely NOT disco hits. But in my head they were. And I loved those albums too.

Raising the bar   I loved what was going on at the time, but I couldn't understand what the words meant. I couldn't understand what they were singing about in the Clash songs or the Sex Pistols because between the production and the accents I had all the words wrong in my head. And New York was much less political. It was a mixture of energy and poverty and fashion and how we were living anyway. We were street urchins, a lot of us, and the older ones were ex-street urchins. The English thing was much more about philosophies I guess. They wanted to change society whereas in New York it was about the fact that we were so far outside of society in any case. Society didn't really want any part of us. They had no use for us. They never do have

I am licensed

by the State

of New York

and I can tell

you that God

does not hate

you and totally

loves you

a use for the poor. Our clothes WERE ripped, but then they became a statement. We WERE a mess so we became more of a mess, at least for me.

My father, who fought in the Second World War always said, "Look at the worst case scenario and work backward. How much can you live with the result? Does it matter? What have you got to lose?" My parents set the bar high, I gotta give them that. They were supportive, but if I did something that was crap they would tell me it was crap. Like they came to my first gig and they said, "That sucked", and it did. They were glad I was doing it but it sucked. But also when I made something that they really loved then they REALLY loved it. If it was good they would say, "This is fucking great!" And they didn't blow smoke up my ass. The reality was that I had a strange voice, but it was a lazy voice. It took years to develop. It's like when they say, wow they're 16 and they are so good; but would you go to a brain surgeon who was 16? [*laughs*] With the arts it takes a long time to get good and that's why you've got to set the bar high. With Adrian [*Sherwood*] there were 500 other singers waiting so you'd better learn how to do it hard and fast and good. With all of the people I worked with they had high standards and my standards are high.

Everybody needs a job   Everybody needs a job. Everybody needs to be of use. The biggest crimes we commit are to elderly people when we sequester them to nowhere, to decay. These people have experience, they have talents, they are problem solving, and have all kinds of abilities that we need and we should be exploiting that. When I go down to Mexico and I see a 90-year-old women out with an infant at 1 o'clock in the morning because there's community and you realise how important community is. And the infant is serving a purpose and so is the 90-year-old woman carrying that infant. And it's not patronising either of them, it's not made-up busy work, it's not a government scheme. There's no gold star for everyone. Not every kid is a genius, believe me they're not [*laughs*] it's just that everybody has a purpose and I do believe that everyone has something to give, and that given the chance everybody does want to be useful. People don't want to be snatching purses. When I was doing syringe exchange, people were always asking, "Is there anything that I could do to help?" We had a lot of people who were hanging out in the homeless community who weren't drug users, but we were a place to go. And every day they were asking for a job. It's a fundamental human need. So you can find the answers to problems in the most unlikely sources, you know? You really can if you keep your ears open.

The accidental pastor   I was born with faith. It wasn't because it was indoctrinated in me. I would pray for hours for everything in the world. I just always believed in God. My mother would take us to a mosque or a temple or church or Buddhist temple in Chinatown, and we got through a lot of Sunday schools. She was always on a search and had such a vast understanding of theology; she could make things make sense really easily. My father was agnostic so we were totally given free reign and for a while I had an anger for religion, but it was never "Fuck God!" it was more "Fuck religion!" Religion is like some sort of pornography, it's identity theft, and it really is. Anybody who thinks that God is talking to them and them only is a dangerous person.

There's no logical explanation because I feel that it doesn't need one, because it's beyond logic. It's like, I don't understand how electricity works, but I know that when I switch the light on it will be there and it's really that. It's that simple for me. And it doesn't keep me from doing the wrong thing, but sometimes it might help me determine the right thing. This is again why I don't like religion, because if you need the fear of God from keeping you from doing something damaging to your fellow man then that's messed up. And we've all done harm, I've done harm, but the difference is that if I thought it through and thought that someone was going to get hurt or someone's feelings were getting hurt here, then I would stop. The thing is that we are all grabbing the moment and we aren't looking at the bigger picture.

The only reason I got ordained is because I was doing a needle exchange and outreach work on the streets and a drunk would fall over and break their arm or something. I would call an ambulance and I would go, "Where are you taking them?" as I knew they would just take them round the block and then dump them because they didn't want them vomiting in the ambulance. And they said, "Who are you?" and I said that I was his minister because I was standing outside of my church [*laughs*], and I said that he was one of my flock. But then the guy's whole attitude changed, and he goes, "Look you've got to understand, I pick up people all day and they are just going to get drunk again or go to rehab and come out again," and he started confessing. He just wanted somebody to listen so I thought, "This could come in handy." [*laughs*]. And the legal aspect is good, I could sign a wedding certificate or a passport application. Or someone might come and ask me if God hates them because they are shooting dope, and I can say to them, "I am licensed by the State of New York and I can tell you that God does not hate you and totally loves you."

Responsibility and redemption   You've absolutely got to take responsibility back, and when you do you gotta take the pain back too. I've done some horrible things in my life and I have to own up to them. That doesn't mean that I'm going to do an Opus Dei and starting flagellating myself but I can't get away any more with denying that they happened either. I've got to own it because I want the other parts too.

And I do believe in redemption and I don't believe in hell. I hope I'm right! [*laughs*]. I think the Kingdom of Heaven is within all our grasps and I think that we're all going to be getting there whether we like it or not, and that's a good thing. I think it's a joyful, happy thing. And it's not a lightshow put on just for me, so that makes every life and every soul of value. So when I hurt other souls then I gotta say that I hurt them, but I don't have to do it again.

Limited notions of gender   I don't recognise gender but unfortunately the world does. For me being a woman is something that I play. I relate more to being a trans female than a genetic female, do you know what I mean? I happen to have been born a genetic female. It was the way I was brought up. I remember this guy hit me when I was a teenager and my dad gave me the dog's chain and dropped me off and said, "Go find him because you can't take shit." Now people don't do that with their daughters, you know what I mean? I didn't have any brothers. My father's thing was, "You don't take crap from people." You don't take crap from the Nazis, or it could be a cop (or whatever), but you don't take any crap. This is where gender comes into play for me. The expectations put on us to behave entraps everybody. It's bad for women, it's bad for men, it's bad for all of us because we're put into such limited frigging categories it's so not what we are supposed to be about. We are souls and we've got so much potential and it's such narrow shoes.

I learned how to be angry and to keep my anger for work purposes. And I won't accept being put out to pasture. Defiance is great fuel and instead of beating yourself up for having human emotions such as anger and jealousy, they become a problem when you deny them or say they are not attractive. And then you find yourself doing something really ugly. One of the ways that you can recruit people into insanity is to prey on the hurt they feel. I know what it's like to be an immigrant and feel like an outsider. That's how pimps work down at the bus station when you are vulnerable and alone. Perhaps one of the ways to deal with terrorism is to make people feel more welcome and treat people nice. A lot of things have to come into play for bad things to happen so perhaps by being nice to people we can remove one of those building blocks.

In punk the idea of beauty could be different. We all hate ourselves, that's a given, and everything is on us, especially when we are young, to turn us into the perfect consumer. So to reinterpret what beauty is and what gifts and talents are and to make a place where they are valued, that was supposed to be what it was about. Seeing what we can learn from each other rather than seeing everyone as a threat; seeing the esteem in everyday actions. Just getting up in the morning is an estimable act, because if you think about it there's no logical reason to do it.

Sid Truelove & Zillah Minx

Sid Truelove and Zillah Minx met at a Crass gig in 1979 and were soon living together in a house with touring partners the Poison Girls. In the summer of that year they formed Rubella Ballet, with Zillah on vocals and Sid on drums. Their first performance was a somewhat impromptu affair when they took to the stage at a Crass/Poison Girls concert.

Keen to offer an alternative to the monochrome and militaristic image offered by many anarcho bands, Zillah and Sid's trademark soon became the brightly coloured Day-Glo clothes that they wore on stage. Sid also found himself drumming for Flux Of Pink Indians during this period and wrote two of the tracks that would later appear on Flux's Neu Smell *EP, which went on to sell more than 50,000 copies.*

Rubella Ballet's first release was the cassette-only Ballet Bag *in 1981. Apart from Zillah and Sid, the line-up constantly changed, but during this period Gem Stone and Pete Fender – the children of Poison Girls singer Vi Subversa – took on bass and guitar duties. Support from John Peel and an extensive tour with Death Cult raised the band's profile further. In 1985, they formed their own label, Ubiquitous, and eventually put out three albums, including* At Last It's Playtime. *The band split in 1990, with Sid already playing in the dance band Xenophobia. But the band reformed in 2000 and has played live sporadically ever since. In 2014, Rubella Ballet – still with Zillah and Sid at the helm – released, to much acclaim, the punk/goth-flavoured LP* Planet Punk.

Zillah Minx: I was 15 in 1976; the Sex Pistols had not been on the TV and nobody knew about punk. In my mind, I was one of the people that helped create punk. I was only 15 but I'd seen a few people around, like Siouxsie [*Sioux*] and [*Steven*] Severin down Petticoat Lane. Siouxsie came up with silver tights on and a long mohair jumper and we used to go to a market stall there called the Last Resort and they used to sell some slightly punk clothes. I used to make all my own clothes and we weren't really sure if we were even called punks. I knew one girl at school who had six earrings in, and she wore straight trousers. The little things that we used to do was change our trousers from flairs to straight trousers and put an earring in and that sort of thing. For me the whole thing was about fashion. At the beginning there wasn't any music.

You couldn't find any of that music at the time, even if you knew what it was. What we would listen to was a bit of reggae, a bit of dub. It was at the same time that Bob Marley was happening. My dad used to work at Finsbury Park as a teacher and he was teaching a lot of black kids, and at the time they all went to the Rainbow. And there would be Bob Marley walking down the street with his staff and his hair, you know this King of Ethiopia, and my dad would come home and tell me about this strange-

looking person and what he was like, as well as me being this strange-looking person. For me it was a fashion thing to start off with. So we went looking for other people that looked like us, and looking for some music, and then as we were doing that, the Sex Pistols came on the TV, and everything just exploded into this whole punk thing.

I was always involved in making my own clothes so it was like an evolution for me. I also liked it because it meant that we looked really different. People would talk to you on the street in East London, and say things to you, but if you looked different, and hard, then they'd shut the fuck up. And while I was only a girl of 15 people would whistle at me and I didn't want that kind of attention.

<u>Sid Truelove</u>: The amount of abuse that Zillah got was beyond comprehension. And it shocked me. The stories that Zillah has told me would make anyone shit themselves. The first time that I went out with her we were outside this pub in East London and this geezer walks up to me, this 4 ft. 5" bloke, and goes "I suppose you think you're tall, don't you?" And he then hits me so hard and it spun me round and knocked me out. And that was our first date wasn't it? [*Zillah nods and laughs*]. I think that Zillah is probably the hardest girl I know. I don't think anyone knows the abuse that Zillah got, the abuse that girls got.

<u>Zillah Minx</u>: And that happened whether you were a punk or whether you were normal. It would be that kind of thing.

Liberation through punk

<u>Sid Truelove</u>: Becoming a punk was different for me. I lived in a village outside of Birmingham, really in the middle of nowhere, and everyone was into Status Quo and Deep Purple and it was driving me insane, and I didn't know what to do. My mum was quite physically abusive to me, and I was getting beaten up at school and I wanted a release. I would go out at night and walk around the town so that there wasn't anyone bossing me around or telling me what to do. I was kind of in a world of my own. And as soon as I heard the Sex Pistols it was like someone had got a key and unlocked this door, and that was it, my life changed completely and I ripped my clothes up, I bleached my hair.

I remember going to the youth club, throwing the door open, walking in and sticking *Anarchy In The UK* on this crappy little record player. And that was it. I then wrote letters to get a job in London. When I got to London punk exploded, and it turned out that where I lived in Notting Hill Gate was where the Virgin Records store was — THE Virgin Records store — it was the only one at the time. And it had loads of posters in the shop and I remember getting about 500 of them and sticking them around my room [*laughs*]. And I met someone called Richard, who was my mate, and we'd go out and see people like Adam and the Ants — we saw a lot of them. Then he came back one night and said "I haven't been to see Adam and the Ants, I've been to see Crass!" And I was like, "You traitor!" [*laughs*] And then I liked Crass and I saw the second gig that they ever did. I think it was at Chalk Farm or Swiss Cottage and it was absolutely… well it's very hard to explain, it was all black, with this barrage of audio-visual work. It was just totally different to anything we'd ever heard, and we thought that Adam and the Ants was quite different.

And the second date I went on with Zillah was at the Conway Hall gig where it all kicked off [*laughs*]. Someone got pushed off the roof and about 200 skinheads turned up. I feared for my life that night.

Zillah Minx: I didn't. I loved it! I loved all the fighting and the rioting [*laughs*] because to me, it was the strength of the punks fighting back against all these stupid people. "I don't want to know about you fascist bastards! We're going to stand up. We are going to be the new force that's coming. Watch out! We're the punks that are going to get you. We're girls and men, and we don't care." And we were all ages too. There were a lot of punks that were 11, 12, and 13. Gem Stone [*the daughter of Vi Subversa from the Poison Girls*] was 11; Pete Fender [*Vi Subversa's son*] was only 14. Honey Bane who was a friend of ours was 15. I was 18 and Sid was 19 but there were a lot people that were a lot older like Crass and of course Vi Subversa who I think, at the time, was about 40. And so I thought that we were a new force of people and that is what we were going to do.

It's important to remember too that before punk came along the typical night out would be at 'Tiffanys', where we'd turn up, all dance around our handbags and, at the end of the night at 11 o'clock some bloke would come up to you and say: "Can I have the last dance?" And you'd think "Oh God! Do I have to?" and that would be it for the night — you've got to dance with one bloke and he's taking you home? So that was boring, and rubbish and sexist. But you'd go to a punk gig and what you could do is buy a pint, talk to the men, talk to the women, and watch the band. And you wouldn't have to be there and stand and become part of a cattle show. At a punk gig there'd maybe be people there who'd written a fanzine that you could read and talk about. So being a punk was so different from following the normal, straight route.

The political movement

Zillah Minx: Punk has always been political. I come from a political background. My mum and dad were involved with removing Reg Prentice from the Labour Party [*who was famously de-selected from Labour, and then defected to the Conservatives*]. That happened around 1975 as I was becoming a punk. It was very controversial at the time. In my heart of hearts, I was hoping that punk would go the 'right' way and become left wing and anti-racist; luckily it did go that way. There was the Clash who did the same thing, and the Sex Pistols, and everyone has seen it now

[*Julien Temple's film* <u>Never Mind The Baubles</u>] that they supported the striking firefighters, with this party for the firefighters' children, and this is when the Pistols were being called the scum of the earth as if they did nothing for anybody.

And so it was nice to see that the other bands WERE political. And it was blatantly obvious with the Clash as they had it written down their clothes, and *Anarchy In The UK*, etc. So it was those sorts of things that started us off thinking that there was a political side to it. And we ALL went and looked at what ideas like anarchy meant. If a word came up that we didn't know we'd go and look it up. To me that proved that a lot of the punks we knew were intelligent. A lot of them were doing degrees, or nothing, it didn't matter, they were still intelligent.

And then when the anti-racism topic came up with Rock Against Racism, that was it. I was on the first demo. There were a 100,000 people that marched from Trafalgar Square to Victoria Park, and there were punks on that parade, and that was the first time that I saw somebody with a Mohican. That was how early it was. And it was with the Clash, Poly Styrene and everybody: by the time we got to Trafalgar Square and there were 100,000 punks there, you knew you were in the right place.

Punk as a way to live

<u>Zillah Minx</u>: And then when Crass came along that was even better. And so what happened in my opinion, and maybe a few others, is that punk started in this whole way and by the time it got to Crass, they gave us this idea that we could LIVE as punks, and that we COULD make a community. A lot of punks started making co-ops, such as going into housing cooperatives and having somewhere else to live. And vegetarianism was another political theme. My sister had become a vegetarian and at the age of 11, everyone laughed at her everywhere she went. No one knew what that was. People would say, "Come around our house and we'll give you some meat when your mum's not looking." But Crass told people about that, and that's really important.

The band wasn't very organised in the early days. It had people coming and going. One time we went to pick up Annie Anxiety (as she was singing for Rubella Ballet at the time) for a gig in Chelmsford and it was me and Sid and Punky Pete and my sister. And Annie just decided that she didn't want to do the gig. It wasn't a problem, we just went off to do the gig, but when we got there that's when we realised that there wasn't anybody there to sing. So I said, "Err, ok, well I'll do it then"… and it's because Johnny Rotten said anyone can do it, get up there and do it. We took that on board. Everybody talked about it. We can just do whatever we want. It doesn't matter what you do. In fact, there was some band that was really silly and they'd get up with children's plastic flutes, people would get up on stage and start reciting poetry that they'd written.

Go fuck yourself!

Zillah Minx: My sister went on to be a union rep and that was because she knew that when she was at work if people said something to her, she'd tell them, "I'm a punk, don't talk to me like that. Don't think I'm not going to have an opinion. Don't think that you're going to be a sexist bastard and tell me to make the coffee, because I'm not. Go fuck yourself!" That's what it gave you: the ability to say what you really meant because people were so frightened of just the idea of punk, from what they'd read in the newspaper — like punks are going to spit on you, or beat you up. What it was actually about was that punk was assertive. We weren't aggressive. It was the normal people that were attacking us that were aggressive. We would stand up for ourselves and be counted. That's what always happened.

The thing is that Sid and I are just ordinary working-class people that would never have been in a band if it wasn't for punk; we would never have had our say if it wasn't for punk. We are being asked our opinions all the time, and it wouldn't have been the same if we'd got ordinary working-class jobs and didn't have a life as a punk.

But, we find it difficult to look at what's happened now. We had hoped that punk would change things and make them better. But what's happened is the political system went against the left and things have become more right wing. And the other thing of course is religion. If people are going to decide that women have to cover up, or women have to do this, or women have to do that, then that has an effect. People are asking, "Why are you wearing that mini skirt, why have you got a low top on?... that's why you're getting raped." No! That was changed in the 1960s, and we'd been changing things since then, but it's going backwards. So yes, we became angrier because I don't like to see the kids of today suffering so much. They are stuck in school and not being allowed out. They are fingerprinted for their dinner money. They're being taught rubbish at school. The curriculum is narrow; they're not allowed to think for themselves. You can't even get a day off school without your mum and dad being fined. They've closed down teacher training colleges; they've closed down art colleges, so where are kids supposed to go? Kids have got no freedom. When I was 14 I was going to gigs. This has got to change.

Sid Truelove: Punk was part of my release for me. Because of punk I decided that no one's ever going to tell me what to do again, ever. And I still live by that now today. And I have never been so happy.

Right at this point, right now, even though I've got two types of cancer that they claim are going to kill me, and I've got ulcers on my feet that make walking so difficult, I've never been so happy in my entire fucking life. I feel contented that I've done something that I wanted to do.

Charlie Harper

Charlie Harper was born in Hackney, London, in 1944. The fact that in 2014 he is still recording music and playing live all over the world makes him one of punk's true enduring heroes. His musical journey started in 1975 when he formed R&B act the Marauders, but an encounter with the Damned saw him change his band's name to UK Subs and their style of music to hard street punk with a rock'n'roll edge. Throughout 1977 and 1978, they played all over London, including punk HQ the Roxy, building up a loyal following along the way.

Championed by John Peel, UK Subs signed to City Records and released their first single C.I.D. *in September 1978. The following year, they signed to Gem Records and scored seven consecutive UK Top 30 hits between 1979 and 1981, including* Stranglehold *and* Warhead. *They also managed two UK Top 10 albums –* Brand New Age *and* Crash Course *– cementing their reputation with a heavy touring schedule that included shows with the Ramones.*

In 2013, double album XXI *was unveiled, leaving the band just two official recordings away from achieving their aim of releasing 26 LPs with titles running alphabetically A to Z. UK Subs still typically perform between 150 and 200 gigs each year.*

When I was younger I had no idea what I would do when I left school, so my mum and my aunt wanted free hairdos and they said to me, "You should go and be a hairdresser." [*laughs*] So that's how it was for a few years. I'd work all winter and in the summer I'd go down to the South of France and busk. I did alright then and when I got back, the hairdressing really took off and because I was arty I could do all these fancy cuts and effects. And I got to the point where I had my own shop and employed people and I was earning a fair bit of money.

Getting into punk though was a great accident. When the pubs shut at 11 o'clock, as they did in those days, we found a pub that was open until 1 in the morning. When that shut we started going to clubs. We were Bowie freaks with coloured hair, and because we looked a bit outrageous, we found a club called Chaguaramas, which was a lesbian club. I could get in there because you couldn't tell if I was a girl or boy and it was fun. One time we went down there and it had changed. There were all these guys in leather jackets and jeans and strange haircuts. It became the Roxy and there were punk bands every night except Sunday and that became the watering hole.

I was still going back to South London and playing in my R&B band when one day I got a call from my friend who had a club in Kingston-upon-Thames and he said, "I've got this record, it's right up your street, you've got to come down here." I went down that Sunday, and it was the Ramones' first record. I thought, "That is it!" We were already playing the really hard and fast R&B and we were dressing in army fatigues so it was easy to make the crossover into pure punk. And one time when the Damned couldn't fulfil their Roxy engagement, they rang us up, and we did a good set, so we ended up filling in for anyone who flunked. We almost became a house band.

So not long after the Roxy thing happened we were asked, "Do you want to come on tour?" and I decided then that I would give up the hairdressing. I just gave the shop to the other stylist and never regretted it. And so in terms of my philosophy, you've got to do a job well and with all your heart. In our music, we don't want big record companies involved. I've got reservations about being radio playable. The stuff that you hear on the radio is so wet, because it's music being made for money, that's the only purpose. I don't want to join that lot because we make music for ourselves. I also think that above us is only shit. You get the business and the corporates interfering in rock'n'roll and it's just shite up there.

Give me a saw and I'll build it myself   My view is work for yourself! Do something yourself, don't go and sit in any office working for someone else. You've got to do your own thing. And for punks it isn't only about forming a band, there was (and is) a thousand things that you can do in punk. Get involved, don't just be part of the audience; take pictures, write a fanzine, grow punk rock flowers and so on — it's a whole alternate world where you can do anything. I've got grandchildren who are in a pretty smart band. They're going down a storm at 16 years old, and the drummer and bass player are 13.

The only thing that pisses me off about DIY from a band perspective is that you sometimes go to places like a squat in Italy to do a gig, and there's just one light bulb and no stage, and they think, "We're Punk Rock, we don't need lighting." But people have paid to see a proper show. And you need a stage. Once I said, "Give me some bloody wood and a saw and I'll make a bloody stage myself!"

Pete Fender

Pete Fender was playing guitar in punk bands from a very early age. Shortly after he had played bass with his mother Vi Subversa for the Poison Girls, he scored particular success at the age of 13 with Fatal Microbes. The band featured his sister Gem Stone on drums and Honey Bane on lead vocals. Small Wonder Records released a 7" single by the band featuring the song Violence Grows, *which at the time was championed by John Peel.*

Pete's next project was Rubella Ballet, again with Gem, although this time on bass. He took time out from the band in 1980 to work with Simon Stockton (who had just moved out of Dial House) on his poetry project, T42. *Pete recorded a solo EP* Four Formulas *for XNTRIX Records the same year and spent much of 1981 playing drums with The Androids of Mu, before re-joining Rubella Ballet.*

Pete left at the end of 1982 to join Omega Tribe, whose first EP Angry Song *was co-produced with Penny Rimbaud for Crass Records. Next they released the LP* No Love Lost *on Corpus Christi Records in 1983 and, with its melodic style and powerful lyrics, the acclaimed LP secured Omega Tribe an important corner in anarcho-punk history. Since then Pete has continued to write and perform music on an ad hoc basis and is currently working on material for a forthcoming album.*

Writing about punk philosophy, I cannot help but write from a fairly unique perspective; both as an early member of Poison Girls, and several other bands on the scene – and as a child growing up in one of the households that, very early on, helped to promote the idea of anarcho-punk.

When punk rock happened, I was not one of the bored teenagers emanating from safe suburban homes who seemed to be in charge of defining what it was; I was several years younger than most of them for a start and both of my parents had been anarchists before I was born. I'd got a guitar when I was eight and had started keenly on the path towards becoming a musician. Still, I had no idea how I was going to do it. I would listen to my dad's folk and jazz records, my mum's hippy records and to the chart music of the time, which was glam rock and Motown. I loved it; it was joyous and funny, sexy and cool. I thought, "That's what I want to do when I grow up."

In the beginning, the philosophy of punk was clear: you can be you, and you can do it yourself; you didn't have to worry about having the kind of entitlement that comes through qualification, you had as much right to free expression as the next person. If you wanted to perform, had something to say, or just wanted to go out and enjoy other people doing it, there was nothing to stop you. The very act of performance, of being there, said all of this quite clearly — and much of the content, while not always very far removed from this ethos, was often secondary in importance to the act of performance itself. "I am a poseur and I don't care," pretty much summed it up. We were having fun – regardless of any statement of rebellion, this was really what it was. Nothing seemed to matter much above all of that — punk meant freedom!

Well, nothing lasts forever and I can remember the feeling — at the end of 1978 — that punk rock was on the wane. We had enjoyed two summers of unprecedented energy, upset many people in the establishment and consolidated in our own minds much of what it was that punk stood for. Nevertheless, as we entered 1979, there was something of a sense of loss. We had made our big statement and it seemed that punk no longer had much that was fresh to say about society or the world at large. Undoubtedly, the desire to confront and to shock a society that was felt to have become too safe and boring ultimately made it harder when trying to effect any real change in the mainstream. The media had assimilated the imagery and turned it around. We could shock no longer. Indeed, we were becoming a joke to the world outside. As a force for change, punk had momentarily run its course in the natural order of things.

The second wave of punk presented a new doctrine, brought about by the introduction of a number of radical ideas drawn from various corners of the counter-culture that had preceded it. Ideas like pacifism, vegetarianism and anti-capitalism that had been close to the heart of the hippy generation but had hardly seemed relevant in the first wave of punk rock. Punk became a banner under which to draw all of these ideas together and to encourage a young generation into becoming politically active. Although I found this exciting to begin with, one of the mechanisms by which this was achieved was the expulsion of mainstream attitudes and cultures that were considered threatening to the doctrine. As an artist and a free thinker, I found this aspect particularly difficult. Punk became isolated from any cultural background and was condemned to continual self-consumption. As a result, I saw the explosion of energy that was manifest at the outset gradually cut off as the frustration and desperation set in – not just because we realised that we had achieved very little political change, but from the realisation that we had sent ourselves up a blind alley in artistic terms through adherence to a set of ideas that allowed little appreciation of the mainstream culture in which we lived; increasingly, we seemed able to comment on the outside world only in terms of negative reaction — there was nothing available outside of 'anti-this' and 'anti-that'. I was sad to witness such a brave new attitude to life turn in on itself in this way.

Somehow, punk had evolved from a simple, almost naïve, approach to self-expression that celebrated a wide range of diversity in both form and content, into something predetermined that ultimately became severely restrictive, even prescriptive, both in terms of artistic style and in philosophical spread. This contradiction, that a movement supposedly all about freedom of thought and resistance to authority had become so rigidly defined, I still find depressing.

What interests me now is the freedom of expression that comes from genuinely free thought — that is, free from doctrine or definition. This, for me, is what the idea of punk still represents. No more, no less. The goal is still the same as it was in the 60s: to try and find ways to have a good time, and let it all hang out. Some of us found different words to describe it when punk rock was first happening, so as to fit in with the vernacular of the day. To me it is all the same thing. I can see a straight line all the way back to my folk/hippy roots, and I rejoice in that.

Pete Fender

Steve Ignorant

Born in 1957 in East London, Steve Ignorant is a singer and artist. In 1977 he co-founded Crass with Penny Rimbaud, and went on to record and release seven albums and 10 7" singles. Since the days of Crass, Steve has written and performed in a series of punk outfits including Conflict, Schwartzeneggar, Stratford Mercenaries and Paranoid Visions.

During his time as a performer Steve has expressed his ideas in a variety of mediums. He has been a sculptor, a Punch and Judy performer under the pseudonym Professor Ignorant, and he has penned an autobiography with Steve Pottinger entitled The Rest is Propaganda.

In 2010 Steve embarked on a tour called The Last Supper, *performing Crass songs from the period 1977-1982. In November of the following year he took the stage of the Shepherd's Bush Empire and was joined by Penny Rimbaud and Eve Libertine – the last time these members of the band have performed together.*

Since moving to the Norfolk coast in 2007, Steve has volunteered as a lifeboat man and has been writing and performing new material with his new band the Slice of Life. He is currently working on a much-anticipated new album.

When asked about the feelings I associate with Crass, I feel pride and awe. Just from that little room in Dial House it started off with me on vocals and Pen on drums and it ended up being what it was. In fact what it is, because you can't get away from it, it IS still around. People come up to me and say, "Steve, thanks for changing my life". And I say, "Well it changed mine as well." If it hadn't have been for Crass I would have ended up getting a girlfriend, getting engaged, getting married, having 2.4 kids and living somewhere like Gidea Park in Essex with a car and Christ knows what. I sort of knew that wasn't for me (and fine for those who do want that), but Crass and punk gave me a way to get out of there. And also from going around and doing the gigs I certainly saw England in the late 70s and 80s, and that was an eye opener for me, and I met thousands of people as a result.

When punk came along I felt, "Shit! I can understand this." I wanted to be a part of it because I got what they are saying. It was exciting. There were poets. There were dramatists. There were filmmakers like Derek Jarman, although I don't know if he could be regarded as punk. And I think that out of all of that you've got your artists like Banksy and a lot of them have been inspired by the artwork of Gee and Jamie Reid and that sort of stuff. And it just goes on. Whereas with, for example, the skinhead era – and I do remember looking like that – the only thing remaining is the Trojan symbol.

Why I'm not stuck in the dressing room   I still feel responsible for the reputation of Crass, even more so now. When we were doing the Last Supper Tour and we were in America, we had a gig in Baltimore that was cancelled because the owners of the club fucked off with all the money. People were flying down from all over the place to see us. And I was thinking [*head in hands*], "Oh Christ! Oh fucking hell. What are we going to do?" Some were on Facebook trying to sort it out. Then we decided it would be in another venue, and then that one was off. And then somehow the people who used to work at this club, along with the security, came in to open it up for one last night. They honoured the tickets but at half price. And one bloke came from Chicago. I was feeling pretty wretched anyway because I just got the news that my dog had died, and this guy from Chicago turned up with this six-pack of beer and said "I haven't got a lot but this is for you." Anyway, after the gig he comes up and said "Steve, could you get the band together?" And I said yes because I just thought it was to have a group photo, and so we got everyone together and he says, "Right, I just want to say that I appreciate you coming tonight because Crass has helped me through a really bad time." And he suddenly burst into tears. And I said, "Fucking hell mate. Are you alright?" And he said "Yes, its just that I saw my dad shoot himself with a cattle gun in front of me and I've been suicidal myself." And I spent the time with him just talking to him. That is the responsibility that you've got. It was the same in New Zealand where some girl said to me, "Are you Steve Ignorant?" And she burst into tears. "Crass's music helped me. I was abused as a kid," and that is the type of conversations you get. So I don't want to be stuck in the dressing room saying, "I'm not signing any autograph or I'm not talking to anyone." I'm always out talking to people, that's the job you do. If people want to talk to you about Crass, if they are bothered to buy your records and if they are coming to your gig, then the least you can do is give them five minutes of your time, even if it is just to hear them say, "Thank you" or to sign their records.

Getting vegetarianism on the menu   I think it's progress that you can now go into supermarkets and get organic or fair-trade food. I know it's all a rip-off in that you pay over the odds for it, but it makes me think of Crass and when we were called weirdos and wackos just for being vegetarian, but people got into that and then more people became vegetarian. Not only because of this but maybe they were inspired by Crass. Maybe by Conflict too. Then you had these little vegan and vegetarian cafés starting off. Now look at the industry of vegetarianism. You have people that go organic because it's healthy, for example. It's got to be a good thing whatever shape or form it takes. Instead of people going to McDonalds and eating that sort of crap. If there was any success from Crass or the ethical punk movement then I think that's where most of the success lies. You can go to basically any pub and get a vegetarian option or any shop or any restaurant and get a vegetarian option.

Talking to racists [*Talking about -isms like anarchism or Buddhism*] I've never bought into that kind of thing. That sort of thing you can do at Dial House, but you can't really be Zen in the middle of Birmingham can you? Not unless you go to a Zen centre or something like that. It's real life, isn't it? If you've got time to do it then fine but a lot of people ain't got time to do it. I'm more interested in going out there and meeting people. I want to meet the racists; I want to meet the sexist bastards. I want to rub shoulders with people like that because that's my life; it's what I do. It's what I sing about and what I talk about. I don't want to go somewhere and have to sit quietly. I guess you could call it realism. And regarding my views on anarchism I really don't know any more.

With Crass what happened was the lefties came over and they'd say, "Do you want to do benefits with us?" and we'd say, "No, we're not left wing" and they'd say, "Oh, you must be right wing then because you wear black." Then we'd have the right wing coming over to us and saying, "Do you want to do gigs with us?" And we'd say, "We're not right wing" and they'd say, "You must be fucking lefties then." So we thought, "Right! What we'll do is we'll put an anarchy symbol on everything so everyone knows we're not political. Then what happens? The only picture that people know is the bearded guy with the bomb. So then, right, here comes the CND symbol to show that we are pacifists. So we ended up with thousands of banners just to sort of describe what we weren't [*laughs loudly*]. Once people picked up on the anarchist thing, they would come to me and start talking about Bakunin and Malatesta and all that sort of stuff. I've read two pages of Malatesta and I've had to put it down because it was so boring. Then these schisms appeared, "Are you anarcho-syndicalist? Are you anarcho-pacifist? And are you anarcho this or that, blah, blah, blah".

Holding the line against bullies and injustice And so, if I am an anarchist, where does my anarchism come from? Well it comes from books like *A Kestrel for A Knave*. It comes from *Saturday Night, Sunday Morning*; *A Taste of Honey*; *Up The Junction* and *Poor Cow*; *Cathy Come Home*, and all this stuff. This is where my philosophy is. I cannot stand injustice and I don't like bullies and I think basically that's it. And I didn't fit in with the anarchist way of thinking because I don't need to know that in 1824 there was a Polish uprising in the salt mines of whatever. I'm sure they died for a worthy cause, but it means absolutely fuck all to me. There's no point inviting me to an anarchist meeting, which I was often, because what needs to be addressed is these racist fucking bastards down the pub.

I've spoken to Christians and they've said, "Are you a Christian?" and I've said, "No I'm not", but my perspective is pretty much Christian, good Samaritan. For example, if my worst enemy fell over in the road in front of me then I'd have to pick him up, or if they were drowning in the sea, I would have to pluck them out. Where I can help out to stop injustice then I'll do that or if see someone worse off than me I'll help them out.

One thing that I would have done differently is related to violence at the gigs and people trying to trash the gigs. In the end we took up arms but I think we should have done it much earlier. I think people like Conflict had that right. The thing about Crass and what everyone forgets (or no-one really knew) is that the Crass audience was made up of the real misfits; the fat kid at school who had the piss taken out of him, the skinny kid, the kid with bad acne, kids who couldn't afford punk clothing, even those that didn't even fit in to the punk thing. And we would get these people that would come to our gigs, and they'd read the lyrics and it meant something to them. And it meant something more than just going to see Crass for them. They would range from being 14 or 15 years old to being 18. And they could come from small villages, say out in Cornwall or somewhere, and the most violence they have ever seen is their dad shouting at their mum or something, and so to be confronted at a gig with big blokes with broken bottles, how can you expect them to fight back? Part of me didn't want to escalate it and have an open war between us and those threatening violence. This is what I would have done differently.

I remember watching a film called *To Sir, With Love* where at one point the teacher says, "Chuck out all the books, it's not working for you kids" and the children say, "What are we going to talk about sir?" The teacher says, "Well about sex, life, death, marriage…" and one of the children puts their hand up and says, "And what about protest?" And at this point the teacher, played by Sidney Poitier, says, "It's your duty as a young person to protest against the world, but to do it non-violently." And I think that it is your duty as a human being to question and to protest.

Allison Schnackenberg

Allison Schnackenberg grew up a fan of the US punk scene and found herself at an early age managing punk bands and working in Rough Trade Records in San Francisco. In 1985, John Loder offered her a job with Southern Records in London, helping him get the label's distribution arm running efficiently. An Anglophile, Allison jumped at the chance and moved to the UK. Southern, which began life as a recording studio, is closely linked with a number of other labels, including Crass, Corpus Christi and Dischord. The association with Crass began when Loder became friends with Penny Rimbaud, who went on to record Crass's first LP The Feeding of the 5000 *at Southern Studios.*

Allison has worked with a multitude of bands including NoMeansNo, Babes in Toyland, Chumbawamba, Rudimentary Peni and Therapy? She once said that, "The only common thread that unites the bands on Southern is attitude."

In 2005, Allison launched the Latitudes Sessions, where bands record and mix 20 minutes of music in one day and release it on CD; vinyl versions came later in 2007. All of the recording sessions took place at Southern Studios. Loder died in 2005 and these days Allison is both owner and director of the label. Outside of Southern and Rough Trade, Allison has had a range of other roles including being manager for Steve Ignorant during the post-Crass years and being label manager for One Little Indian in the late 90s.

I grew up in the States but I've been in the UK for some 30 years, so I have a kind of crap cross-Atlantic accent. It's difficult to say exactly why punk was so important to me, but I think, initially punk was about community. I grew up in suburban America and my early exposure to punk was through a magazine called *Creem*, which was a rock magazine. They were one of the first mainstream magazines that covered punk. They started writing about the Ramones, Blondie and Patti Smith, and the New York scene. Hearing that music was really hard to do at the time, we didn't have the Internet or anything like that. Occasionally a rock station in Philadelphia would play a track by the Sex Pistols and I would be like, "Oh my God, this is so exciting," so I started mail-ordering the stuff. Then I went out to my first couple of gigs, which were the Boomtown Rats, and I think the Clash with the Undertones. The New York bands would come play clubs but I couldn't get in because you had to be 21. After a while I discovered that there was a smaller scene, and I thought, "These are my people!" There was a sense of community. That's always something that has been really strong with me.

In high school I was in a band and promoting shows in Philly. There was a band called Crucifix who were from San Francisco and they wanted to tour on the East Coast. We somehow got hooked up with them and a friend and myself helped them book a tour for the East Coast. They were playing in Boston, it was my 21st birthday, and I got on the train up to Boston, and John Loder was there too because he wanted to do a record with them [*on Corpus Christi, an offshoot of Crass Records*]. I don't know what I did or said but I guess he liked me, and it was because of John that I then got a job with Rough Trade. Basically, he called them up and said, "There's this girl and I want you to give her a job at the warehouse or something." It's funny because I was so excited, and I went and had an interview and got hired. And when I was working in San Francisco at Rough Trade, I started out packing boxes. I was getting paid $7 an hour and I could have a pink mohawk. John and I became friends as a result.

I moved up in Rough Trade and became a salesperson and actually ended up becoming a director of Rough Trade in the States, all in a very short period of time. It was very chaotic. But John started to get really upset with Rough Trade in the UK. It was John's view that Rough Trade had this master plan to swallow up all the independent businesses, and he was really unhappy about it. He said to me, "We're going to pull out of Rough Trade and start our own distribution house," and I was like, "Great! Have you got a job for me?" I found myself applying for a job within a month, and that was it. I thought I'd come for a couple of years and work with him, and I'm still here [*shortly after the interview Allison returned to the US*].

I got really involved and I had the best of both worlds. I was an Anglophile, I was really excited about Britain, and really into British music. But Crass was the thing that drew me here, full stop. John Loder and Crass were one and the same. Although I came in 1985, which was just after Crass finished, it was still very much alive. I was really into Poison Girls too and lots of other stuff. But Crass was the thing that blew my mind. To be working within that organisation was incredible. It was the best job in the world, why would I leave? I had everything.

Punk and the Creation of Opportunity   So I got involved with punk because I saw a community and that community was one of opportunity: your background didn't matter, your gender didn't matter, and your education didn't matter. That was really exciting to me; it was this opportunity. You'd go to a gig and it would be like, "Let's start a band! Let's start a fanzine! Let's start a venue!" I did all these things before I moved. I was 22 when I came to the UK and I had done all that stuff, and fought battles with the police and the town hall, and done bands and tours and fanzines, all this really great stuff. And I'd created the world that I wanted to see.

As I've gotten older my values have extended into things like ecology, animal rights, and things like that. I'm not a vegetarian anymore, but I believe strongly in how we treat animals and how animals are raised, animal husbandry and so on.

I have really strong feelings about that. I'm forever driving people crazy about recycling stuff around here. I care too about family values and people being able to have a good work/life balance, which is something that we didn't have. I think John deeply regretted that; he talked to me about it when he was ill — we worked so hard.

Feminism in the mosh pit   [*In relation to Crass*] Probably the first record I really got excited about was *Penis Envy*. It was the same for most women who were Crass fans. There weren't that many bands saying that kind of feminist thing at the time. I try and think back and there was a really interesting article in *Maximumrocknroll* in late the 80s/early 90s. They had this series where they covered women in music, and I got really angry about it because I felt like they were pandering to the idea that women get marginalised in the punk scene. So I wrote a letter to Tim who worked there, and who I knew, saying, "You're pandering to this idea that doesn't really exist, and by doing that you're reinforcing the idea that it DOES exist." And we had a heated debate back and forth about it. I never really encountered that. I don't know if that's because I've always been a loudmouth, or strong person, but I was brought up to believe I could do whatever I wanted to do. I never really encountered that kind of macho thing.

My friend Nancy from Philly and myself went up to see Bad Brains, and we go into the mosh pit, and the look on the guys' faces was really funny, but they all respected us and came up to us afterwards saying, "You're in the pit!" And it's like "Yeah, we're in the pit at home, why wouldn't we be here just because you guys are scary?" To me that barrier never existed. That was the thing that I liked about punk, I felt I was on common ground. Even in my dealings in the business, the only time I really encountered sexism or machismo is when I've been dealing with people who are outside of the music business, like peripheral service companies. Like the shipping company that calls and says, "Oh, all right, love, you can talk to your boss about this," and I'd say, "I could do, but I am the boss!"

Seeing things and wanting to change things has always been a large part of punk. I still feel really angry in a lot of ways, and I have what's become a motto: if I were ever to win the lottery I would drag MCPS [*the organisation that licences reproduction rights and collects royalties*] through the courts because it's a terrible, bloodsucking organisation that persecutes independent business, etc. This is an example of what infuriates me, still. There are people doing all kinds of things though and standing up for wider political ideas. There are these people that embroider a puzzle piece about world hunger, and it's created this huge installation. And with things like that I think, "My God, this is punk!" There's a lot of women doing things, organising their own businesses, they're banding together and creating little collectives. This is grassroots punk stuff.

Taking control of your situation The more you look at it, the more interest there is in people taking stuff back to a personal level. For example, growing your own food, making your own clothes and so on. Wanting to know where their food comes from. I think that a lot of the politics is being brought back home, if you will, and rather than people marching and saying, "I'm really pissed over this" instead they're saying, "I'm controlling what I can control. I'm making decisions about how I raise my children, what kind of clothes I buy, and what kind of food we use in the house." It's almost a return to a couple of hundred years ago when people did this kind of thing because they had to. People are making these decisions because they don't want to detach themselves from these decisions and they're not happy about what's going on.

There's a lot of kids who want to be in the music business and at Southern Records we'd get people asking to come do work experience all the time. And so instead of doing work experience we developed an internship, which is slightly longer and they would get a little bit of money, and they would have more opportunity to learn something of value, rather than make the photocopies, make the tea, and stuff the envelopes. As that went on, and business started changing, it became really evident to me that a lot of these kids didn't understand that there was another way. I always thought of Southern as being another way. So there was one kid who was working at a record store that was known for selling records really cheaply. So we asked, "Do you like working there?" and he said, "Yeah, it's really good, they sell stuff really cheaply, just £5 for CDs." And I said, "How do you think they manage to sell that stuff for £5? They squeeze the record company so much, and pay it maybe £1.50 on a sale. So, how much do you think the CD cost to make, and how much do you think the band get?" And his face went white, he hadn't thought about it. He just thought, "That's great, the CDs are cheap," he had imagined that the band would still be getting £5, somehow.

But I do think (and hope) that the public consciousness is starting to swing back that way and people are much more aware of how they're spending money. There's a whole movement to eat less meat, for example, but eating a really good piece of meat that's been humanely produced once a week rather than having something cheap five days a week can be better. That's the kind of thing that will impact the corporations, and they have to listen a little bit. There are people like Jamie Oliver, with his campaign for chickens, who is fighting corporations. That is a kind of activism that people can relate to because they can see that it's having an impact. Those UK supermarkets like Morrisons are stocking more locally produced goods. With Waitrose, Sainsburys, and even Tesco, you go in there and they have certain food lines where they identify the farm that the food comes from, and then explain what their values are. Don't get me wrong, I don't think any of them are going far enough yet, but they've gone there because they've been pushed. If we continue to push then I think they'll continue to get better.

And I think it gets pushed down the food chain too, as farmers are educated that they don't have to cram that many chickens in to make a living, they can produce a nicer breed of chicken that grows more naturally, and they'll get more money for it because the consumer is willing to pay. We didn't use to care that 50 people died in a factory in India, to make a pair of £5 jeans. But now we have to take responsibility, as individuals, for the fact that these corporations exist and are exploiting people.

I can't really change the banking system, but I can change where I bank, where I spend my money, and how much dependency I have on that system. Whether or not that's even conscious for a lot of people I don't know, but I see it happening.

No experience that I've had of corporations has been positive, particularly in the music business. Personally I don't think that they should exist. I think there should be some kind of an upper limit on the growth of business. I think the world would be a lot better place if we had 50,000 banks instead of five, and if we had many more local businesses.

NoMeansNo were on tour recently, and one of the guys in the band had been brewing beer at home since the 70s. They had made a joke brewing video at one point that was included with one of their records. He was telling me that after this tour he was going to this brewery in Bavaria. Apparently, some kids who had bought the record, had then got interested in brewing, and they'd started a brewery in Canada, setting up their own business, and they'd invited the band to come and play at this brewery in the middle of nowhere. That's the new punk, that's amazing. Through this joke beer video the band inspired some kids to start a brewery. Those kinds of stories show how a legacy is being handed down. It's a philosophy – do anything you want to do, and that doesn't only mean starting a band, it means do ANYTHING you want to do.

If I had to distil what punk taught me down to the most base level, it would be: think for yourself. That's something that they don't teach you in school, they don't teach you to think for yourself; question it, think for yourself, and if people can learn that, then that's enormous.

Disruption

From the Sex Pistols' subversion of the Silver Jubilee to Crass's *Penis Envy*, the language, imagery and subject matter of punk has always been invested with a radically confrontational power; a power that is designed to jolt the audience out of any comfortable received notions or hardened political dogma.

The natural order of gender roles, the inevitability of war, and the "freedoms" of capitalism have all been mainstream ideas that have been taken on with a disrupting intensity that has become a distinguishing feature of the movement. At the heart of this is a belief that one cannot live an authentic and self-determined life by following the directives of an organised religion, or a political ideology or any other of the ideas and institutions that seek to influence our behaviour.

True engagement happens when these moments of 'un-thinking' are disrupted, and places of uncertainty are created that demand a response from the individual. **Graham Burnett**, a key member of the scene from the beginning and a permaculture teacher, remembers the effect that Crass lyrics had on him when he was a young socialist.

"The epiphany for me was when it said on the album *Feeding Of The 5,000*, 'Do you believe in Marx? Marx fucks'. And I was reading *Socialist Worker* and this, that and the other and I thought, 'You can't say that!' And I wrote this letter to Crass saying that you can't dismiss the work of Marx and all this doggerel that I'd got out of the *Socialist Worker Party Handbook*. I never sent the letter, but I played the record over and over and it was like the Zen whack on the side of the head. It opened up a whole load of questions, "What is this anarchy? What is this do-it-yourself stuff?" That was the moment for me that really opened things and made it clear."

When we asked **Penny Rimbaud** about the many contradictions that seemed to characterise the Crass body of work, like the delivery of pacifist ideas with intense aggression and anger, he told us:

"Contradiction is essential...You present somebody with an impossible contradiction and they're forced into themselves. That was a technique that Gee and myself developed within the avant garde: everything had to basically contradict itself, be self devouring. It's something that's deep in my creative consciousness, everything said must be then removed."

Situationism and Surrealism Malcolm McLaren is well known for referencing Situationism as a key idea in his pop culture attacks on the Establishment through the Sex Pistols. Situationists contend that we are currently living in a period of advanced capitalism where individuals express themselves through the acquisition and consumption of commodities rather than lived experiences. This phenomenon is called The Spectacle and the rise of aspirational lifestyle marketing would certainly fit this idea. They argue that this is damaging to the quality of human life and the wider society. As such they see the construction of liberating 'situations', disorientating and destabilising set pieces, as a way for individuals to reconnect with the moment and their own experience of living.

In Iceland we spoke to the Mayor of Reykjavík, Jón Gnarr and to Einar Örn Benediktsson, in charge of Culture and Tourism, who describe themselves as Surrealist Punks. They have recently created a situation on a grand scale by forming a protest political party, the Best Party, and becoming the majority in the coalition council for Reykjavík. The Best Party grew out of the outrage that was felt in Iceland after the mismanagement of their banking system led to a financial crash. The party was intended to expose the hypocrisy of the career politicians who had allowed this to happen while claiming to represent the electorate. It had no policies and was 'ideologically opposed to ideology'. Party members used surrealism to deliberately puncture the notion of what a political party should act like, using costumes and stunts. Their hope was that their disruption of the election process would open up space for new, more representative grass-roots parties to come through the system. They didn't expect to be elected, and could have declined with the excuse that they were not serious contenders, but they found themselves in a situation and decided to respond by going through with running the city.

Without the comfort or constraints of a political manifesto they were forced to make council decisions based on 'human rights' and what would most improve the lives of individuals in the city. This has not been an easy road and they had to make tough compromises along the way. They continued to use surrealism to create situations throughout their time in office, all the time allowing the possibility for redefining council politics. Jón Gnarr famously came to work dressed as his mother for Gay Pride week and could often be found roaming the halls of City Hall dressed as Darth Vader while continuing with the business of being Mayor.

Crucially they declined to run for a second term of office despite having very high popularity ratings. The new coalition council that took office in 2014 has representatives from the Pirate Party and Bright Future Party which was created with Best Party ideas at its heart.

"I said I'm stepping down because I want more people in. This power is not mine to hold. It's not mine to own. I'm not a subscriber to this power... It's everybody else's so please come in, use it, be part of it because it's ours to share, to feel good." **Einar Örn Benediktsson**

The thorn in the side of the smug   No ideology, no matter how well intentioned it might at first appear, is safe from **Gavin McInnes**, who uses his position in the US media to attack and disrupt the comfortable paternalism of the liberal agenda. Gavin rails against the assumptions and abuses of power made by liberals on behalf of those they seek to protect. He argues that their political correctness and overcompensations only alienate and rob people of their self-determinism.

"Regarding PC, it's become more than policing...When you don't know if you are supposed to say African American, person of colour or black, you just go, 'I'm just gonna avoid them. Entirely. I don't wanna say the wrong thing.'"

Gavin specialises in saying the unpopular and unsayable, and challenges the ideals that most of us would take for granted as reasonable, as they are often the least subjected to scrutiny. He is a particular scourge of the left as he believes that all politicians are self-serving, no matter what their political hue and yet the left are often portrayed as the 'good guys' by the traditional opponents of government. In his words, "Sunshine is the best disinfectant."

He takes on the unthinking literalism of anti-establishment ideologues who resort to an oversimplified view of the world in order to bolster their own political position, rendering their opposition ineffective. He also sees off-the-peg belief systems as a barrier to free thought, as they provide all the answers without the need for individual engagement with the ideas. They condition us to drawing the same conclusions and creating consensus within the group rather than taking in the fullness of the situation and seeing all the ramifications of our actions. Worse still, we use these received ideas in place of taking the full responsibility for our decisions.

"They've taken the metaphors literally and they think it's men in pig suits just eating money while starving children go, 'please, more gruel?'"

From launching a tirade against a disability advocate on a television news program to making short films baiting feminists, Gavin forces people to fully examine the motives behind their comfortable moral positions, even those who would think that they were ethically beyond reproach. He is continuing in the punk tradition of disruption by challenging everyone who would seek to have some power over our lives, no matter how seemingly innocuous they appear. All political perspectives have the potential for tyranny if left unchecked.

Self-Disruption   In some of our interviewees we saw disruption applied almost as a discipline of thought. Where they found themselves becoming too entrenched in a certain idea they deliberately took the opposite view or derailed their own argument in order to find a more authentic perspective. Each thought and opinion had to be constructed anew.

"There's constant changing, there's constant questioning in my head... it's this constant switching. Yes-no-yes-no-yes-no-yes-no, polarity switching, questioning questioning questioning questioning." **Mark Stewart**

This mental rigour seems to fit with a commitment to the principle of taking full responsibility for your own thought processes and is a way of guarding against unconsciously adopting positions or making assumptions. We saw Mark Stewart constantly challenging his own conclusions. Gavin McInnes expressed a belief that we only learn in the mental spaces created by disruption because that is where our thinking is freed from our usual habits and crutches.

Sleeping agents Although some of the people we spoke to expressed a desire to disengage from 'the System' and escape its corrupting influence, others saw the disruptive potential of punk ideas infiltrating the mainstream. Gee Vaucher talked about the importance of punks taking up positions in the police force, education and health work as they were in positions to influence the discourse and make positive changes.

Mark Stewart is fascinated by this idea and talked about the need to engage with the Establishment, not only to take it on, but to provide alternatives, otherwise you have lost control of the narrative.

"But what I'm finding quite interesting is there's actually some really really cool – I call them sleeping agents – kind of people who are sympatico inside the machine. Like Matt Groening is really cool. There's people way up in Sony Film, there's amazing directors. So it's not really them and us... You have to break the narrative, and provide an antidote."

The idea of disruption has come a long way from the cruder attempts to shock and 'shake the frame' that were seized upon by the press in the early days of punk. We now see it being used in more considered and positive ways to create opportunities for people to experience the world authentically, or to free up mental processes so that learning can happen. On a larger scale, disruption can be regarded as a tool to bring about changes to our social services and even our culture. In keeping with the DIY principle, disruption is a device that is accessible to everyone, to be used in the moment, and is both simple and profoundly sophisticated in its philosophical basis.

Dominic Thackray

Dominic was born during the Summer of Love in occupied West Germany, the son of a priest. The family moved back to England just as the Red Army Faction's campaign was getting interesting and he grew up in a cul-de-sac (French: arse of the bag) in a small town about 50 miles from London.

After a series of low-rent jobs he went on to study typographic design at the London College of Printing and has worked fairly consistently as a quite excellent graphic designer since the closing stages of the 20th century. His book My Tsunami of Euphoria, *a slim volume, was published by Exitstencil Press in 2011 and* Mr Cunty *in London 2012, even slimmer, was released by Arigâteau Press the following year. He remains a big fan of the work of Ulrike Meinhof.*

Some of the people that we have spoken to have talked about certain -isms (existentialism, buddhism etc) that have influenced their thinking. Do you have any?

Er, not really. Or maybe I mean yes. Probably I mean yes. When I was around 14 I was turned on to thinking about anarchist thought, mostly that would be down to Crass of course, who were quite serious about it, but also because of some of the lighter currents among the subculture that were interesting to me in those days. I thought the Situationists were really exciting, the visual stuff was thrilling even if the texts were a little bit impenetrable. I tried to read *Das Kapital* when I was 15 but gave up due to a sort of emerging attention deficit and a lack of revolutionary economic grammar. I became interested in some of the Existentialists around that time too, which probably started with having to read Camus for French A level. I liked their world view; their stuff was a bit of a treat to read, it made sense and helped as a sort of way to deal with a harsh world. I think all good people, of whatever stripe, are good Existentialists at root. That's not a value judgment, Existentialism basically precedes essence and whatnot.

When I first went out into the big wide world, around 17 or 18, I thought I self-identified as an anarchist, but the only anarchists I met were wankers, or grumpy auld men who wouldn't talk to you unless you bought their book. But I fell in with some groovy communists who were doing top dollar stuff including running the non-stop anti-apartheid picket of the South African Embassy in London's Trafalgar Square in the mid to late 1980s. And that was that for a few years. And then 1989 happened and things went a bit weird on several fronts. It turned out that the Soviet Union was in a bit of a mess here and there, and sweet Nicolai Ceausescu had been something of a buffoon all along, the de facto Gary Glitter of the socialist countries. And Dee Dee left the Ramones. It was a terrible year really.

<u>What were the ideas in punk that attracted you? Do you identify as a punk?</u>

My dear auld dad used to take the *Sunday Times*. One time the colour supplement had a pic of some teenage punks at a 'punk ball' on the front cover and a titillating sort of exposé within. This must have been around 1977 I think, I would have been 10. I've never seen or heard the words 'punk ball' used in any context anywhere since, but I remember the outrage among my parents and their friends, especially since there was a sort of implicit suggestion that punk meant gay and that the collapse of the auld world was just around the corner.

I used to draw punky rockers after that, all haircuts and earrings and goofy sneers, this sort of thing. You know that cliché about how there's always one really kind and super teacher among all the mediocre ones. Well it's sort of true. My art teacher, Mrs Metcalfe, was really enthusiastic about my drawings. She talked to me about the Surrealists and got me to do a Surrealist painting, which she entered in a national competition. Thing is I liked the stuff, especially Giorgio de Chirico and his discarded banana skins in deserted railway stations, all this business, but I didn't necessarily get it. My surrealist painting was quite rubbish and it didn't get placed but none of that dampened her enthusiasm. Mrs Metcalfe was the first bohemian I ever met and a couple of years ago I became virtually reacquainted with her through her son Hugh Metcalfe (who runs the notorious Klinker club), a towering heavyweight genius avant-gardist absurdist performer/filmmaker friend and collaborator of Penny Rimbaud's. It's a funny auld world.

Do I identify as punk? I don't think so. I'm well on the way to 50. I'm a parent. I'm s'posed to be a graphic designer. I kind of hate all kinds of musique, I mean kind of. I still like the Ramones of course but what can you do, and Hard Skin are brill. Jello is still very wonderful and I liked that Jeffrey Lewis album of Crass songs a lot. I went to see Kid Congo a couple of months ago. That was life-affirmingly good. It sort of turned into a bit of a 24-hour bender, which in turn was more or less followed by a week of recovering with doughnuts so, you know, is that punk?

<u>How have those ideas informed the way you have chosen to live your life?</u>

Oh I don't know. A bit I s'pose. I moved to Paris for a couple of years in the mid-1990s where I worked as a receptionist in a shitty, zero-star hotel in the Rue de Buci on the Left Bank. I really liked it there. I was kind of a bit touched to see there was somehow still a lot of love for Johnny Thunders in Paris, among all the indie record stores and those kinds of places I mean, I don't know if there still is, this was a while ago after all. I'm still working on getting through those Situationist texts. I thought Debord's *Comments on the Society of the Spectacle* was a much more rewarding read than *Society of the Spectacle* and Raoul Vaneigem's *Revolution of Everyday Life* turned out to be totally ace – "You wanna fuck with us? Not for long!"

Oh actually I've just remembered a bunch of stuff which maybe answers the question better. I took some photos of Dee Dee Ramone when he released his autobiography *Poison Heart* in 1997. I used them for a college project that got a terrible mark, which maybe should have been obvious enough if you're building a project around photography when you're s'posed to be studying typography. I wrote my BA dissertation about Dee Dee and it got a better mark. Later, when Dee Dee died, *The Times* took one of my photographs for their obituary and *The New York Times* took another for their website. It was very sad that Dee Dee died, but I was pleased that my photos were used in the way they were.

And I made a new typeface for subtitling Lech Kowalski's Johnny Thunders biopic *Born to Lose – The Last Rock & Roll Movie* and his Dee Dee Ramone memoir *Hey Is Dee Dee Home*. That was kind of fun, in a way I mean, I mean we type nerds are not the sort of people who need to have a good time in order to have a good time.

Lech was exhibiting D.O.A at the BFI's *Never Mind The Jubilee* film festival in I think Summer 2002. Dee Dee had just died and so we put together a short 10-minute tribute, made up of his footage for the Thunders movie, for the festival. It was called *Gabba Gabba Dee Dee Ramone*, which was coincidentally the same title as my BA dissertation. The former personnel of the mighty Crass were at the same festival, doing an all-day event of films and performances which was, as you can imagine, pretty terrific. The lady who was organising the festival asked me to write it up for the BFI website so I got to meet Penny and Gee and some of the others in the Green Room afterwards.

I was working at the time for another, much grungier film festival and we arranged with Penny and Gee to do a slimmer version of the BFI event at Raindance later in the year. And we went on to become friends and collaborate here and there, with Gee on festival posters and what have you, and Penny took a role in my super-awesome-yet-mildly-flawed 2006 short film *Girlfriend in a Kimono*. I separated from my wife earlier this year and I'm currently living with them at Dial House in the Essex countryside so yes, on reflection, that brief period we called Punque Roque did go on to inform my life in some or many respects.

What gets in the way of living your life in the way you choose?

The perpetual crises of capitalism don't help. Turns out capitalism is just one great pyramid-shaped Ponzi scheme, made out of raw sewage and with full trickle-down effect, who knew? And at the present moment Israel is fully engaged in a murderous assault on the people they've kettled into the concrete and desert hell-hole of Gaza. I'm not sure that liberals in Bromley, Croydon and Dorking, engaged in a process of scoffing luxury-length quinoa vol-au-vents while constantly resharing memey graphics on the internet of Palestinian children and Israeli children holding hands like so much harmony on a piano keyboard made out of two different materials in a Paul McCartney song helps anybody very much, except to keep things ticking over on the business-as-usual front. I'm probably not answering the question properly.

What has changed in your beliefs over the years?

I don't think I know how to answer this in a fully formed grown-up way. I don't think any of us were ever wrong about how we saw capitalism or imperialism or the nature of the State. I mean I don't think so, even if we sometimes had our doubts about what we were doing from time to time. We were probably wrong about some of the bands, I mean who can explain the enormous popularity of, say, GBH in America?

What difficulties have you encountered in enacting your beliefs?

Oh you know, the usual, cops, roughnecks, lawyers, dentists, architects, local government bureaucrats, corporate types, all manner of filth really.

Some of the fans seem to have a very rigid idea of how 'punks' should act and can be quite hostile to anything that they see as going against those values. What are your views about this aspect of the punk scene?

Yes, I think it's kind of embarrassing, that stuff. But it sort of depends. There's aspects of it which are very lovely of course, young and not-so-young people getting dressed up, dropping out, dropping in, not participating in the status quo, rejecting the Liberal-Fascist Complex, all this kind of business. That's proper nice. When folk get all sanctimonious about it then it becomes less interesting. Straight Edge, for example, was kind of painful.

Have these ideas brought you contentment in your life?

Yes and no, probably in equal measure, so that's kind of a result, isn't it?

Dominic Thackray

Mark Stewart

Mark Stewart is a sonic trouble-maker and cultural agitator who first came to prominence as a member of the Pop Group, formed in 1977, making powerful and confrontational music that traversed punk, dub, funk and jazz. Mark felt the call to action of punk, but was not inspired by the artistic limitations that he saw in the music of that scene.

He has stated that his intention with the Pop Group was to form a funk band, but the resulting fusion of intensely political and uncompromising lyrical content with disruptive and genre-busting music was to prove powerfully influential. They released their debut She is Beyond Good and Evil *with Radar Records in 1979, but they were signed to Rough Trade by the time of their most well-known single,* We are all Prostitutes *released in the same year.*

After the demise of the Pop Group in 1980, Mark embarked upon a series of collaborations with like-minded musical pioneers such as Tricky, Trent Reznor, Keith Levene and Lee 'Scratch' Perry. One of his most enduring creative partnerships has been with Adrian Sherwood of On-U Sound, working together as Mark Stewart and the Maffia with a loose collective of musical artists. In 2010 Mark reformed the Pop Group stating that the world was probably more fucked up than when they had first formed, and they were definitely fucked off.

He continues to work on solo music projects and in 2012 released The Politics of Envy *and its dub version* The Exorcism of Envy. *In 2013 he collaborated with visual artist Rupert Goldsworthy to produce the installation piece* I Am the Law.

In Bristol, we were going to funk clubs, and doing this really heavy weird kind of funk dancing and going to funk gigs, like War and Fatback Band and George Clinton. And suddenly, I think it was in *Sounds* we saw this little tiny picture of these London kids, and they had the same clothes on that we had, and so we immediately felt part of the same thing. Years later you end up meeting some of these people – Doug from the Mary Chain for example, Bobby Gillespie and Ian Curtis – and you're talking to these people, and you're finding out that in a tiny suburban part of Manchester or a tiny part of Glasgow, there'd be three or four kids that'd be walking around with *Metallic KO* by Iggy, or getting into the New York Dolls or whatever and it was in complete isolation, but they were all doing it of their own volition. But then of course when the Pistols started coming up everybody thought, "Oh, right, this is it!" And when we saw Paul Simonon from the Clash, with Letraset stickers on his bass – that act was an enabling act. It made us realise that we could pick something up – a weapon – and do something as a means of volition.

Engaging with the machine   We had this idea of an explosion. It was a Situationist idea that the Pop Group used, of an explosion in the heart of the commodity. It was Malcolm McLaren's idea of engaging with the military industrial complex that helped make it happen. Our view is that if you're separatist and not engaging, it's kind of like vanity publishing. For example, I was having this conversation with some really hard-core German punk band mates of mine who wouldn't use any kind of social media. But it's with these very ideas that we have to engage with what you call the machine. What I'm finding quite interesting is what I call sleeping agents – the kind of people who are sympatico inside the machine. Matt Groening is really cool. There are people way up in Sony Film like this too. So it's not really 'them' and 'us'.

But with some English punks they stay back and think it's not punk to get involved. You have to engage to make an effect, otherwise it's just *The X Factor* people that are going to be seen. If the New York Dolls hadn't signed to Mercury and Malcolm McLaren hadn't used all those shock tactics in what we call the Murdoch media now, I wouldn't have seen it. So I wouldn't have been changed. You have to break the narrative, and provide an antidote.

There's constant questioning in my head. It's like an art provocation or something. "Who do you think you are to say that?" It's like my research into history and politics; if you keep on digging and questioning and question why and who you are, then you start to understand who you are. It's like conspiracy theories. If you look at the extreme right and the extreme left, and the economic terms, you start to encounter the same names. You can start to get something. The funny thing is though that you've got to engage somehow.

For me, the point of punk was about this idea of deference. Before punk, for boys and girls it was this deference of somebody's-better-than-you-because-their-family's-got-money. But the whole thing is breaking down. And the world can change in the moment. The old elites are constantly being threatened, and replaced, and the people who the people think are in control are puppets. For some reason I find myself moving in these spheres.

In Rough Trade wearing an army helmet   Morality was the point of punk – because it's an immoral world. We wouldn't sign to EMI because they were arms dealers. We found out Warner Brothers were arms dealers. I mean there is that moral imperative. At the end of the Pop Group I thought music was a complete and utter waste of time. I thought it was immoral, I thought it was decadent. John Pilger was exposing all this stuff in Cambodia, I'd just met this Situationist guy and I'd just made this album called *For How Much Longer Do We Tolerate Mass Murder?* and I'd just got to this stage where I thought it's all a bit wank, and I wanted to actually go out in the field and do something.

So I went and volunteered. I was there in Rough Trade with a bloody army helmet on because we thought there was going to be another world war breaking out. Well, I did, although nobody else seemed to, in the music business anyway. We ended up as 500,000 people. There was a massive march – a CND march. Crass were coming down through Downing Street, I was there with Tony Benn and the head of the Metropolitan Police, Paul Condon. It was the last ever Pop Group gig, and the beginning of Mark Stewart and the Maffia.

Moral weight loss plan   And I know this sounds like hippy bollocks, but you've got one life and it's good to sort yourself out, and we've got this whole aspirational shit that we've got round us about wanting the prettiest girlfriend, the prettiest boyfriend, objects, possessions, and stuff. And you can get locked into that. So many of my mates got locked in this thing and it's so easy just to give up, and go and work in the call centre. But if you've got a spark in you it makes you feel even more alive. Knowledge is a nutrient. It gives a lot back. It's good for you. I've got no intention of preaching my morality to you. But after this 'morality weight loss plan' I do feel a lot better. It's the end of the game if I know who I am. I think part of the thing for me is that I've got to really really throw a dirty dice and play the blind card against myself to stop, to keep clean. I've got to twist.

If I am ever forced to look at what I do from a distance, then what I like being is part of a community. I find it quite hard to maintain a big community of people around me because I'm travelling so much. I'm used to having a load of mates in Bristol, and we're all having parties and going to pubs and working together. Or somebody's helping doing up somebody's squat or house or whatever. It's that whole thing that you can sit back and somebody else carries the party. And we take turns carrying the energy. And around the world, there's a dialogue, and you're kind of comrades. That's what I get from music. I get this feeling, even from free jazz, that there's someone who's feeling this dissonance. So it makes you feel that you're not mad. Because a lot of people around the world will try and convince you that you're mad. I mean, the other day my mum said to me, we were talking about how this Polish guy I know was making really good money building, and he was going to re-train as a plumber. And she was, "I've always told you to get a trade. Why don't you do that?" Still! I just do music as a hobby – still!

The future is there to be built. It's a blank canvas. It's a place to dream into. And anybody can make tomorrow. Tomorrow is open. We're not trundling down a dark tunnel created by these people who think they run something when in fact they're owned by somebody else. And the people that actually own it want change as well. And the imagineers (or whatever I call them) are really interested in maverick people with crazy ideas because that's how they can get stuff catalysed. Your morals come with the making the things. Like if you're making a piece of wood – it's a Taoist thing. In making the thing you start the process.

It only takes good people to do nothing for evil to prevail   I think what Alan Watts did in the 60s, relating to Zen and the haikus are crucial. But I'm sick and tired of new age bollocks with people going off into some fucking new-age healing selfish kind of thing. They're putting all the energies that could, for example, help some cooperative in Palestine, into pilates or healing flowers or something. There's a selfish new-age righteousness that is coming with money. And with digital media everyone's zoning out to their own worlds. I think Macintosh is a new kind of hierarchy. Capitalism is the most barbaric of all religions. I mean everybody is becoming addicted to getting the latest kit. And they're doing shitty jobs just to fund a fucking Macintosh. And nothing is fast enough. But that's cost you two grand. We're becoming digital slaves. We're becoming enslaved, and the people in those awful Chinese places are suffering, and you know that's the reality.

It only takes good people to do nothing for evil to prevail. And this is what happens if people want to be in their digital 21st century bubbles – being responsible for awful regimes around the world. I've heard that the war in Afghanistan is over lithium for mobile phone batteries. It's all completely connected, it's all completely simple. China runs the world. But, what I've learnt is it's not 'them' and 'us'. We're all the same, even the richest kid in some awful family that's done war crimes or whatever can be a really cool kid.

Career opportunities   What a lot of my friends got from punk was the conviction not to go in as infantry. There's this saying that I've got; there is the arrogance of power, but we had the power of arrogance. Which means you just walk into a room, push the doors open, even if it's full of bankers or whatever, and you're as good as anybody else. So immediately you can break those class ceilings, those sexual ceilings. And with that confidence it's like a racehorse. People can see that confidence. It's like a glow around you. They can see that aura, and sometimes it's invincible.

And with those ripples around the world, people have become enabled by punk and are now in fact running cool companies, they're working in prisons, they've got energy that goes throughout but they're not necessarily musicians. It's like with the Clash's song *Career Opportunities* – that took the lid off what we thought we had to be, or who we were. Or how we were kept down.

Punk changed all of that.

Jello Biafra

Taking his stage name from the war-ravaged African state then called Biafra and appending the name of a popular dessert, Jello Biafra formed the notorious US west coast punk band Dead Kennedys. In 1979, a year before the release of the band's iconic album Fresh Fruit for Rotting Vegetables, *Jello ran for mayor of San Francisco with a provocative platform that included holding auctions for high-ranking government positions.*

The Kennedys' first album suffered distribution problems owing to the band's name, and later in 1981 they encountered a similar fate when they included, in their album Frankenchrist, *artwork by H.R. Giger depicting a penis landscape. The band and label were prosecuted under California obscenity statutes for distributing "harmful matter to minors" although the trial concluded with a hung jury. This marked one of many instances when the work of Jello and the band was the subject of controversy and attacks from Middle America.*

The Dead Kennedys released five studio albums before disbanding in 1986, after which Jello used his skills in oratory and method acting, to deliver scathing and politically potent spoken word lectures across America. Jello engaged in frequent collaborations with other artists, such as the Lard project with Ministry's Al Jourgensen and Paul Barker (1988), and the D.O.A.-backed Last Scream of the Missing Neighbors *(1990). Numerous collaborations of this sort continued for the next two decades up until the formation of Jello Biafra and the Guantanamo School of Medicine, which saw the release of their album* The Audacity of Hype *in 2009 and the acclaimed* White People and the Damage Done *in 2013.*

From an early age I was a very engaged newshound; I saw [*Lee Harvey*] Oswald get shot live in the living room, I saw the Berlin Wall go up and the civil rights demonstrations, and the Vietnam war, and many other things. Luckily I had parents who were not quite as extreme as I am. However, I guess you could call them radical for their age group, as they chose not to hide reality from their children. So, in other words, if bloody race riots came on the TV news, which came on right after the cartoons, I was able to watch both with equal fascination. I guess my favourite cartoon characters were Bullwinkle the moose and Senator Everett Dirksen [*smiles*], and we're talking mid 60s by this time when I was six or seven years old. My parents explained it all to me and they tried to engage with us about what was going on rather than change the channel so as not to 'upset the kids'. It means that I missed out on some really awful TV shows that people around me still quote to this day. But I think I was very fortunate in terms of both what I was exposed to and what I chose to expose myself to and this fed in to the method acting training I had later in middle and high school.

I'm really grateful for, maybe the conscious side of the 60s and the cool, wild shit that went on. This is a much deeper, tangible memory for me, than it seems to be for a lot of other people my age. As soon as I heard the wilder side of rock'n'roll that my father accidentally blundered into on a radio station, when I was about seven years old, I was HOOKED! And I knew "THIS IS WHAT I WANT!" And I gravitated to early Rolling Stones-type stuff as opposed to the Beatles. I was just about the first kid in my elementary school to have long hair and kind of paid for that [*mimes a fist going into his face*].

The same feeling came back when, in a fit of what I guess you'd call inspiration, I cranked the Sex Pistols up with my door wide open to annoy the entire floor of my college dormitory and I then took out my scissors and cut off all my hair and put it in a bag and nailed it to the door, and suddenly people were scared of me, and disturbed by what they saw and I thought, "Wow! This is just like having long hair in the sixth grade." And of course it wasn't all about fashion to me because I had come through the 60s and I remembered the SDS [*Students for a Democratic Society*] when attempts were made to throw them off the Colorado University campus. And in Boulder, where I grew up, my parents kicked Coors beer out of the house because of Joe Cruise's political views and because of all the nasty people that Coors have funded to this day. So that was kind of ingrained.

Police riot   My dad was a psychiatric social worker and was eventually going across the western United States into ghettos, and what were called the Indian Reservations at that time, and, as he put it, teaching people how to teach. And he set up social work and continuing education organisations of their own... And I didn't realise until I did his eulogy last Fall that my father was an unwitting participant in the civil rights movement. You know, we fought so much when I was a kid that I didn't really appreciate it. I remember him coming home and talking about the LAPD putting a sawn off shotgun in his belly which was in reaction to the anti-Vietnam protests... this was when protesters burned down a Bank of America in Santa Barbara. The next day, the LAPD came up and basically ran wild in the town. I heard the term 'police riot' from my father of all people.

I realised at age 10 or 11 that the smiling storybook policeman was just a storybook, and had nothing to do with how the Chicago police were behaving at the Democratic Convention in '68. So I always had that fire in me, and as soon as I realised the role of giant corporations in all of this, I wasn't very into them, either [*smiles*]. And I had realised that even before punk started that the really wild sides of rock'n'roll and 60s culture had been systematically dumbed down by the music industry itself by the mid-70s, and so it was like [*using gentle voice*], "Now it's time for soft rock, for adult rock. Now we're all going to listen to the Eagles and FM DJs, the new Scientology Jazz fusion album..." And that kind of thing made me MAD!

I'd already unplugged from commercial radio in eighth grade when I bought the Blue Öyster Cult album *Tyranny and Mutation* on a hunch that it would be cool, and it became my favourite album for a year or two. And then the rock critic of the big local Denver paper, *The Denver Post*, wrote a review of Alice Cooper who I really liked, and it was like we finally got rock'n'roll with interesting lyrics that shock people and I thought, "I like this!" And I still believe in shock value in a very big way and he wrote how bad it was, saying, "If he wanted to, he could write pretty ballads" [*does mocking voice*]. So then a little while later another review comes up entitled "Black Sabbath is almost as bad as the MC5," so I started looking for MC5 albums the next day and I lucked out. And that opened up a whole new world with *Kick Out the Jams*, the Stooges and so on. It felt a bit lonely being the only person into this while my friends were into prog rock, Emmerson Lake and Palmer and the worse band ever – Yes! And then Alex Harvey, of all people, said in an interview that people were getting too secure and too into arena rock, and getting away from the audience and he said that some day soon there were going to be some young people that would kick down the door and replace them. Little did I know that was about to happen.

Gabba Gabba Hey!   I guess it's going to be traced back to the Ramones here [*in the US*]. The Ramones record was available long before there was a Pistols record, and so I'd go to the store and [*mimes looking at a Ramones record sleeve*], "So who's this here? They don't look like some kiss ass wimpy band so lets bring this home." And at first I thought it rocked but it was FUNNY. "Look at how short these songs are, and there are no guitar solos on them, and beat on the brat with a baseball bat, what IS THIS?" [*laughs*]. And I'd play it to my pothead friends before we'd trip out on Krautrock and we'd all laugh. And then the Ramones came to Denver and those of us who knew who they were lined the front row. And this was back in the day when nobody danced at shows – you weren't allowed to. You HAD to sit down. And so out come these four degenerate looking guys in leather jackets and when you heard a chord on Johnny's guitar you knew it was going to be louder than you were prepared for. And THEY WERE GREAT. And at least half the fun was turning around and looking at the country, rock and jazz-fusion glitterati with their feather hair and their shades and their corduroy jackets with patches on the elbows and the women with 20s hairdos with a flower because Joni Mitchell did that, and they were HORRIFIED. With them going, "No, no, no" and me going [*rubs hands together*] "Yes, yes, yes."

Hey CAN'T HAVE ME! And that means WATCH WHERE YOU SPEND YOUR MONEY

i'm not going to cooperate with corporations anymore,

An act of insurrection! And the people that got it thought, "Wow! This is so powerful, and it's so simple, that even I could do it! I SHOULD do it." And out of that one Ramones show came Dead Kennedys, Don Fleming, Velvet Monkeys, Gumball, the Wax Trax label, the Ravers, the Nails, the SST bands. Al Jourgensen from Ministry said he was there too. And the Ramones were doing that all over the country, planting those kinds of seeds. And even though the Ramones said that they weren't a political band and of course Johnny became more and more far right conservative as he went on — even writing a letter objecting to what I was doing [*laughs*] — to me, in a way, it was political because it was such an act of insurrection. Both in terms of simplifying the music so that anyone could play it, which brought back that all-important spirit of rock'n'roll that the major labels were trying to stamp out once again, but also the lyrics of the Ramones, even if they weren't directly political they were TOPICAL in a way that was JUST NOT DONE. Such as trying to turn a trick at *53rd & 3rd*. Or *Commando* when hardly anybody was talking about Vietnam even as a humorous aside. To me that was political, topical or at least interesting and it established that 'tradition' of topical lyrics and the idea that you can do it with rock'n'roll and make it interesting. And the idea that you could use humour to make a point as well, which the Ramones were very very good at [*laughs*].

Saying the unsayable When punk came in, suddenly, I wasn't born too late, I was born at the perfect time, and it was a blank canvas. And the political side came back in when I came to California and the first real, authentic punk rocker that I met in San Francisco was Will Shatter who would later be in Negative Trend and Flipper… and punk was very topical. Within weeks of a mass shooting involving gangs in a Chinese restaurant in San Francisco, out came the song *Chinese Gang Wars* by the Nuns. So we had bands singing about things other than endless boring love songs, which I never related to. I thought they were stupid when I was seven, and when I was 17 I realised how much they lied about how real human and romantic interaction actually happens, either everything will be solved by falling in love or the sex, drugs and rock'n'roll version, and both of them were totally bogus to teenage me, and they still are. Punk again was a whole blank canvas of what you could write about and how you could do it, and the more twisted and sick-humour orientated it was, the better, at least on the American end. And you got some of that in England too like *Gary Gilmore's Eyes* [*laughs*]. Nobody would have put out a song like that one or two years earlier.

Painting a target on your back One of the songs I wrote for the Dead Kennedys, which I wrote in about 20 minutes, and it was just done, was *Nazi Punks Fuck Off*. And at the time it was aimed against people that I thought were acting like a bunch of fucking Nazis who would jump on the stage, run, dive, hit somebody on the back of the head and run away. That was not what punk meant to me or what we wanted to happen at the shows. And sure enough somebody got on stage on the night we debuted it, wearing a "White Power Niggers Beware" T-shirt and a swastika. And he went on about how we were a bunch of commies and all the people in the room, which might have been some 600–800 people, saw what I was talking about. It also meant that some people who did have deeply racist or fascist beliefs felt violated about that song and in turn wanted to violate me and violate my band, and so there was a lot of tension there including dynamite going off in front of my house (which is another story). So that meant that being so overtly in your face, full on, radical and not subtle in my beliefs or vision in any way, well that caused trouble. When you get known there are two types of known people in this world: there are stars and there are targets, and on a kind of underground level I hit both simultaneously, and not everybody likes my personality anyway. And so there was always 'stuff' going on, and later on Dead Kennedys tours I never knew if someone would want to argue, if not want to fight me, either because I was too political or not political enough – no middle ground [*smiles*]. I mean it is a volatile kind of music, especially hardcore, and it brings out volatile people from all sides.

Taking punk ideals forward for regular people If you want to, one place you can start as an individual, without having to get your head cracked by the cops, or sit up all night with a bunch of 'more radical than thou' people talking about 9/11 conspiracies or anarchy, is to decide that, "I'm not going to cooperate with corporations anymore, they CAN'T HAVE ME!" And that means WATCH WHERE YOU SPEND YOUR MONEY. And try to give them as little as is humanly possible – no chain stores, no chain restaurants, spend your money with local businesses so it keeps the money in the community. It's a start. And it's really easy to spread that message without preaching at people and coming across like an anti-abortion zealot or a militant übervegan who turns people off vegetarianism or whatever. And I tell people I haven't eaten in McDonalds for over 35 years. So how hard is that? And this is like drugs or tattoos, the more you do it, the more you want to go further.

And then we can encourage people not to work for corporations, but if you do, the digital age ushers in a whole new frontier of sabotage on the job [*smiles*]. I always try to appeal to that inner prankster and stuff. You're supposed to outgrow that after about age 13, but I never did.

John Robb

Blackpool in 1977 may not have exactly been a hotbed of UK musical talent but that didn't deter John Robb. He was inspired by punk's DIY ethic and formed the Membranes, a post-punk outfit who went on to release six studio albums before going their separate ways in 1990. Four years later, he unleashed Goldblade, who quickly became a fixture on the live circuit with their "punk rock hooligan blues."

John has also written several books including, Punk Rock: An Oral History, and has worked as a journalist for numerous publications, including Sounds, NME and The Sunday Times.

In 2011, he launched an online music and pop culture blog called Louder Than War, and later that same year he won the UK Association of Independent Music 'Indie Champion' award. He also set up Louder Than War Records, with the aim of releasing new music from up-and-coming bands.

I was into music before I was into punk – such as glam rock in the 70s. And you'd watch it on *Top of the Pops*, but it just felt unattainable. It was either made in London – and I lived in Blackpool so London could have been as far away as New York – and you never went there, or in the case of David Bowie it could have been outer space. It was that unreachable. You really wanted to get involved, but you couldn't because you were a nerd in a small town that nobody cared about.

When punk started it was really exciting because anything that takes on the establishment in music is exciting. There were a lot of strands and messages, really early on, which we connected with. Even though we were 14, 15 or 16, we did have a sense that things weren't quite right in the world. Punk addressed a lot of those issues. The generation demanded punk and punk came. I don't think that punk drove those people because they already felt like that – it was a rallying point.

There was a sense when you were growing up that the 60s was a period of idealism, and that you had missed out on something. The Pistols came along and everyone loved them because they were an exciting rock'n'roll band. They opened the door for everyone. You saw a picture of Johnny Rotten before you heard them and you just knew what the band sounded like. The clothes looked amazing. After the shapeless denim of the 70s everything was tight and linear. The hair looked amazing. I know every footballer in the world has spiky hair now, but in 1976 spiky hair was a powerful image.

Make Your Own Culture   In the whole of Blackpool there were probably only 50 punks. It was pretty heavy being a punk and it wasn't really a mass movement

− more of a cult. You couldn't really get the records either. The one that really blew our mind was Buzzcocks' *Spiral Scratch*. Someone had brought it into school and it was so obviously home-made. You'd never seen a record like it. And that was quite inspiring, that you could make your own records. I'd never thought of that before, and for me that was one of the most revolutionary things that came out of punk. More than anything, it empowered you to create your own culture. That was a key thing. Whereas before we just received culture or bought into it, now you could make your own.

I know it's a cliché and everyone says that, but to hear that you don't have to be a virtuoso and that anyone could be in a band is an amazing thing to hear when you are 14. We got the fanzine *Sniffin' Glue* so we saw how you could make your own media too. It was a really creative time and everybody was interpreting a narrow template in their own ways. It's like the big bang when the whole universe just scatters all over the place and you get completely different versions of stars and black holes etc. For my part of my generation, punk was a cultural big bang.

It's funny how punk has percolated culturally, it's like everywhere and nowhere. You won't see a punk anywhere unless you go to a punk festival, but punk attitude is everywhere you look. It doesn't matter if you ended up a plumber. For me there should be no snobbery in this. If you've still got the punk attitude then it's still in there. It's still in your eyes.

A broad church   You need systems. If you've got millions of people, you've got to organise it somehow. Even people who tried to live outside the system were inside it in the old days. As soon as you pressed a record, you were pressing it on vinyl, which comes from oil. So you were still buying into the system. You know Apple pay shitty wages to people in China, but none of my friends can make mobile phones. But, there are a lot of things you won't buy into and there are great things that came out of punk for me personally. For instance I'm a vegetarian, which is not a big deal, but it is personally important to me. I still adhere to all those political ideals. A lot of old punks have become MPs and that creates a space for a certain type of debate.

I've got a few personal 'isms' (like pacifism and veganism). But I hate it when people say, "Oh, you're going to tell us what to eat now." I'm not going to do that, I don't think I'm better than you. It just makes sense to me; this is my way of dealing with the world. Whereas eating steak may be your thing; I don't really give a fuck about what you do. It's not like it's some sort of 'ism' contest. Anarchism is very hard to define; it's Greek for 'chaos' [*laughs*]. I think the idea of finding a way to determine how you will live your life is good.

There's a very caring element in punk. It's amazing how many became social workers or worked in drug rehabilitation. A lot of people went in the direction of service careers, because not everyone can play music. It was a different time in 1976 and it was a lot easier then because you could go on the dole. You can't do that now because you are a "scrounger". It's all that language of hate we hear these days. You're a scrounger if you don't want to do a job for half the money you would have earned a year ago. They're not scroungers, they're just proud and they don't want to do a shit job for shit money. And the money they are taking out of the system is pretty miniscule compared to the amount the banks have taken out recently. [*laughs*]

Feminism in punk   Punk fractured the pop template of four lads against the world, with the women that there were. Poly Styrene was an amazing woman, and the Slits were hugely influential on us. We wanted to hang around with strong, tough, intelligent, scary looking women. We weren't interested in the dolly birds down the rugby club. Punk did challenge, to a certain extent, the stereotypes of the strong male warrior and the weak woman needing to be rescued. I found the female musicians really inspiring and how the Slits talked about feminine rhythms in the music. They weren't confined to being singers either. They could get involved in the music making process. They showed that you didn't have to act sexy to be in a band. You could if you wanted to, but you didn't have to. It was a redefinition of the roles in pop music. And I don't have a problem with artists getting a payday. In the 70s people paid to go to gigs and bought the records. Now they blag into gigs and nick the music off the Internet. They can't expect you to create this stuff and just starve. You can't make art out of thin air. Stuff's got to come from somewhere. You need the money to make the art. As an artist you'll do anything to make your art exist as you hear it in your head.

Ideas in Flux   Punk tore a hole in the fabric and all these people and ideas got through. Without it our lives would have been very mundane. We liked the fact that there were these people who were a lot older than us who were being affected by it as well. Punk should be for everybody. We liked the fact that Joe Strummer had been to public school and threw it all away to be in a punk rock band and sing songs that made sense to everybody. They want you all split up, but when the kids from the estates with all the great ideas are getting access to the system through the money and the contacts of the kids with the posher education, that's when it gets dangerous. It's the flux of ideas with people from different backgrounds that creates an interesting space.

Tony Drayton

To create a voice for London's exploding punk scene, Tony Drayton launched <u>Ripped and Torn</u> fanzine in October 1976 and it ran for 18 issues until he quit in 1979. Living in a squat and short of cash, he scraped together £6 for a typewriter in a second-hand shop and thus a new fanzine, <u>Kill Your Pet Puppy</u>, was born. It ran for six issues between 1979 and 1984 through a period that saw the birth of anarcho-punk and the rumblings of a goth subculture. Groups featured in <u>KYPP</u> included Adam and the Ants, Crass, Bauhaus, Southern Death Cult, the Mob and Sex Gang Children.

<u>KYPP</u> was written and designed in an 'anarcho-situationist' style by a fluctuating group of around 12 members of the so-called Puppy Collective and they could sell up to 1,000 copies of the fanzine in one day at the right event. Tony was also heavily involved in the Centro Iberico Anarchist Centre and another venue, the Batcave, that opened in 1982 in Soho. After <u>KYPP</u>, Tony wrote a few pieces for <u>Sounds</u> and <u>NME</u>.

For much of this time Tony was a highly successful and sought after fire-eater and juggler, touring around much of Europe.

I was living in Cumbernauld, a satellite town of Glasgow, and left school at 16 in 1974 and I was really getting into music at the time. David Bowie had his *Aladdin Sane* album out, and there were Mott the Hoople, Roxy Music, Sparks and all the bands that eventually became glam. I think with David Bowie especially, he was introducing people to Lou Reed, the Velvet Underground and the New York Dolls and that was the natural route through to all that side of things. And then American punk was coming through. The Patti Smith album was being written about a lot and I was buying the music papers every week and hating my life.

I was commuting between Cumbernauld and Glasgow and these music papers were my life. I was really aware of everything that was happening. And then when I got the Patti Smith album and the Ramones, it was even better than they wrote about. So I was a punk straightaway. When I first heard there was this British punk thing I thought, "I'm part of it, I don't understand what it is yet, but I'm with it." I went down to London in 1976 and saw the Damned play at The Hope and Anchor and I came back and wrote the first *Ripped and Torn* on the back of that. It was so powerful. I wasn't a musician, so I couldn't express my thoughts and feeling into music, but I was quite good at writing so I wrote the first issue of *Ripped and Torn* quite quickly. I was going from the whole spirit of punk thing to actually being part of the movement. I made 10 copies on the work photocopier and sent them out to Rough Trade and Compendium. They both ordered 200 copies and that was the beginning of a whole new adventure.

By March 1977 I'd moved down to London. I was even more a part of it and that summer of '77 to me was absolutely magical. At that point people were saying that punk's dead. The Sex Pistols had split up and the Clash were playing big venues and the original crowd were dropping out. But actually it was an incredible time. There were lots of free gigs and I saw bands like the Lurkers, 999, Adam and the Ants and X-Ray Spex — the amount of bands I saw that summer was amazing. The fun we had that summer was sensational. THAT was the summer of punk, not just the summer before [*laughs*].

Squatting in London   Some of the people at Rough Trade were living in a squat in Frestonia which was a big squatted area of West London. From there, I moved to another squat in Covent Garden, which was all warehouses. You see, at that time in London everything was so run down. It's hard to remember that areas like Covent Garden, where the Roxy was, were derelict and all around there were boarded-up buildings and hoardings. And so we quite easily moved into this great big block of houses. Nowadays, if you see it as you come out of the Covent Garden tube station you can't believe that the whole area was squatted. Covent Garden Market itself was closed down and there were a couple of pubs there with entertainment in them and that was all there was. So there was a community of residents who still lived there.

My punk world was expanding from liking the music, to liking American music, to writing the fanzines. This lifestyle became more and more important to me. It wasn't being written about, there were no lines to it; we were making it up as we went along. This was new territory, and we thought we were pioneering.

In 1979, I went even further. I chucked everything in and got a bus to Paris. I met some punks in Paris and stayed there. We hitchhiked up to Brussels, then from there to Amsterdam and back down to Paris. And so the summer of '79 was quite sensational too. [*laughs*] I was definitely there for punk purposes, just seeing if you could live like this. I then came back to London and started squatting in a fire station. I seemed to have given up on houses. My first squat was a pub, the second a warehouse, then a fire station and then from a church to a hospital. [*laughs*]

Increasingly living on the outside of society   Around that time, people were asking me when I was going to start doing another fanzine, because I'd stopped doing *Ripped and Torn* when I went off at the beginning of the year. And then I started doing the *Kill Your Pet Puppy*. Joly of Better Badges said he would pay for the printing and I would just buy the ones I wanted at cost price, which covered the start-up costs. And he would print and sell as many as he wanted. And all that started up again in '80/81. And at that point I went abroad again; I thought the first trip wasn't long enough. And I went a long way out for a long time, six months. When I came back I put together the unfinished elements of the fanzine. I was beginning to put some things in about squatting and how-to-do-it guides for living the alternative lifestyle. That sort of stuff was coming in now that the Thatcher years were starting to bite. I had started living in houses at that time and got involved with housing co-operatives. They took us on as tenants and we became West Hampstead housing co-operative people. That was called Puppy Mansions Number One.

In anarcho-punk we felt we had really formed our own society and that it was going to last. We thought that we had broken away from normality and this was it. We'd done it! I was completely removed from society. All of that travelling and living in commercial buildings I really had little idea of the way that society operated. I had very little communication outside of the punk world. And that became even more so when I got involved with the Stonehenge festivals through Mark of the Møb and the other Wiltshire bands.

There were troupes of people there, who would play music, juggle and perform circus skills and they would go round Europe and Britain and do that, and they'd be staying on the 'outside'. Mark and the Puppies moved into a housing association house in Grosvenor Avenue and we started to develop these ideas of travelling and going off in a troupe on a big tour, which in the end was just me and my girlfriend. We went off to this juggling convention in Belgium and did that tour which took us to a circus festival in Spain, which was like Stonehenge relocated. From this little trip we ended up doing full-on tours, around Spain and Gibraltar, and back up to France. At that point I took ownership of a giant bus. We were living completely outside of society.

After that I had to come back to England to get a driving license and got back to Hackney and met up with some people I knew before. And so I squatted again. I started working in Covent Garden to make money while I got the driving license and I realised that I was making more in Covent Garden by myself than we were as a 20-strong troupe in Spain [*laughs*].

I got work performing at the premiere of *The Phantom of the Opera* which was another side of life that I'd never heard of. This was a world where you get paid £100 to juggle in the street before Princess Diana would show up. I thought, "I like the sound of that!" The guy who'd asked me was an agent and he said we could get more of these jobs and so Spain was drifting further and further away. I'd left the bus in Toulouse and I met this guy with a smaller bus. We decided to swap so he went down to get it and it had been squatted by punks! [*laughs*].

Getting a more regular life   The whole consumer society had passed me by;

I can't see the point of it, but I do have a mortgage. I went from being the chairman of the Mace housing co-operative to deciding that it was time to buy somewhere. We decided that we were going to have kids and if we were, we weren't going to have them where we could be evicted at any moment. And so I started to move into more regular employment by accident. I was still performing as a juggler and saw this job in the library working for the Electoral Services Department getting people to join the electoral roll and from that I was offered a permanent job. I'm happy where I am now [*working for the council with market traders*], I can cycle to work and speak frankly to my clients. So I will happily drift along here until something comes along to catapult me elsewhere. I think all that has come from not being afraid to try things, from leaving to come to London.

I think that the punk philosophy that is still with me today is not to be afraid to have a go; don't panic because it doesn't matter if it fails. I think that's something that I've brought with me. I'm not so sure about the sense of community now although I do have control of 300 traders at the market, for the council, so maybe that's my New Model Army now [*laughs*]. Perhaps I'll take them on a march down to Downing Street throwing their fruit. I suppose, though, the frankness and outspokenness of the traders and their individuality, reminds me of the punk spirit. They don't give a damn either.

It has made me happy to live my life this way. I would have been incredibly unhappy, maybe turned criminal, if I had been stuck in Scotland without a way out. Punk was a creative and productive avenue, I'm sure the other route would have been criminal. A lot of criminals are very clever, just bored. I've been quite lucky and I'm thankful that punk was there for me at the right time. I've never been sorry for anything that I've done in punk.

Construction

Perhaps the most commonly expressed feature of the punk movement, mentioned more often than disruption, or freedom – or even political activism – is the notion of Do It Yourself. The DIY message could not be clearer. It means that you do not need to wait for the permission to act. You do not need to have the required credentials or experience or education in order to take action. You do not even need to possess the resources, the money or the know-how to create something of value. You are enough within yourself, and what you practically need by way of help or assistance will come to you if you search for it. The DIY ethic though is not an idealistic or unrealistic fantasy, far from it in fact. It is a grounded approach to taking action and making a contribution, and it manifests in a variety of ways.

Educate Yourself   Very many punks might also be described as autodidacts, in that they take particular steps to self-educate and to discover for themselves how they will construct a view on the world and their role in it. This goes well beyond being a consumer of the news or regular channels of information, rather punk has often been about looking beneath the surface and seeking to understand, to a deeper level, the dynamics that are at play.

"As my English was limited I had no idea for example what *Alternative Ulster* [*by Stiff Little Fingers*] meant [*laughs*] so it was kind of meaningless. And I kept coming up on the words 'anarchy' and 'anarchism' in the Crass lyrics and I had no idea what it was. And so I was at the library each day, often many times a day... I had this thirst to know more... As a confirmation present I was given a book that I didn't think much of. It was the *Tao Te Ching* by Lao Tzu and it was from a relative. And I thought [*pulls face*]. But I was a compulsive reader and I would read anything. So I started reading the *Tao Te Ching* and it fascinated me. And I felt a resemblance between it and Crass, in relation to non-violence. And being a victim to constant violence that was something that interested me at the time... And later I read *The Bible*... and while I have great respect for many religious people, I couldn't honestly believe in God. But I can have a sensible conversation with religious people about *The Bible* and about God." **Jón Gnarr**

"You have to question things and look for the subtext and if you can't find out what's going on, at least find out more... Malcolm X, my hero, talked about the ability to change and make change. He studied philology in prison; he studied the dictionary. And doing that opens up the whole world to you. You have to search. I can't spell, and I'm going through the world with a 14-year-old's education, but I had people who said, 'No, I'm not going to fill out that form for you, you do it'... People made me go and chase things that I was entitled to because I was intimidated by it, and that was a punk thing, 'You do it and you do it now.'" **Little Annie**

Heal yourself A particularly interesting manifestation of the DIY concept is the idea that we do not always need to rely on the state or the established health system in order to treat ourselves for illness. And this refers not only to physical illness but also to areas of mental well-being. We also find, in areas of the punk community, alternative accounts of what constitutes mental and physical health and the philosophies sitting beneath treatment.

"I had cancer and I treated it through vibrational medicines and the help of a Chinese herbalist who also works on a vibrational level. That worked for me and I came out of it blessed. It might not work for other people and they'll find their own form of blessing. I do believe the old Yogic idea that we are what we eat, and if we eat pharmaceutical drugs that's what we are, in part. Our thinking is affected, our being is affected. On a molecular level we start acting differently within the molecular world. We become a different energetic force. That's a matter of where people want to be." **Penny Rimbaud**

"I strongly believe that we have a responsibility for each other and I don't want to go into it on a personal level, but I try and work with people that other people wouldn't work with. People might say, 'Why do you put up with that guy? Why do you work with junkies around you or whatever?' And it's because somebody needs to look out for these guys. They're great people and that's just something that they didn't wish upon themselves... in many ways we're all in need of hospital treatment but we could avoid that hospital treatment by being looked after in the community." **Mark Wilson**

Typically underpinning much of the DIY thinking behind self-treatment is a set of alternative doctrines related to health management, which might for example include herbal remedies or, as in the example of Penny Rimbaud, vibrational therapy. And in addition to this body of thinking on which an alternative approach can sit, there are also the individuals and experts that are skilled in these areas and can offer assistance. We discuss this later in the context of Alternative Worlds, but it is worth highlighting the broadening out of this concept from a perspective of DIY, to a community-focused response which carries a different idea of Do It Ourselves (DIO).

Feed yourself, house yourself, manage yourself Against the backdrop of a growing interest in Western vegetarianism and veganism in the late 1970s, punk also explored the DIY aspect of food supply. In many ways this has been one of the more tangible successes of punk, whether this has been to literally grow your own food, or to effectively lobby suppliers to provide food that has been subjected to different standards, for example, relating to animal treatment.

"I think that it is progress that you can now go into supermarkets and get organic food, or fairtrade food. I know it's all a rip-off in that you pay over the odds for it, but it makes me think of Crass and when we were called weirdos and wackos just for being vegetarian... It's got to be a good thing whatever shape or form it takes. Instead of people going to McDonalds and eating that sort of crap." **Steve Ignorant**

"Buy organic! Buy local!... It's the small things, but also major things like the food you eat why not go vegetarian? Hell, go vegan! Go as far as you can on your own personal level towards a better way of existence for the people that have suffered, or the animals that have suffered as a result of how the food is produced." **Dick Lucas**

It was at many of the 'punk communes', for example where bands like Crass and Poison Girls lived, that the practice of growing your own food was adopted. And still to this day we see this DIY model of self-sufficiency being successfully practiced, with continuing developments being found, for example, in areas of permaculture and so on. Once again the DIY design is in fact a DIO response and if we take it as not only a method for achieving a certain aim, namely feeding ourselves, but as a basis of constructing a society, we see the power that is contained within it.

It requires a move away from an individual set of skills related to resourcefulness that are exhibited so effectively through DIY, to a set of more complex DIO activities associated with collaboration, problem solving, communication and taking responsibility. This is what we see in punk as the deeper seam to the DIY principles, which entertains a more thoughtful engagement in how we construct our lives.

And the list of applications of the DIY and DIO ethos goes on. **Mark Wilson** of the Møb offers a version of this in relation to where we might live, which has seen him create his own shelter whether in the form of the travelling Peace Convoy that he joined, the properties that he squatted in London in the late 70s, or the house he has just built himself:

"It's funny because in relation to punk, DIY tends to stand more for things like gigs and so on, but for me it's everything. I believe that everything that needs doing, we can do it ourselves. While I didn't build all this [*looking around at the house and surroundings*] I did build it all in my brain. I said, 'this is what it's got to be like. We've got to use second-hand wood, we've got to get this wood from here.' These windows are all second-hand and all begged or borrowed. I watched *Grand Designs* and they would spend £40,000 on windows and I would think no, you could build a house for £40,000 [*laughs*]. I am PASSIONATE about doing it myself."

And the DIY ethic has been deployed particularly keenly in the punk movement in order to support artistic effort – from making a record, to gigging and everything in between.

"From a practical standpoint, what I admired about the punks was the self-reliance and creativity and the making-do aspect, and that's been embodied in everything that I have ever done. My band books its own shows, organises its own business, records its own records. My studio was built by the people who work here. We taught ourselves how and we built the studio." **Steve Albini**

"What was quite inspiring to me was that you could make your own records. I'd never thought of that before, and for me that was one of the most revolutionary things that came out of punk, more than anything was that it empowered you to create your own culture." **John Robb**

"For me a huge inspiration was the book *Our Band Could Be Your Life* by Michael Azerrad which came out in 2001, which was the first year that I started touring. Although I'd been making music for a few years before that, I had just started doing tours, and everybody in the record label told me, 'You can't do it that way! How can you go and play a show if you don't have a hotel booked?' I was like, 'Isn't it possible? What if I just show up? If we're only getting paid $150 and a hotel's going to cost like 100 bucks then we're not going to make any money, so why can't I ask the audience if we could sleep on somebody's floor?' Like, 'shouldn't that be able to work?' When that book came out it justified all of my imaginings about ways it could be possible. Not only is it possible but this is about all the bands I love. This IS how they did it. From the Minutemen of course, Sonic Youth and Beat Happening. I knew that it seemed that logically there should be this other way to do it than everybody was telling me." **Jeffrey Lewis**

Putting DIY in a broader frame   It is the extension of the DIY notion explored so far, incorporating a broader DIO frame, that takes the punk movement on a more mindful, and less instrumental, journey. In widening the focus in this way, we invoke the duality represented in the principles of freedom AND responsibility. Or put another way, we see how an individual and self-orientated perspective on existentialism must ultimately imply a connection to, and responsibility for, others. Simply finding a way to more effectively do whatever I want to do can only survive for so long before the consequences for others, and the obligations to others have to be taken into account.

But this is where punk does, and must, stop short – at the point where the design or ideology for carrying this forward enters the fray. To propose for others what they should do, or how they should live their lives, at least for most of the people interviewed, is beyond the punk script. Challenge, yes! Disrupt, yes! And take personal responsibility, yes! But for most, this is end of the line and the work that remains is the construction of oneself as each individual sees fit.

Jón Gnarr

Jón Gnarr's life has been quite a journey. Wrongly diagnosed with "mental retardation" as a child, he eventually went on to become the elected mayor of Reykjavík, Iceland, in 2010. In between these two significant events, he has tried his hand at punk rock, taxi driving, acting and comedy, and has also been known to dress in drag when attending public events.

As a teenager Jón played bass in a punk band called Nefrennsli, and during the 1980s he became close friends with members of the Sugarcubes, whose singer Einar would turn out to be an important political ally in later years. In the 90s, Jón became well known in Iceland as a stand-up comedian and also worked as a creative writer and actor.

Jón's interest in politics was ignited in 2008 when Iceland went into financial meltdown. He put together the anarcho-surrealist Best Party with his old friend Einar and announced that he was running for mayor. He says he initially formed the party as a joke, to expose the inadequacies of those he blamed for Iceland's problems.

The joke backfired somewhat when he was elected – and so, a gang of ex-punks, poets and pop stars took control of Reykjavík City Hall. Jón and his team ran the city successfully, and with a great deal of support, for four years before he stepped down in 2014. He has authored a number of books, most recently Gnarr! How I Became the Mayor of a Large City in Iceland and Changed the World.

When I was five years old I was institutionalised because of behavioural problems. I was judged to be mentally disabled, or 'retarded'. My mother was 46 when she had me and my father was 50. My father was born in a turf house in 1918 and was uneducated – intelligent but still a very simple man – and so to him I was retarded. So what was so interesting, or peculiar, about my upbringing is that my parents didn't have any expectations and it's very strange to grow up that way. They were just happy if I could just put my clothes on or something [*laughs loudly*]. They were always waiting for the 'retardedness' to really kick in.

After two years with a paediatric psychiatry institution my diagnosis was 'maladaptiveness'. That had no meaning to my parents, no meaning to anyone in fact – the meaning was that I was incapable of adapting… the assumption was that I would never be a normally functioning person in society, and that was the diagnosis.

When I was 13 years old I was sent to a boarding school, but not a normal boarding school, it had bars on the windows like a correctional school, a 'borstal'. It was in the middle of nowhere in Iceland and I had no idea because I had never been anywhere. I didn't even know if I was still in Iceland [*laughs*]. I could have been in Greenland, I didn't know. I was there for two years.

Finding Crass   I was sitting in my room and I was SO alone, and I had Crass, and I sat in my room and I listened to *So What* on repeat and I cried my eyes out [*laughs*]. I carried a knife for protection, and I was aware I could always use that knife. It was quite emotional. The lyrics and the artwork meant so much to me. When I discovered Crass I barely spoke or understood English but I had a dictionary, and I read the lyrics and saw the artwork and I had no idea, many times, what they were referring to. Of course I knew the Sex Pistols, and that was brilliant, and 'Punk is Dead' and Ronald Reagan and Margaret Thatcher and all that. But I didn't follow news here. I had limited knowledge of what Margaret Thatcher was doing and so I had all this background information to gather [*laughs*] from different sources.

For me, when I discovered and started hearing about punk I related to it because it was something that sounded like me. I was kind of outside and not a part of what was going on. I didn't follow what was going on. For example with *Grease* the film, I didn't understand it. It was a song and dance movie and it was 'period' and I didn't understand it because I thought that people in different countries lived in a different period [*laughs hysterically*]. I had the album because it was given to me and I was puzzled. And Danny, the high school guy. It was like something from outer space.

I've always had difficulties with music. I cannot stand music [*laughs*], which I know is a pretty strange thing. It's not that I don't like music it's just that I cannot listen to music. It makes me feel uncomfortable. And I've tried going to concerts but I have to leave because I get so overwhelmed somehow. It's some kind of over or hyper-sensitivity. I've walked out of every concert I've been to and I've tried. It doesn't depend on the music. It doesn't matter if it's Sigur Rós or death metal – it has nothing to do with that.

And so I have this problem that I can't really explain. However, I was reading Crass like poetry. I also had a difficulty in writing and it was an embarrassment and I was teased. But Crass wrote in a different way. They didn't use the classical way of writing. They would have a slash between sentences and big capital letters and so on. At first I was fascinated with the artwork and how they used graphics and words. I was fascinated with punk. My first fascination was when I saw the Sex Pistols on TV – *Anarchy In The UK* video – and I saw this lead singer in a band that was not good looking and he had red hair. I connected with him. There is somebody that looks like me. I thought, "I could be him" in a few years. And I don't have to be a loser. I could be a front man in a band that is part of something, and is dangerous and challenging. And before that my only musical experiences were with my mother, because she liked music and she loved Meatloaf. My mother was fascinated with Meatloaf and *Paradise by the Dashboard Light* and she would go "Oh! It's Meatloaf... he looks disgusting but he has the voice of an angel." [*laughs*] I would just love being with my mother and seeing her happy. So what I mostly relate to is the message of BE WHO YOU ARE. You are the only you. "He is he and she is she but you're the only you" [*reference to the Crass song* Big A, Little A]. And I read this through my dictionary interpreting the message and I got goosebumps thinking "yeah, I can be me." And I decided I have to learn English to understand this important message so that became a side project.

Getting out of the maze   I kept coming up on the words 'anarchy' and 'anarchism' in Crass's lyrics and I had no idea what it was. And so I was at the library each day, often many times a day. At times I had a quota on how many books I could read because I really like to read. So I went through the shelves and read everything. I had made friends with people working in the library and they liked me because I had an interest in reading. And they got *Melody Maker* and with their permission, like a special permission, I got to keep articles on punk. I went there and I asked the librarian about anarchy and what it was and he sat down with me and explained "It's a political theory; it's like everybody gets to do what they want to do as long as you don't harm others." And I was fascinated. That's how I've always thought of myself. So I must be an anarchist. So I had this thirst to know more but there wasn't that much literature in Icelandic. And the books on anarchism in English were way too heavy for me. I wanted to know everything there was to know about anarchism and that is due to Crass.

It became a door that I could not have imagined. And I opened the door and I walked in there. At the time I felt stuck in a maze and everybody was finding his or her way through the maze. And I knew it. And everybody knew that I would NEVER find my way through it. I saw it on their faces. I saw it in their eyes. They'd be thinking you're never going to find it. We're going to leave you behind because we have to find a way for our own sake so, "Bye bye!" Crass was a door in that maze. You don't have to go through the maze. There are different options. And that's anarchism. I became totally obsessed with Crass and the lyrics and I longed to be a part of this. I used to be a punk but punk arrived here at the time it was fading out in Europe, I suppose. Punk was dying when it arrived here in, say, 1980. I had a tough time in school because I was bullied a lot. Instead of going to school I went on the bus and I hid my books somewhere and I went around on the bus because I didn't want to go to school and they didn't care for me there. That bus led me to the central station in Reykjavík eventually and there were other kids, the same sort as me who didn't want to go to school.

Making sense of anarchy   When I went to school it was hell because as soon as I arrived I was bullied and they would ask, "Are you a punk?" "Yes", I would say,

"Can I spit on you?" "No". "Well, if you're a punk then it's OK to spit on you, right!" "No, it's not." But they would spit on me anyway and beat me up. And I would wear a badge with an anarchy logo, and they would see it and say, "So are you an anarchist?" "Yes," I'd say. "You don't know what anarchism is do you?" Then I'd say, "Yes, I do", "No, you don't... what's anarchism then?" "Well, it's about being against the rules and for freedom." "So, if you're against the rules are you against traffic rules?" "Err, no." "Well then you're not an anarchist." So this is what they'd do, and I really wanted to figure out good answers to their questions [*laughs*]. But in any event it usually ended in a beating so it didn't matter what I said. And when we were hanging around with these punks we were fairly harmless and would just smoke cigarettes or sniff glue... we would go into the toilets and sniff glue or gas. And we were not dangerous. We were harmless. But people were afraid of us and we became quite notorious which was slightly beneficial in some ways. So we stuck together and I think many of us were being bullied. And because of this I didn't attend school and so I was sent to this correctional school.

From anarchism to Taoism   As I got older I was supposed to have a Lutheran confirmation and I told my mother that I didn't want to do it because I don't believe in God and she said: "You're having confirmation like everybody and there'll be no exception. There will be no discussion about it and you will DO AS YOU'RE TOLD, this time." So after the confirmation there is a party and you get gifts so I made an agreement with my mother that I would get a bass guitar as a gift, because I wanted to be a bass player in a punk band, because it looked simple enough to play... I had a lot of attitude at the time and I used to walk around with a copy of the *New Testament* of the bible and people would ask me, "Aren't you supposed to be a punk? Why are you carrying around a copy of the *New Testament*?" I would say, "I use it to wipe my ass." [*laughs*] So it was kind of a statement but it was also a joke. And before the confirmation the priest took me aside and said, "If you behave in the ceremony, I will have a party for you afterwards, a special party". But he lied, there was no party. And I behaved so well thinking I would have a special party. As a confirmation present I was given a book that I didn't think much of. It was the *Tao Te Ching* by Lao Tzu. It was from a relative. And I thought [*pulls face*]. But I was a compulsive reader and I would read anything, and so I was going to take it to the store and change it for something else. I wanted to exchange it for the *Anarchist's Cook Book* that I thought I was going to get for the confirmation but I didn't. I was quite disappointed [*laughs*]. I started reading the *Tao Te Ching* and it fascinated me. And I felt a resemblance between it and Crass, like non-violence. And being a victim to constant violence, which was something that interested me at the time. It said be kind to your friends and thus increase kindness. It also said be kind to your enemies and thus increase kindness. And I felt there was a similarity. I have read this book more often than any other book. It's the only book I've had all my life, the same book I got at my confirmation.

Becoming a surrealist mayor   When my English improved, I started reading into serious anarchist theories like Bakunin, Proudhon, but, I didn't relate to it. I felt Crass was more anarchist than Bakunin. I've read about different types of anarchism; contemporary anarchists – David Graeber, Noam Chomsky, and so on. On the other hand Taoism is anarchist, it's like anarchistic philosophy. Through Lao Tzu I got into Zhuang Tse who I think you could say was the inventor of anarchism and the idea of anarchism. Being an anarchist is, for me, just a part of what I am as a person, and it doesn't have anything to do with where I am or what I am doing in life.

But in discussing all of these 'isms' like socialism and feminism and anarchism and Taoism, I've got kind of tired of it [*laughs*]. Like the "are you a…" questions. What I discovered later as I got older, was that anarchism was becoming a prison. It was a systematic prison. So like, "if you are a vegetarian then why are you wearing leather trousers?" I remember an interview with Flux of Pink Indians in *Melody Maker*, which I read using my English dictionary [*laughs*], and the journalist pointed out that they were wearing leather and they were vegans and they couldn't explain it and I had these moments all the time. "You're an anarchist and you're against rules, but you accept traffic rules. Ah! So, you accept SOME rules and reject other rules, so it's just selfishness really!" "No, it's not!" I felt that anarchism had just became one more theory. And the next step would be where we would need to build something – a big building where we hand out the rules on 'how to be an anarchist.'

I like to say that I am an anarchist because there is no such thing as a perfect ideology. There is no perfect system and we should look in the opposite direction for the 'non-system'. For me, as an adult, I like what the Surrealists were doing when André Breton wrote the *Manifesto of Surrealism* [*laughs*]. Because people ask me, "Where did the manifesto for the Best Party come from?" It's from André Breton's manifesto. And it's kind of chilling because THERE was the manual for how to run the Best Party. The Surrealists were political and in serious times. And out of the Surrealists came the Situationsists and they were also political. The hippy movement was in many ways born out of Surrealism and Situationism. AND Crass. And for me, the Best Party was the next step. How can you take Crass further, this idea, this state of mind and this work? How can you take it further? It's been very complicated taking all of this forward and hard work. It's been frustrating really because the idea is to have no idea. [*laughs*] It's the 'nothing'.

Anarchism is freedom. But it's not freedom without responsibility. There is no freedom without responsibility because then it's chaos. And chaos is not anarchism. People sometimes confuse the two

The death of ideology   We formed a majority with the Social Democrats and they were a bit cautious and didn't quite trust us to begin with. But the minority detests us. They simply don't like us. The strange thing is that the minority consists of the conservatives and the left. So we have both the left and the right against us. When it comes to different issues like tax, for instance, they don't have to think because they have their ideologies. So if you're from the right, you're against tax – you don't have to think about it. If you're to the left you're for tax. What I hope that the Best Party means is that it means the beginning of the death of politics – politics is dead! And I say that. I like to say we are the first mammals in the world of dinosaurs. The dinosaurs are so big and so sure of themselves [*laughs*] and they think they rule the world, and they don't. It's like the fight of the underdog. Fewer and fewer people have more money and more people have less.

As Crass say, like in *System*, systems are not made of stone, they are made of people. Bombing Number 10 [*Downing Street*] makes no difference, as they say. That was something I had to look up too [*laughs loudly*] because I didn't know what it was. I was thinking, [*continues laughing*] "Bombing number 10? That makes no sense… err… and that won't change anything… err… what's wrong with the number 10?" [*laughs*]. So there have always been hindrances of language.

I have used this unique position to fight for human rights. And we have given people all around the world hope that there is an alternative. There IS hope and I have no idea how this is going to evolve, what is going to be the next step. It is something that has a beginning and an end and we are not finished yet. I became mayor more than three years ago. And according to all polls I was very popular and the majority wanted to see me as the next mayor. I think it was 37% of people that wanted to vote for the Best Party. That was according to Gallup. But I never had any intention of any political career because I don't believe in politics, so I said I am very thankful for the trust but I am going to go do something else and I want to close down the Best Party because it is nothing. It doesn't exist. There are no members. It's not a real party. It doesn't have a manifesto or an agenda or ideology. There is NO ideology to the Best Party, and if we come up with an ideology we kill it. So it's a conceptual thing with a beginning and an end. It's like we still haven't delivered the punch line. We are not there yet. What I want to achieve is to be able to make Reykjavík the first military-free city in the world. To declare it a military-free zone. And I think that's going to be of huge importance. I don't know if it's possible or HOW I'm going to do it but that's something I would really like to do.

There is a big political party in Kosovo now called the Strong Party which is inspired by the Best Party and I would like it to spread like a virus. I hope it spreads. And if one party promises 20,000 new jobs, the Strong Party promises 30,000 jobs [*laughs*]. It's the same nonsense as the Best Party. You create an option in the maze, like Crass did for me. Because we can make holes in the maze, so what we did was coming up with this option. And of course we didn't invent it. This thought has been around for 10,000 years, this idea. I get thousands of letters from people all around the world telling me what we did, what I did, what the Best Party has done has helped them or given them something and it can be almost anything. I get post from Kosovo, from Palestine, from Ukraine, from Spain, from the States, from Colombia and so on. Things like, "Thank you for existing, you give me hope." "I've just heard about you, you are awesome, thank you. You give us hope." I don't know who these people are... I get some people saying that I give them reason not to kill themselves... Inspiring people to carry on a little more.

Make the changes you can   We all live under the reign of capitalism whether we like it or not. That's the dominant system. To be able to do certain things you have to accept the terms. You don't know what they are really, you just agree to them. I personally don't agree to the terms in theory but when it comes to it [*hand action as if signing a contract*] I do. I think we tend to be over-ambitious. A change doesn't have to be huge. A change is a change. Like a mouse is not inferior to the elephant even though the elephant is bigger [*laughs*]. So just making a difference is enough and, maybe, first and foremost it has to do with oneself. To make a change in your own life rather than change the world. People have a slogan 'Peace on Earth' but I'd be happy with Peace in Reykjavík... It's hard and also we have to prioritise. First things first.

For me the first thing is human rights and equality. If you can achieve something of value in that respect, you are making a change. And I doubt that we are anywhere close to the end of capitalism because it's SO effective. Even in its generating status it's effective. Even re-inventing itself all the time. And now after the crisis we are facing a re-born capitalism. It's like advanced capitalism. I think that what they will do next is limit our access to the Internet. They will do that within five years. They will localise like the Chinese model. They want to keep us local. To divide. They don't care about what happened in Egypt, and Occupy Wall Street and social media. Not the corporations and not the government, they don't care about it. They are working on it and I know that for sure. Like tapping in on e-mails and stuff. I write all my e-mails and I think that somebody is reading all my e-mails [*laughs*]. I sometimes write e-mails to the people who are reading my e-mails. I'm quite sure about that.

And if not me then many of the people I correspond with. It can be quite terrifying and in my mind, like now, I have been a part of something and been the creator of something like the Best Party and it's anarchism, it's direct action, it's against politics right in the belly of the beast. Where do we go from here?

Where next Columbus? [*laughs*]. I don't know. It seems to me that most people who are actively working for peace usually wind up getting killed. There's no meaning in peace, and there's no [*laughs*] future in peace. It's dangerous, it really is. I think the number one on the priority list IS human rights. And the BIGGEST obstacle is religion; organised religion. And so you will make a lot of enemies and many of them are complete lunatics and they believe in stuff that is not real. I am scared of those people. I am scared about where we go from here. I think if I were to take the next rational step it would be religion, for me, and that's far more dangerous than politics because at least in politics people have some ideologies based in reality [*giggles loudly*]. But in religion it's based on imagination and fiction and hate. And the Pope is man of the year. Are we really that stupid? We've been evolving for 100,000 years and we make this person the man of the year, because what? Because we are gullible?

Twelve steps to heaven   People are entitled to have their own beliefs. Maybe, because I am an anarchist at home, my children have had the freedom of opinion on religion. And I have had that freedom too. I was involved in the Twelve Step programme. We came to believe that there was a higher power, and I came to a stage in my life where it was like death or destruction, so I decided that I would try this Twelve Step thing. And I was told that I should go to this meeting and pick someone I liked to be my sponsor. And he will guide you through the steps. That's what I did. I sought out what seemed to be the most intelligent, appropriate man in the meeting. After the meeting I walked up to him and asked him to be my sponsor. "Sure!" he said, "but do you know what that includes? It means that you will have to contact me every day and obey what I say and follow my advice because you're lost and I am your direction." And I said, "Yes. I'm prepared to do that."

Then we went to his car. He asked me to have a talk in his car. And I was sitting there and thinking to myself, "I'm going to be humble. I'm going to be humble because arrogance and selfishness has put me in this situation that I'm in." And we sat in the car. I was in the passenger seat and he was in the driver's seat and suddenly he goes [*mimes clasping hands*] "Dear Jesus, we are together here, etc." And he was having his personal conversation with Jesus and I was thinking "Oh! Fuck!" Then came a thought to me "Jón, this is arrogance. Give it a chance and see if it works." So I decided to give it a chance.

I read the Bible. I read the whole Bible as well as the Apocrypha. I read that too. The bonus chapter [*laughs*]. It's crap! [*laughs*] Except for one book which is very adventurous, very surrealistic. I did an honest, intelligent, effort to try to believe in God, to be religious. I participated in masses and everything and I tried to adapt it into my life. One of my idols is Leo Tolstoy. And many of the people

I considered to be the greatest people that have ever lived have been religious: Mahatma Gandhi was religious, Leo Tolstoy was very religious and so on. And Tolstoy was an anarchist. He was the inventor of Christian anarchism. He merged the two and said there is no authority but God. He wouldn't recognise the church or government. And Tolstoy's theories on anarchism were the inspiration for Gandhi, because he read Tolstoy's theories and they corresponded. So in a way, Tolstoy was responsible for what happened in India. So I have great respect for many religious people. But I couldn't honestly believe in God.

So I can have a sensible conversation with religious people about the *Bible* and about Jesus and God and all that. I believe in religious freedom and I respect people's religious and spiritual ideas. I've been involved in death and dying and I know spirituality plays a big role in death and in the face of death… Often people will turn to God as the last resort. So I have great respect for religion; however, at the same time I think it's our greatest obstacle. So it's a paradox. It's an oxymoron… That's somehow where you are always destined to always be… in the middle of this paradox. People don't seem to care much about deep thoughts, they're more interested in fame. That seems to have lot more importance [*laughs*].

Anarchy, freedom and responsibility   Anarchism is freedom. But it's not freedom without responsibility. There is no freedom without responsibility because then it's chaos. And chaos is not anarchism. People sometimes confuse the two. Like neo-conservatives would point to some country, say in Africa and say "that's anarchism, right?" "Err, no!" I think the system becomes an excuse for responsibility. It's also like group responsibility. Everyone and no one has responsibility and that can make good people evil. These are the tools of evil. Everyone is just doing his or her job. That's what the Nazis said. Eichmann said, "You don't have any right to charge me. I didn't do anything wrong. I was simply doing my job."

In Iceland, right after you die, official letters have to be written to the state; you know, the banks and the government, everyone is sent letters by the estate of the deceased. Two weeks after my father's death he got a personal letter from social services. And I have this letter and it's so beautiful. It said "Dear Mr XXX, your application for an emergency button has been discussed at the meeting, etc. Decision: denied. Reason: applicant is dead." And it's an actual person that wrote this. So the thinking is that we're writing you a letter and because you are dead we don't see a reason why you need an emergency button. And it was written to HIM not to the estate. Personally addressed to him. Can you believe it?

Einar Örn Benediktsson

Einar Örn Benediktsson entered the punk stratosphere at the start of the 1980s as a singer with short-lived Icelandic outfit Purrkur Pillnikk, who clocked up a UK tour with the Fall in 1982. A couple of years later, he joined anarcho-punk band KUKL, along with singer Björk Guðmundsdóttir. Moving to the UK to study at the Polytechnic of Central London, Einar made contact with Flux of Pink Indians and Crass. With a relationship established, KUKL's two studio albums, The Eye and Holidays in Europe, were released on Crass Records. A mixture of goth rock, punk, free jazz and rhythmic music, with a good helping of free spirit thrown in for good measure, one review said of the KUKL live experience: "This concert cannot be described. Those who lived it will have it with them for the rest of their lives."

In 1986, Einar and other members of KUKL formed the Sugarcubes – Einar sharing vocal duties with the fame-bound Björk. The band signed to One Little Indian in the UK, released three studio LPs, and enjoyed critical acclaim in both the UK and USA.

After the breakup of the Sugarcubes in 1992, Einar stepped away from the musical spotlight and, among other projects, wrote a newspaper column about daily life in Reykjavík, co-founded the city's first cybercafé, and collaborated with Blur's Damon Albarn on the soundtrack for the acclaimed Icelandic film 101 Reykjavík.

In 2003, he embarked on a musical project, Ghostigital – electronic beat music with elements of dub, hip-hop, rock and noise – a collaboration with Curver that continues to this day.

Taking an unexpected turn in his career, and in the wake of the banking crisis that severely affected the country, Einar created the Best Party with fellow punk and anarcho-surrealist Jón Gnarr. In 2010, following the unprecedented success of the party, he was elected to Reykjavík City Council where he was responsible for Culture and Tourism.

I was playing outside my house, I guess I'm 14 then, and a friend of mine tells me about this English music group and the singer has green teeth and they're puking on an airplane. I remember thinking, "Oh that's very exciting." At the time, my friends were listening to something called ELP and I asked them, "ELP, what is that?" and I realised that ELP stood for Emerson, Lake and Palmer and so I asked for the album *Tarkus* for my Christmas present. And when I got it and I put it on, I just didn't get it. It was like, "What is this?" And so I was trying musically to find out what was going on and it was in 1976 that I just started hearing about punk music and started listening to *New Rose* by the Damned and *Spiral Scratch* by the Buzzcocks.

At the time, my father was living in London, so I sent him a list of records and he brought them to me or sent them over. I was buying a lot of music from mail order catalogues. Every week I went to buy *Sounds*, *NME*, and *Melody Maker* in the shop. I was just reading up on all of these new things. I spent the summer of '77 in London for three months. I was walking down the Kings Road looking for punks and just trying to sort of work out what this was. When I came back home, I cut my hair short and had stripy trousers and I just flipped over into punk. It was so interesting for me; the music, the style of everything. I had a dinner jacket and I sprayed the word "Rat" on the back but the spraying was very white so you couldn't really see what it was.

Listening to John Peel in the snow   In photographs from that year in school, I am the only person that stands out like that. The short hair I had was basically longer than I have now. It wasn't that drastic, but it was regarded as quite extreme then. It was like I was a loner in the punk thing here in Iceland. There was another group of people in the next town, who did covers of Sex Pistols songs, and they're still going today. There was a small affinity between us. Then late at night, I would go out in my mother's car, which was an old Sunbeam, as it was the only way I could tune into BBC Radio 1. I listened to John Peel in the freezing cold and sometimes the reception wouldn't be too good, because there were cloudy skies…

Then, when I went to college at 17, I got asked to be the manager of Utangardsmenn. They were like a revolution in a way because the band featured two brothers, Mike and Danny Pollack, who tuned their guitars in the Detroit style. They recreated the sound of MC5 and the Stooges. Here I was, involved in rock music in Iceland, which was fantastic! What was also fantastic with them was that they were singing in Icelandic, with powerful social lyrics that could be understood by Icelandic people.

White Riot in Reykjavík   On my vacations I went to England. In 1980 I got a phone call from the Reykjavík Arts Festival and they asked me, "Can you find us a band to play in Iceland?" Speaking to my friends in England, we called the Clash and that is how the Clash came to play the Reykjavík Arts Festival in 1980. I was driving them around here in Iceland with a Tannoy system on top of the car. Mick Jones and Paul Simonon were singing on the Tannoy as we were driving around the centre of Reykjavík, and then I saw the police right behind me. The police pulled us over and said, "What are you doing?" I looked at the police officer and I realised it was my old boy scout leader and he said, "My dear Einar, you don't need to be doing this." I excitedly said, "Well I've got the Clash here and they're just singing, they are doing a gig here." I then had to drive the Clash in the car down to the police station and I was taken inside. They said, "Look, can we just dismantle this kind of a sound system?" I said, "Yeah, no problem." Then I walked out, dismantled the Tannoy system, got into the car and I drove the band back to the hotel. It was my little white riot in the centre of Reykjavík.

Anarchy in the post office   On the 8th March 1981, I formed a band with my two best friends who I'd known since I was 12 years old. Then on the 1st April, less than a month later, we went into a studio to record our first 10-track single. All our songs were like 20 or 30 seconds long, but because of punk the format of the music could be short. It became apparent to me that you can actually be really straightforward in telling the story of how to approach things, not how to think, but how to provoke. To be different was okay. You didn't have to go with the norm. With my first band I was just going to do noises because I didn't know how to play instruments and had never sung before. They handed me the microphone and said, "You're going to sing." And so I had to do something and I started writing down words, about my daily life, how mundane and exciting it was. And about notions of being scared. Why are you scared? What does fear do to you? And what happens if we don't give emotions a name, such as anger or joy; what would happen if those things didn't have names? Would they even exist?

That's basically how I started. I just got involved with music and got thrown into having to deal with being the manager of a band at 17. I wasn't allowed into some of the venues that I booked the bands into because you had to be 18. I would be sitting in the foyer selling tickets but not be able to go and see them because that's where alcohol was being served. It was all about being part of a movement, which was doing something; which was different and was being noticed. I was, of course, being noticed with a bowler hat and Doc Martens, short hair and all of that. I was working as a postal driver and I had a white shirt that I decorated myself by splashing red paint all over it. I was called into the office and they said, "Einar, you're giving people registered mail and in those letters can be something serious. Do you really think that it is wise that you look like you have just killed a person?" I had to dress down a little bit for work, and just put a sweater on, but still I was wearing my red shirt underneath [*laughs*].

Authenticity through punk   With punk, I felt I had found the key to being creative because there were no barriers. There was nothing that was predefined in terms of how I should be writing things. I was writing about my reality in the city of Reykjavík, seeing a peeping Tom or later more abstract ideas like standing on a lamp post and asking should I jump? Should I jump? Punk was the key to unlocking my heart. I'd say, "Here you go. This is me. Take it or leave it." And

I see a system where everybody is equal and everybody feels great and there are no wars. There's no famine and everybody is basically doing what they want to do

say, "Okay, bring it on. Bring it on." One of my songs was, "Shall I punch you out? Shall I punch you out?" That was the lyric. I was just, "Come on. Do it. Do it!!" Nobody came. And it's like, "Okay, here I am. Punch me out." Actually, I did get punched out for it one time. [*laughs*]

For me, punk opened the door to expressing myself, to writing and to working, and to carrying on. But also I developed the ability to work with other people, to listen to other people, and to cooperate. So, this was a new era where I took on the ethos of punk, which was about expressing yourself, publishing what you wanted, publishing it the way you wanted it and connecting punk and surrealism in a way that created art. And without all of this being 'highbrow' or anything like that.

Then this evolved into the Sugarcubes and this was like going into an empty space in the music scene with avant-garde, abstract ideas of what pop songs should be about. Our lyrics were not normal; they were different. But they were reflections on us saying and doing what we wanted to do. We set up camp in Iceland. We started bringing in other Icelandic bands to help them along, very much the way Crass helped out with their label.

This got more people involved and more Icelandic music was put out through various offshoots of that movement. We continued to do that here until the Sugarcubes finished and then I didn't do any music for eight years. I did one record in 1992 and then nothing until 2000, when Damon Albarn and myself were asked to do a soundtrack for the film *101 Reykjavík*. Damon said, "Okay you take care of the backing track. You do the drums and bass." And so I said, "Okay yeah sure." I'd never done that before, but I got a computer and I had to learn how to program things but it's like, "Okay I'll do it." We managed to finish that and afterwards, I started Ghostigital in 2001, which is still going today.

Punks in government More than three years ago I formed a party called the Best Party and we got out the dissident vote in Reykjavík. Since then I have been a City Councillor. Everybody was like, "What are you? You're not a Socialist Party." We said, "No we're not." And I'd say, "I am a punk." It's like proclaiming, "Oh I'm an alcoholic." But I AM a punk, and I say that because I haven't changed in the way I regard the right to express myself and I'm not only talking about freedom of speech. I'm an anarchist and people say, "But you're not an anarchist because you work within the system. You are part of the system now." Okay, I may be part of the system, but what I learned through punk was to listen and to take on board ideas, to try to understand and not to make up my mind that things should be only one way. There is good in possibly every political system.

If I were to label myself, I would label myself more as a Situationist. I like to create situations and we're definitely in a situation here with the Best Party. Punk is a situation — you take the moment and you create something that you have to deal with. Pogo dancing was a situation. You had to deal with it. And since I've been in government] people say to me, "You're empowered now" and I answer them back, "I don't want power... instead we want more of the idea of free democracy or open democracy." I want to give away my power in this process. And what this entails is that you then have to take responsibility for your actions and you have to become a responsible person. Some people say that their responsibility is limited to voting every four years and then spend the next four years being vitriolic towards the people they voted for. Or they say, "This is not who I voted for" and so the discussion becomes forever polarised in terms of for or against.

Sidestepping dualism   In Iceland, it's very interesting because we have a state religion that is Lutheran, but our old religion, associated with the old Norse gods, is still rampant here. You get people who are called Thor, and even people who are called Christian Thor. You get this duality of religion in their names. And this often leads to being either 'for' or 'against'. And I'm never 'for' or 'against'. I want to find proper solutions. To fight the system, or to be the system, that is my biggest question! We started here with a pilot project where citizens can put in their ideas for the city to create. But it is quite extraordinary how people are always asking or coming up with ideas for the city to do, but it's never ideas they want to do for the city themselves. It's never "I want to do this. Who can help me?" But rather it is, "I want the city to do this." I'm interested in bringing about a fundamental shift in the way we think. How do we start? We have started this process here by entering the Best Party into the political forum. We don't answer back when people slag us off. We are not violent in that we don't talk badly about people, like people usually do in politics. I heard last week broadcasting from the British Houses of Parliament where one MP was deliberately trying to upset another... what kind of role model is that? That's a total bastard. We try to solve things and do it in a friendly manner, not in a hostile manner.

I was attending a conference in the Faroe Islands and I was talking to a Danish delegate there: a Danish politician who was actually a far, far left politician. He said, "What kind of a system do you see?" I said to him, "I see a system where everybody is equal and everybody feels great and there are no wars. There's no famine and everybody is basically doing what they want to do." He said to me, "That's very utopian of you." Then I answered him, "If I don't say it, it will not be heard and therefore nobody will notice that this idea is there. If I go and say everybody is valued, that everything should be valued as equal, it is important to maintain that dialogue, and not to forget that this must be the end goal." For me, that's anarchy and if I don't say it that way, even though

111

they say it's utopian, then it will never materialise. If you don't say it, if you don't do it, it will not happen.

Step up, take responsibility, and make a difference   More people come to me asking whether I am running for a second term, because I said I'm stepping down. But I don't want the power. It's not mine to own. It is everybody else's so please, please come in, use it, be part of it because it's ours to share, to feel good. I don't think it's naïve to say it. You have to say it. I try to say that as simply as I possibly can.

That is one of the lessons I've learned from punk is that you CAN do it. Anybody who tries to say that you cannot do it, that you're not clever enough, they're just trying to get you away. They don't want you to be part of the ruling system. I think the thing to do is to say, "Hey system, here I am" and refuse to say, "No." Just say, "Yes, I will do it." This is the biggest thing for me to have done; this, and to say that anybody can do it. You just have to have an interest in rekindling your sense of responsibility. You have to say, "I am responsible and I am ready to take responsibility."

When we went forward with the Best Party we had strange slogans, like "Adopt A Bum". People said, "Oh you're being negative. This is not very human of you." But what has been done for the homeless? Not very much. So if we say "Adopt A Bum" then people start thinking about it and their responsibility for homelessness. We said that we wanted polar bears to come here, which also sounds like a silly slogan. The issue though is climate change – we are getting polar bears on the icebergs drifting away from Greenland and when they land ashore here in Iceland, we don't have a method of capturing them or a means of trying to send them back or anything like that. We just shoot them. We're just highlighting climate change. This is happening. It's about opening up, in a different way, and speaking about the situation and about what is happening.

Negotiating with the Hidden People   I built a house 12 years ago here on the outskirts of Reykjavík. I built it myself with these two hands and with five friends all building five houses together, as part of an artists' commune. So, as we were building the houses we started to encounter some problems. We had made the decision to build them away from the road because we didn't want to disturb the meadows where the elves and hidden people live. But because we started to encounter problems, I thought that I needed to negotiate with the elves so that we could actually live here with them. In the summer, how slow the building process was frustrated me, so I got in contact with an elf seer. The elf seer came in and I explained to her that I've been speaking to the elves when I'm brushing the foundations and doing all jobs around the building of the houses and that we are building away from the street so as not to disturb the rocks because that's where we believe the elves live. She said, "You're a good boy Einar. This is absolutely the correct way of thinking, but there are no elves here. It's hidden people. Hidden people are a bit taller than elves and they're more human looking than elves. There are three meanies here who have got a mean streak in them and they're not very happy that you're actually building here. But, you have made all the necessary preparations and there is plenty of space here for you all to live. So I will speak to them, but I ask of you that you go into the meadows and you ask for good weather." And I said, "What, I should just ask for good weather?" She said, "Yeah just ask for good weather and get all your neighbours to ask for good weather." Further to that, I got to learn the day after, on a Monday, that the guy on the truck who was digging for the sewage system had quit because the hidden people had been teasing him. Also one of my neighbours had been threatening to dynamite them so I had to ask him to speak to them and he said, "I don't know how to speak to them." I said, "Here follow me." I taught him how to speak to them and to address the hidden people and they listen. You might not hear them, but you can speak to them, which is, fair enough.

What this taught me is that by going into the meadows and just asking for good weather, it's not about whether there actually are hidden people or elves there, it's about whether you are content — if you are content with yourself, and if you are content with nature. If you are fucking up nature, you are not content. You will not have good weather. For me, in the bigger picture, it doesn't matter if I'm a punk or a conservative or generally a fucker. What matters is that you are at peace with nature and human rights. If you are, then everything will fall into place.

Graham Burnett

Graham Burnett has been a political activist, punk, and for almost 20 years, a teacher in the discipline of permaculture. He first heard about the concept in an article in Peace News *in the early 1980s and, following extensive research and training, he went on to found Spiralseed in 2001. He works with projects and organisations including Comic Relief, Capital Growth and the Vegan Organic Network, as well as cultivating his own garden and allotments. He also co-runs permaculture courses at Crass's Dial House in Essex, and is the author of* Permaculture: A Beginner's Guide *and* The Vegan Book of Permaculture.

The word permaculture was originally coined in the mid-1970s to describe the design system pioneered as a response to what many people saw as serious challenges to our survival. It has now moved on from these roots and looks at strategies to create sustainable food-growing methods that will enable us to live harmoniously in relation to Earth and its resources. It's a holistic approach that can be applied in all aspects of life. As well as providing the tools to create greater sustainability within our lifestyles, home environments and on our land, permaculture is also about finding ways of promoting community and rebuilding fragmented societies.

The whole punk thing was happening around the time that I was in school. It was kind of in the air. My punk peer group and me had been into Genesis, Yes and Emerson, Lake and Palmer and that kind of stuff. I had also became aware of avant-garde jazz through the older kids at school and there were a lot of older people around, lefty types and arty types all doing different things. So punk was just part of that whole thing. We were a little bit sniffy about punk at first, because the whole thing was violent, with people spitting and all that kind of business, and we were quite scared of the local punks down their end of the high street. We all still had long hair as well. And so one day, one of our crowd went to their crowd and asked for a fag and we thought we were probably going to get beaten up, but then we thought, "Oh, they're just kids like us." That, for me was the moment when I opened up to what it was all about. That introduced me to things like Rock Against Racism with the Clash and opened up the whole political thing really.

I suppose it's a cliché, but it was Crass really that made it all change. A lot of the older people were socialists and I got into that socialist milieu and would sell *Socialist Worker* outside the local record shop on a Saturday morning. I remember one day going into Projection Records, which was our local indie record shop, and there were these punks in there hassling the guy who ran the shop and they had this new album that had come out called *The Feeding of the Five Thousand* and they were saying, "Play it! Put it on mate!" and he did. I was mooching around the shop at the time and I thought, "What the fuck is this!" [*laughs*] and I bought a copy there and then. Crass always had that influence from the avant-garde, and I got that straightaway because I was into that kind of stuff already. And I picked up on the fact that this was merging punk with music that was not of the rock'n'roll tradition. I got it home and was playing it and I remember thinking, "This is great, all that swearing" but the epiphany for me was when it said, "Do you believe in Marx? Marx fucks." And I was reading *Socialist Worker* and I thought, "You can't say that!" And so I wrote this letter to Crass saying that you can't dismiss the work of Marx and all this dogma that I'd got out of the *Socialist Worker Party Handbook*. I never sent the letter, but I played the record over and over and it was like the Zen whack on the side of the head. It opened up a whole load of questions, "What is this anarchy? What is this do-it-yourself stuff?" That was the moment for me that really opened things and made it clear.

I had always been politically active. Rock Against Racism was the 'in' to it for me, and throughout the 80s I got involved in direct action. The people I was around were certainly protest culture and ALF [*Animal Liberation Front*] type people. There was the Anti-Nazi League, then the CND [*Campaign for Nuclear Disarmament*] and that led into Anti-Apartheid. And I suddenly became aware that this was all 'anti', it made me think what was I FOR?

That's how I came to permaculture really. I did have an allotment and I was growing vegetables. I heard this word "permaculture" that I thought was about herb spirals and things like that and I saw a book called *The Permaculture Garden* by someone called Graham Bell. And I bought it and read it and it didn't have anything about herb spirals, but I thought, "This is what I've been looking for." Permaculture isn't just about growing stuff; it's a whole philosophical approach. It's almost like the practical application of anarchy, or one description of it.

Some people think that permaculture it is a completely new thing, but it's all just pulling together ideas that have been around for centuries, thousands of years in some cases; I think it was Bill Mollison who coined the term. He's had a very colourful and interesting life and he worked in the logging industry, I believe, in Tasmania and he was seeing the environmental devastation that was causing — all the fertility in the land disappearing and the soil washing away. He was also seeing that it was dehumanising the people who worked in that kind of industry. They were becoming quite brutalised and not caring. A few years later he found himself living in the rainforest in Tasmania and he was observing the way that everything met the needs of everything else in that system. Everything that the creatures needed was provided by the plants, and everything the plants needed was provided by other plants and the droppings of the animals. And he thought, "Why can't we set up human systems that run like this?" So that was the beginnings of it. He wrote a book with David Holmgren, who was the other key player in those days. They wrote the first text, as it were, called *Permaculture 1.*

At the very heart of permaculture is the prime directive that is that we take responsibility for ourselves and for future generations. Around that are the core ethics of permaculture, which are about caring for the earth, caring for people, and fair shares – a fair distribution of resources, and sharing surpluses.

An alternative design for living   At the heart of any society is a stable food-growing base and that's the heart of permaculture, but there's so much more around it. There's the built environment, that's how we organise as communities. Bill Mollison offers the view that, taken in their totality, small gardens were much more productive than acres and acres of wheat growing, because you've got people paying close attention. The whole issue about monoculture is that it actually consumes more than it produces in terms of the oil that's going into it to make the fertilisers and the tractors that turn the soil over. It's not only destroying the soil but it is also using more energy than it is making in terms of calories produced as food.

By contrast, with small intensive growing, the argument is that small intensive farming is more efficient. Obviously my back garden is not going to grow that much, but if you took all the back gardens in this street and put them together, with everyone spending a bit of time growing food every day you can see the totality. It's much more resilient, because if some strain of virus goes through all our wheat and wipes it out, we're fucked, but if we're all growing and producing food then a lot of the land that's around could be turned to productive use.

We're all entrenched in the prevailing culture, everything in this room is part of the oil-based economy, and in a way what we're discussing in terms of permaculture is tinkering at the edges. But it's a bit like the punk thing, I suppose – acting by example. And it's also part of that taking responsibility for ourselves and future generations in that we're not saying, "This is wrong" we're just doing it like the punk thing. If you don't agree with what the government is doing, then you've got the model for the alternative.

Mad Max versus transition   I've got a regular life and until fairly recently worked a nine-to-five job. Five years ago I went part time in my day job because I found that I was doing so much teaching work around permaculture that I couldn't fit it all in. And it started bringing in an income. And I've got four kids. I don't see really why there should be a dichotomy between work and home. There was always that tendency with anarcho-punk, of finger pointing – you should do this and you shouldn't do that. I try not to do that. I'm aware that people are just struggling with day-to-day life. What's wrong with sitting down and watching bloody Eastenders if you've been doing some job you hate all day long? It's fine. There is that, particularly in permaculture circles sometimes, people can be a bit disdainful if you watch television.

I suppose there are the choices you make when you are buying or consuming. You might decide to support your local greengrocer rather than a supermarket. We don't always succeed, but we try. So there is that whole thing about localising economies which is very much a key thing in permaculture. It's not about you growing your own food, or the street growing its own food. If there is an organic farm nearby then you figure out ways that the community can be supported by that, rather than all of your stuff coming from Kenya or wherever – or some unsavoury multinational. It isn't about criticism, it's about people doing the best they can. It's about supporting people in the steps they are taking, no matter how small, rather than telling them, "You should be doing this" or "Why aren't you doing that?"

Permaculture is all about climate change and peak oil, not necessarily that the oil's going to run out, but that it will become a lot scarcer in the future. And it's about what kind of society we want to see when that's happened. There are a number of scenarios. One is total collapse and chaos and we'll all be running around like Mad Max stealing the last drops of petrol from each other in these tribal bands. There are some other scenarios, but the transition one is that we all become much more self-reliant and the world could actually be a better place. It's thinking about how we do that and how we get from here to there in a way that's inclusive and sustainable and everyone's a part of it. And no one is excluded or shot against the wall.

It's interesting to see that the demographic keeps moving. 10-15 years ago it was your fringe hippies and everyone would turn up in dreadlocks, but now you're seeing much more, I hate the term, "normal" people. I did a course in London a couple of years ago and the people who were organising it invited along the local town planners, which was an interesting one. So there were people from the Parks Department and people who were quite hard-nosed and level-headed about things and they really got a lot out of it I think.

There are people who are right on the fringes who'll have nothing to do with 'bastards' and there are people who are in there and engaged and I think there's value to both approaches really. In a way, I would draw a parallel with the animal rights scene where there were always those arguments. Do we smash the doors and take the rabbits out or do you engage and try to change the law? I think you can't have one without the other, you always need both ends of the continuum. They are a kind of mutual necessity even though they may not want to have anything to do with each other.

Looking after apple trees Looking back, I remember there was always something being fought, whether it was racism, CND, the roads protest and so on. You'd either win or you'd lose, and then another thing would come after it. We won on the poll tax and suddenly we had the council tax instead. There's always the next hurdle. "They" would always have the next thing lined up, and it's exhausting really, isn't it. And I thought, "What am I for?" I met one of the guys from the band Karma Sutra at an anarchist book fair or something, and there was a big march coming up. And he said, "Are you going on the march?" and I said, "No, I'm going to stay at home and look after my apple trees." And it was a conscious decision to focus on the positive. The whole thing about permaculture, and working with nature, and people care and the fair shares, is that we can meet all of our needs. There is enough for everyone. You don't have to be screwing people to get what you need.

Mark Wilson

As punk gripped the UK in 1977, Mark Wilson was just about to finish school in rural Somerset. Taking on vocal and guitar duties, he immediately formed the Møb with Curtis You'e on bass and Graham Fallows on drums. The three anarcho-punks, inspired by ATV and Crass, decamped to London squats, where they forged an alliance with fellow anarcho band Zounds, toured the free festival circuit, and quickly built up a loyal gig following with their unique goth-punk sound.

The Møb's most notable release was the 1983 LP Let the Tribe Increase. *The band's music appeared mainly on its own co-operative record label, All the Madmen, although the classic* No Doves Fly Here *single was put out on Crass Records. All the Madmen also released records by other like-minded bands including the Astronauts, Blyth Power and Flowers in the Dustbin.*

The Møb split in 1984, after which Mark spent his time working and raising kids – and hardly touched a guitar in 20 years. He runs a strangely beautiful scrap metal and recycling yard in the woods near Bath.

However, a party arranged by Mark's wife, at which all the original members regrouped and played, gave them a taste of what they had been missing. The band reformed in 2011 and has since played extensively across the UK, Europe and the US. The Møb's first new recording in almost 30 years – the 7" single Rise Up!/There's Nothing You've Got I Want *– was released on the resurrected All The Madmen in 2013.*

I was born in Manchester and we moved to Canada when I was a kid. We came back when I was about 13 years old, and ended up living in the West Country in Somerset. I thought at the time, "What the hell are we doing here?" It had nothing to do with how I felt. I felt that I had a much wider view than what I was seeing there. Although what's very interesting, I suppose, [*laughs loudly*] is that I've come back here.

When I started reading about punk in the NME, everyone around us was listening to Deep Purple, Led Zeppelin and Black Sabbath, which was all very well, but it wasn't anything to do with me. When I first heard about punk I had no idea what it would sound like but I knew I was punk, from the second I'd heard about it. And I kind of prayed to God that I would like this music because this is everything I'd dreamed of. And it turned out to be the case. And we'd spend a lot of time travelling here, there and everywhere to watch, and trying to play, punk gigs. We'd all pile in the van, drive to gigs, thinking, "Can we play? Can we get on the bill? Please can we play?" "No, fuck off!" [*laughs*] would be the usual response. And eventually we'd get a few gigs doing this. And through doing all this we ended up meeting a lot of the people we know today – basically by gatecrashing gigs, showing up and saying please.

It was completely against the status quo, both Status Quo the band and status quo the situation. It was like, "Fuck that!" [*laughs*] and that was exactly how I felt. I'd been angry for a long time. I'd been going to football, and there's no pride attached to it, but I was going to football and getting into trouble. I always felt like I was at odds with the world and punk gave it some focus which I hadn't previously had. It was good to feel that there were other people who weren't happy with the world and not in a football violence sort of way. It was coming out sideways previously and it gave it a way to come out that was meaningful.

I am still passionately opposed to the status quo. There is just no way in the world I feel I'm going to ever fall in with it. I suppose the description of myself as an anarchist works better than any other description. I'm not a deep reader of books. I don't know much about the theory, but I do know that's what I believe in. I don't have to rip it apart into small sections; I know that's how I feel. I feel that the world needs people to change it. I need change. I need it for my children, for the people around me. We all need to do something to improve the situation as best we can. People should be much more angry about the situation than we were back then. But the reverse is the case.

The things that are being done to people are outrageous. The bank system needs overthrowing altogether. One of my crazy things that I'm working on now is that we need this peer-to-peer lending because some of the people involved in this scene have a few quid and a lot of us have not-so-much. But even so I'm sure that a lot of us are relying on the banks when we should be relying on each other. The only real way, in my mind, to deal with the disaffection with society is to create our own society and just fucking ignore them because their world doesn't work and it's been proven time and time again. So I just disregard them and pretend they don't exist. You might say that I have a 'head in the sand' attitude but it's not. I'm willing to confront them head on. And that's what I think people need to do: face them − bankers and the government − head on, and say "FUCK YOU! We've had enough of it. You've robbed us. You've robbed my grandfather, you've robbed my father, you're robbing me and you're robbing my children and FUCK OFF!" But as with everything, I've got a foot in both camps in the sense that part of me pulls away as I live in the middle of nowhere, on a hill, in a fortress away from them and I'm also at war with them [*laughs*]. So in some regards I could be regarded as hiding away from them, but I'm also in court with them and I'm happy to fight them in court or wherever they want to fight. And on any level.

Punk or a regular life? Something that I have done for the last 30 years is to be part of the 'Peace Convoy' or whatever the New Age Travellers situation is, and the squatting scene in London. I've always been in a community situation. Apart from a spell when we lived in a house when the children were younger. Although even then people would laugh and say, "Your house is still like a trailer" [*laughs*]. It didn't look like anybody else's house. I've consciously stayed outside of society and I'd be happy to stay out forever more. I was never going to get a 'regular job'. I once went and worked for the Gas Board for six months when I was living in Yeovil. You could either work at Westland helicopters, which entailed working for an apprenticeship in Weymouth, or you could be with the Gas Board working for an apprenticeship in Plymouth. In 1977, all the punk bands played in Plymouth, so I worked in Plymouth to become a gas man. And so when I came back from Plymouth that was the end of being a gas man [*laughs*]. My only interest was in punk bands. And the world was a much better place without me working for the Gas Board [*laughs*].

Don't DIY, do EVERYTHING yourself It's funny because in relation to punk, DIY tends to stand more for things like gigs and so on, but for me it's everything. I believe that everything that needs doing, we can do it ourselves. And I didn't build entirely all of this [*looking around at the house and surroundings*] but I did build it all in my brain. I said, "This is what it's got to be like. We've got to use second-hand wood, we've got to get this wood from here." These windows are all second hand and all begged or borrowed. I watched the TV programme *Grand Designs* and they would spend £40,000 on windows and I would think, "No, you can build a house for £40,000 [*laughs*]." And these windows cost £300 [*looking at massive surrounding floor-to-ceiling windows*] and then we made the wood to fit around the windows. I am PASSIONATE about doing it myself. If you want to do something different you HAVE to break some rules, go out on a limb, and put yourself at enormous personal risk. Everything I've worked for, and the things people have lent me, has been thrown into this house, and we could lose it all. But you have to take chances. And you have to stick your neck out and do the things that you believe in.

Punk changes lives The Møb are obviously a lot different from the so-called anarcho-punk bands. We share the same history and friends and experiences, but we're a miserable, slow-paced band, apparently [*laughs*]. What I know more than anything now, having gone for 30 years, is how much we make people smile with our misery [*laughs loudly*]. It almost feels like we laid our hearts on the line and opened right up and came out with all this misery that was going on in everybody's heads, and now it feels like this explosion of "Fucking hell! We made it through all that." We see that constantly at gigs with people in tears, and they're still there listening to it and we're still there playing it. It has been immense doing it [*the Mob*] again, and it's far, far more important now than it was back in the day for me.

Coming back was an emotional experience and it's had me in tears on many occasions. With hindsight, you might think that we played huge events back in the day but in actual fact it was 30 or 40 people and a couple of dogs [*laughs*] in a field somewhere watching you do this gig. And now you'll be playing to 3 or 400 people and they know these words and they mean something to them. They've carried that with them for maybe 20 or 30 years. Some of them maybe for only two years. But those things mean a lot to them, probably a lot more to them than it did back then. We're still here. We're still fighting and they DIDN'T beat us down. We didn't overdose and we didn't commit suicide like so many did, and we're still here. When I think about all these magical things that have happened to us. All these people that have come out of the woodwork. And we had no idea we'd impacted on these people. No idea at all. It's the stories they tell you about, "How I was going to kill myself." It has just been amazing.

Caring for people that others wouldn't I strongly believe that we have a responsibility for each other and I don't want to go into it on a personal level, but I try and work with people that other people wouldn't work with. People might say, "Why do you put up with that guy? Why do you work with junkies around you?" or whatever. And it's because somebody needs to look out for these guys. They're great people and that's just something that they didn't wish upon themselves. In many ways we're all in need of hospital treatment but we could avoid that hospital treatment by being looked after in the community. That's sort of what we do. And I'm no different to anybody else. I need a support mechanism too. People can put their arm around us and say, "It's alright Mark." Because you're up and your down. And I don't think this is necessarily specific to a certain group of people who are suffering from a mental health issue. I think we're all dealing with some sort of challenge. We just need to help each other and support each other.

Fight back, make a difference Thatcher was much more scary than Cameron. I'm not scared of him at all. I was TERRIFIED of her. She was a very, very bad person that would do very bad things to anyone she wanted to. Perhaps I'm older, perhaps I'm tougher, I don't know, but I'm not scared of them. I'm happy to punch any of them straight in the face [*laughs loudly*]. And don't be fucking scared of them. To some degree that empowers you. And I just keep trying and I keep bouncing back, and I will continue to keep bouncing back.

To make us feel powerless, and that we can't do anything, is obviously in the interest of the powers that be. And they're entirely wrong. It's only through listening to them that we've ended up in that position; we know in our hearts that we ARE powerful and that we CAN do things and that we CAN change things. Somehow we let them believe that we are helpless, and that we should give up. And little, tiny things can make a huge difference. I always quote this example of this guy who was living in a truck opposite me at Glastonbury festival around 1985. Somehow at that particular time he got interested in windmills and he now runs this company called Ecotricity and we buy our electric from him. He basically produces electricity from alternative energies and you can pay for your energy from Ecotricity rather than from the major suppliers. It's guaranteed to go into renewable energy. And this guy from Glastonbury is now the biggest employer in Gloucestershire. He comes from a New Age traveller background, and a punk rock background previously. You CAN make a difference. He's making a fucking big difference, and people shouldn't believe that they can't.

Build a community and Do It Ourselves   So, you might be a graphic designer, and somebody else is a website designer, and somebody else is a technical engineer or a structural engineer. Therefore, if you have some project that you want some help with there are always people you know who can help. For example, I could have done with a structural engineer here, but I am sure within the 5000 friends that you've got on Facebook or whatever, some of these people can help, and whatever project you've got someone will be there. If you need an accountant, you can trust this guy, he won't fuck you about. I don't know how you'd 'police' it, I only come up with the ideas [*laughs and pretends calling his daughter*], "Tess! I've got another one of my ideas." [*laughs*]. I can't help thinking that there are people who would want to fund things; people who perhaps can't do things themselves, but would like to think that it's their money that is helping to change things. Perhaps some people would be better off in London earning £100 an hour funding someone that is out in a tent somewhere, fighting on some frontline. Neither thing needs to be exclusive of the other and I'm sure this happens all over the place. It occurs to me that there are plenty of people living in central London who don't have any space to put up a windmill, but who might want to fund one out of London for instance. And they will get a warm feeling inside knowing that there is a windmill going around somewhere that is down to them.

No regrets   I believe even more passionately now in the things I did 30 years ago. All that time has done is hardened my belief. I am probably more radical now than I've ever been in my life and I'd like to think I'd be more radical again in two or three years time. For a period, I suppose I toed the line a bit, in as much as it suited me, otherwise we'd never ended up in the place that we are now. I worked like

I'm willing to confront them head on. And that's what I think people need to do: face them – bankers and the government – head on, and say "FUCK YOU! We've had enough of it. You've robbed us. You've robbed my grandfather, you've robbed my father, you're robbing me and you're robbing my children and FUCK OFF!

a dog for a long time, but I did enjoy it. I was doing what I liked doing. I would never work at something I wouldn't enjoy and I don't think that anyone needs to. There is plenty of interesting work to do and plenty that can make a difference. So you shouldn't really constrain yourself with some job you don't like.

Regret is a bit of a waste of time, isn't it? You can only deal with what you have got now, what cards you have got to play with today and I don't see any point in looking back and saying, "I should have done this, or I should have done that." I'm very happy with where I am now. People are very fond of this "In the end" saying [*laughs*], but the end is a disaster, you don't want the end, you want a continuation. Things don't have to balance today and they don't have to balance tomorrow, and hopefully you don't have to balance ever because it continues. You can change all of it if you have the time. If you are not happy with something that you did there, then change it.

I'd like to think that if that's what I do – to make it OK to talk about feeling really bad, or feeling lots of love, or feeling lots of anything – then that is great. To make it OK to talk about feeling scared, or being vulnerable – because we are. As much as anything, that is probably what brings us together in punk. That's where we get our greatest strength from, in coming together.

Alternative worlds

Many of the people that we spoke to have told us that in the early days an appreciation of the music brought with it a sense of community and kinship with other fans. There was a sense that, if you had found your way to a gig in the first place, if you had gone on the journey to seek out other punks, then you had done enough to show that you could be trusted and were part of the tribe. We have heard about how people experienced the tolerance and respect within the punk community that they struggled to find outside of it. The women that we have spoken to, in particular, talk about punks being refreshingly free of the sexist assumptions that were very present in the 1970s and 1980s.

Furthermore, punk provided a collecting point for people who felt different in some way: for people who felt that they didn't fit in. Some of our interviewees describe the genre as offering music for misfits, although it is clear that as much as it was for misfits and outsiders, it also offered a place for the curious, dissatisfied or defiant. Jón Gnarr, Sid Truelove, Dick Lucas and many others describe how they had felt that punk spoke to them as people that were disaffected in one way or another.

And for many punks, where this has involved exhibiting different beliefs, dressing alternatively, or refusing to conform, this in itself has attracted violence of one degree or another, which in turn has reinforced a sense of 'otherness.'

"One thing about being a punk is that you emblazon on yourself the mark of the enemy. By becoming a punk, even cutting your hair was a political statement at that time. You put yourself in a position where you suddenly reveal the bias, the bigotry, and the ugliness of the dominant culture. And that's a really shocking thing to learn about." **Ian MacKaye**

In light of all of this, many of the interviewees were eager to take the ideas that they had been exposed to through the scene, and try to translate them into living. They have described how punk had provided them with the opportunity to create whole alternative societies around themselves, and places where they could work out how to put into practice the principles of anarchism, self-sufficiency or communal living.

Creating an outsiders' community   **Little Annie** describes her early life in a depressed New York, where her lack of an education beyond the age of 14 and high unemployment meant that access to success through the usual routes was closed to her. Finding ways to support herself was a struggle and she had little possibility of developing and expressing her creativity and no chance of getting a place in art or theatre school.

At that time, the New York punk scene was re-defining a new paradigm of success for itself that was based upon creativity, glamour and the ability to be provocative and challenge cultural norms. Things that had previously been a disadvantage, like wearing thrift store clothing, became the basis of a kind of outsider chic and the unconventional was embraced. Life was very hard and precarious, but notwithstanding this, Annie was committed to developing as an artist and performer and was encouraged by the community around her. The scene attracted artists and thinkers and Annie received a kind of alternative education within the terms of this new cultural context.

"At the time I thought, 'Who is Kerouac? I don't care what William Burroughs is talking about. I ain't never heard of him. I ain't interested in what you are saying, you're just an old speed freak.' I thought they were all lying, but I was being mentored, whether I wanted to or not, by some top notch mentors."

People within the punk scene in 1970s New York created communities that provided the support and nourishment needed for artists to develop their ideas and find audiences that they couldn't easily access in "normal" society.

Chicago-based **Steve Albini** builds upon this idea of finding a milieu of like-minded people through punk within which to construct your own terms of reference that are independent from the cultural norms.

"Punk was evidence that people outside your immediate peer group, or friends, don't matter... you are your own barometer. You and your friends know what's cool and what isn't cool, or what is and what isn't fun, what's an asshole move and what isn't an asshole move. You have to trust your instincts about this stuff and not worry about external yardsticks, because you are the one who is living this life experience from which you derive this philosophy that you want to be consistent with. Other people that have an opinion about it from the outside? Fuck all those people, they're not in the room at the time."

Testing the Alternatives   For some, a punk way of life has meant much more than a set of interests or artistic endeavours. It has offered an opportunity to explore genuinely alternative ways of living that have involved a particular kind of experimentation.

Crass's Dial House in Essex, UK, is one such example. It is designed with a specific philosophical and libertarian underpinning in mind, where residents and guests are free to negotiate how they live and work together and structure their own time and activities accordingly. It is an 'open house' in that no introductions are needed to visit, although it may not always be easy to find. There are no rotas or rules, or expectations made of people, rather the emphasis is on negotiation in the moment to determine how the people present might live together.

What tends to happen is that individuals pitch in with the work that needs to be done without any formal intervention. Unsurprisingly, in the Do It Yourself (DIY) spirit, the emphasis is on self-sufficiency and most of the food is grown on-site and chickens are kept. It is a place for creativity and meditation and everything within and around the house has been made or decorated by the people that have been involved with the living experiment over the years. Dial House is not remote from the community within which it sits and the site is used as a venue for permaculture courses, music recordings (there is a recording studio) and creativity events are provided for local children. Since its creation, almost 40 years ago, hundreds, possibly thousands, of people have passed through Dial House from famous artists like Banksy to unemployed bankers and their families, and a whole host of individuals in between.

Working in this way for decades, it has demonstrated that, on a small scale, people are perfectly capable of living in a productive and mutually beneficial way without the need for strictly imposed structures. And this has worked alongside, rather than outside of, the local community.

In contrast to a more fixed residence approach, Mark Wilson from the Møb aligned himself with the new-age traveller community. He saw this as a sustainable means of living outside the system, and lived on the road with his family for many years as a part of the Peace Convoy. The focus away from accumulating possessions, the strong community ethos and the daily disruptive challenge of life on the road, seemed to him to provide the conditions he needed to enact his anarchist ideas and fully engage with the business of living his life.

In a similar vein, **Tony Drayton,** creator of the fanzines *Ripped and Torn* and *Kill Your Pet Puppy* travelled deep into unknown territory in a bid to escape conventional society and live a more authentic life. From the London squatting scene to living on the road as a juggler in a troupe of circus performers in Europe, Tony managed to stay on the outside for years.

"With this anarcho-punk micro climate we really felt that we had formed our own society and that it was going to last. We thought that we had broken away from normality and this was it. We'd done it! I was completely removed from society. All of that travelling and living in squatted commercial buildings, I really had little idea of the way that society operated. I had very little communication outside of the punk world. And that became even more so when I got involved with the Stonehenge festivals through Mark of the Møb and the other Wiltshire bands. There were troupes of people there who would play music, juggle and perform circus skills and they would go round Europe and Britain, staying on the "outside" but making money, which was one of the big problems to live."

Life on your own terms Although this may not be overtly acknowledged, or even consciously intended by the individuals that we have spoken to, it is possible to see within the creation of these alternative worlds, a practical application of existential principles. It is not enough for Steve Lake, Mark Wilson or Penny Rimbaud to sit and think about how they might change society and bring about greater freedoms for those within it, they must also act upon those ideas to give them any value or substance. If words are loaded pistols, as Sartre is famously quoted as saying, then actually living the ideas are the flying bullets that create an effect in the world. Not only is there the idea that the real value of radical ideas lies in the doing rather than the thinking, but also when they enact these ideas out in the material world, they can inspire and communicate by example to others.

We see the DIY ethic here too. It is not enough to feel dissatisfied with the injustice that you see around you, or the limited opportunities available to you, or the lack of freedom you may feel – you can do something about it. The people we have spoken to take on the responsibility of creating a social context that allows them to flourish, develop their creative expression and live in accordance with their values. In some ways it is the antidote to the deadening 'anti' stance that we can sometimes find in the punk movement, as it provides answers to the question, "If not this, then what else?"

The punk movement saw value in outsiders and 'rejects.' And it handed them the challenge of making their own choices, rather than accepting received ideas about the acceptable routes to happiness and success.

"The thing about Crass is that what everyone forgets or no-one really knows is that the Crass audience was made up of the real misfits, the fat kid at school that had the piss taken out of him, the skinny kid, the kid with bad acne, and kids who couldn't afford punk clothing, and they didn't even fit in to the punk thing." **Steve Ignorant**

"What punk rock meant to me was that the parts of culture that had previously been dismissible, that is young people, crazy people, people on the fringes of society, people of abnormal behaviour, abnormal tastes, abnormal standards – those people had to be taken seriously now because they could do amazing stuff. And punk was the first time where I thought that people who thought like me, people who had the same sort of background as me, the same sort of world view as me, were taking themselves and these preposterous notions of theirs seriously and they were expressing it." **Steve Albini**

"So to reinterpret what beauty is and what gifts and talents are and to make a place where they are valued, that was supposed to be what it was about. Seeing what we can learn from each other rather than seeing everyone as a threat. Seeing the esteem in everyday actions." **Little Annie**

Fuelled by this challenge to be responsible for your own well-being and contentment, we see people like Little Annie and Steve Albini creating a new context for themselves that makes sense to them and their peers. They define the terms against which their lifestyles and achievements are measured and they surround themselves with people who can support and nourish their creative endeavours.

One of the truths of revolution is that there is no waiting around for the big event to sweep away the barriers to freedom, no doubt only to be replaced by new barriers, or for gradual cultural change. To do this would be handing over responsibility to others to act on your behalf. Instead we find people who have acted in the moment to create the conditions that they need to live their lives authentically and on their own terms.

Penny Rimbaud

Born Jeremy John Ratter in 1943, Penny Rimbaud is a modern polymath – a writer, poet, painter, musician and philosopher. Penny enrolled at art college in the early 1960s where he met a number of the individuals, such as Gee Vaucher and David King, who would later come to be associated with the band Crass. In 1964 he appeared on the TV programme Ready Steady Go! *where he received a prize from John Lennon for winning an art competition.*

In 1967, Penny set up the open house and 'living experiment', Dial House – a 16th century cottage that he found tucked away in the depths of the English countryside, that over the years has become a creative community of musicians, artists, and radical thinkers.

In the early 70s Penny developed a close friendship with visionary and free thinker Wally Hope, with whom he helped to found the Windsor and Stonehenge Free Festivals. Both shared a mystical take on philosophy and living, until Wally's death in 1975, amid suspicious circumstances – about which Penny has written. Shortly afterwards Penny worked with local lad Steve Ignorant in creating what would be come to be described as the quintessential anarcho-punk band   Crass.

Penny continues to be a prolific creative force, offering radical ideas conveyed through a variety of media. He has authored scores of articles and books, recorded with artists including the Charlatans, Japanther, and Bloody Beetroots, and amongst other things performs regularly with Louise Elliot, an Australian saxophonist, as well as a wide variety of other improvisational jazz musicians. Nowadays much of Penny's work reflects a disciplined study, and a preparedness to continue a lifelong journey of philosophical experimentation.

To me, I don't like the notion of 'punk philosophy' because it exclusifies a particular era within the bohemian tradition. Punk was no more than an extension of or a part of it. In fact, it was a part of an ancient tradition that goes back to pre-Greek times. It wasn't a new philosophy, rather a very profound known philosophy juggled in – in my case – with a great deal of mysticism. That whole business side of it, the music side of it, bores the arse off me to be honest. It was a way of expressing oneself, and I don't actually think that Crass was very punk. It was far more avant-garde than it was punk. It was art punk, really, and it's beginning to be recognised as such because it sounds so weird now compared to the trajectory of rock'n'roll that the Sex Pistols and Clash belong in.

But I am relieved really at the interest now in the philosophical side of punk. The only thing that's ever interested me in any social engagement is philosophy.

The reason I do things is always this, and the reason anyone ever does things is philosophical, it's simply that they don't recognise it as such.

I learned a negative lesson from Wally Hope in a way, if you understand what I mean. [*Penny credits Wally with much of the inspiration behind Crass, and believes that he did not commit suicide in 1975, as the official story argued, but was murdered by the state for political reasons*]. He was a profound mystic and a profound shamanist. He certainly was capable of alchemic projection, and I enjoyed that. It was a confirmation of my own journey, which had been much more through eastern philosophies. His journey had been through that strange western shamanistic thing that sometimes comes from acid. Usually it doesn't, but I think he'd created it into some form of magic. I learned a lot from that western form of my own Zen mysticism. Something that, in a strange way, was more applicable. I felt quite on my own with my own form of Eastern thinking. It was very private, not because I chose it to be, it was private because no one fucking understood anything about what I was talking about.

My most profound conversation with Wally involved no words. We simply beat a fire and described the future. I wasn't aware that we were doing that at the time but, in retrospect, immediately afterwards (when we stopped beating the fire) we realised that we'd actually been planning the Stonehenge Free Festival and all of the outcomes. Possibly not the Beanfield, it wasn't quite that good [*The Battle of the Beanfield took place on 1 June 1985, when Wiltshire Police prevented a convoy of several hundred New Age travellers (known as The Convoy) from setting up at what would have been the 11th Stonehenge Free Festival in England. Members of the police attacked the procession by forcefully entering the field in which the vehicles were contained, methodically smashed windows, beat people about the head with truncheons, used sledgehammers to break and damage the interiors of their vehicles and arrested the convoy members*].

Up until what happened at Stonehenge and specifically what happened with him made me realise that the dream wasn't going to work the way I'd been projecting, and we had to move in a different direction.

I had the great benefit of not having a father initially, and when my father came home from the war he brought all the horrors of the world with him. That was where I started rebelling; I thought, "If that's the world then I'm not going to play." At a very early age I wasn't playing. Not playing entailed saying "why?" to everything, like most kids do. They're natural rebels, kids, because they don't actually want to know, they don't want to have to deal with all this shit, and they know better because they come from somewhere else.

Everything is attitude and choice   Since Wally's death I've come to realise that anger is an unfulfilled form of compassion. I like to think that I've arrived at a far more compassionate place that understands and accepts. Everything is simply attitude; the external world is merely a set of attitudes. And there's a profound existentialism in that. The world is simply what we bring to it; it can be no other way. That's not a whimsy, that's not a piece of mysticism; it's an absolute truth.

The only manner in which that can be corrupted or violated is through attachment of any sort. I can get attached. I'm getting better and better at not doing that, but it's not because I'm trying to do anything, it's simply programming. It's like how you get a new computer and you learn how it all figures together and suddenly it all starts working, whereas before it's like, "Fucking machine, never works." I think the human psyche is the same. If we program it right, it's so easy. Although easy for most people in the western world actually means difficult. Easy is making your own bread, cutting the wood, being your own doctor, being your own psychiatrist, being your own all of these things where we've given away our own power. To have your own power is a massive existential responsibility.

I had cancer and I treated it through vibrational medicines and the help of a Chinese herbalist who also works on a vibrational level. That worked for me and I came out of it blessed. It might not work for other people and they'll find their own form of blessing. I do believe the old Yogic idea that we are what we eat, and if we eat pharmaceutical drugs that's what we are, in part — our thinking is affected, our being is affected. On a molecular level, we start acting differently within the molecular world. We become a different energetic force.

My entire body of work has been engaged in trying to help people make a choice, and on its most simple level it's saying, "None of this is real, so why are you suffering from it? Within it? It is actually an illusion." The Buddhist will simply talk about it as illusion, but the illusion is one's attitude. You alone are your attitude, no one else can be held responsible for it. Blame your teachers, blame whomever you're like. If you're in a position of being able to blame, you're also in a position of choosing no longer to be engaged.

On a path to healing   Philosophy is a scientific attempt to heal the world through the intellect, through juggling of words to find the irrefutable, to find the great fire.

Likewise, so is healing. In healing others, one is healing oneself, because you are others. There is no other. That, if you like, is the devastating existential responsibility. That's the process that I have become engaged in and I recognise other existentialists as having become engaged in. And I view it on a quantum level. I love the multiple possibility of quantum, and that offers almost a parallel to the whole attitudinal perspective. This is the current projection, but actually we can jump now, and that's a very Zen thing. We can jump now, at the click of a finger, we're free!

At the next click we may then draw back all the sort of darkness that we like to inhabit because liking it is the only reason we could possibly want to do so. There's no excuse, there's absolutely no excuse. "I was abused as a child", that's no excuse. It's a reason. The very people who most seek psychiatric assistance in a Freudian sense are the very people who should click their finger, because they've actually got a reason to.

We exist, and we can't not exist. We are of the world, and the world gives as much as we do. The love you take is the love you make. It's as simple as that. The world is profoundly self-governing, and self-healing. That healing might mean the eradication of the human race, but that's the process. Either one is engaged in that process, or one is not. The material world, as represented by the western democracies, is profoundly not engaged in that. It's engaged in determinism, projection, and futures. It's funny that 'futures' is used as an economic term.

I am the whip and the back being whipped   All my life I've been haunted by the Holocaust, and that started with seeing some pictures [*of the Sobibor or Treblinka death camps*] when I was 4 or 5 in my parents' library and thinking' "Jesus fucking Christ, that's it. No thank you." I've read so much and continue to read about the Holocaust, just looking for a clue. The clue came when I suddenly realised that it could only have been that way, and here we are, and how ungracious it would be, if I were to not recognise, as I do, and be a manifestation of which I am — this exquisite moment. And I don't mean exquisite in the X factor sense, I mean exquisite in the divine sense. We are here. We are here because of those Ukrainian guards [*survivors of Sobibor and Treblinka remembered the Ukrainian guards as being more brutal than the Germans*].

We are here because of every cruelty. And because of every beauty   It wasn't so much the symbiotic nature of the victim and the victimiser. They profoundly became unified and at last I found forgiveness. There's a lovely Chinese saying that "they who cannot forgive, dig two graves." I think that's beautiful, and it's so true. It's only in the last two years that I have been able to utterly and completely forgive the Ukrainian guards who were the manifest, grossest element of the whole Nazi program, because they were the people brought in to do the dirty work.

Seeing that is becoming it. That is our potential; we have the potential to be either or both, and therefore self-negating. As much as we might be the victim, so we might be the victimiser. If we can be both, and we manifestly can, then we can be neither and we exist free of that. That's the whole thing that I've come to realise profoundly in the last two years. My whole life has been a struggle towards realising that, and I certainly wouldn't claim to be enlightened, but I feel free, at last; at least, to exist. And when I could at last forgive the Ukrainian guards, there was the duality I was trying to destroy in myself. I just couldn't see how to do it.

There's one particular face in the pit, one girl looking out. Profoundly beautiful, and I've blown up pictures of her and I've given her makeup. I've tried my own acts of re-engagement, restatement, and they'd always failed. They didn't work, because I wasn't looking in the right place. I was looking in the pit, not out of the pit. I needed to paint the face of the Ukrainian guard, which I managed to do and we were free at last, all of us. They were free from their victimhood, he was free of his victimising, and I was free of them both.

So, I now can exist, not even faced with the existential problem of how I manifest within the existence because I simply am manifesting within the existence. I still have moments of doubt and fears, and that's one way in which the ego enjoys a presence.

1, 2, 3 Go, I've got an ego, it won't let me go   The ego is every bit as much an external manifestation as any other part of the material world. That in itself is fantastically liberating. People manufacture and manifest in whatever ways are useful to them in whatever situation they're in. Egos cannot connect. They do not connect. They simply manipulate in a way that is genetic, as in Dawkins' interpretation of it, with *The Selfish Gene*. It's not motivated by intent as such, it's deeper than that, but there's a parallel there.

The needs of the ego are projected from the very start, and the beginning of our consciousness is the awareness of needs. Actually we're not aware that they're other people's needs, we feel they're our own needs. The names we are given are an example. Who are you? I'm Jeremy John Ratter. No I'm not Jeremy John Ratter. That's someone else's name for me. I'm Penny Rimbaud. Claiming my own place.

I was freed through existentialism by realising actually you can reverse all of that. You can create your own choice. You're no longer protected by a sort of moral framework. What the parent likes to believe is that they're offering not only agency but also a moral framework in which their agency can operate. These are the conditions, but don't worry too much about them because actually you're protected and you're safe. These are the parameters; although they don't say it like that. They say this is God or this is the state. I'm using those two conditions and I know there are thousands of others like them; this is the village, this is the community, this is whatever you want. These are the things that will protect THIS particular way of thinking that WE'VE given you. Don't step outside it because you'll be in danger and it's true that you really are in danger if you step outside. From the very start you are completely defined by it and you believe in that definition.

Universal love   I think of the self as an entity, or even an identity, that can exist without the ego. But, it doesn't like doing so because the ego is so incredibly embroiled within its own thinking.

One of its major controls is love. That's why we have such a sort of dreadful manifestation of love, that's why love means so little within our society. It's the subject of crass pop songs and all the rest of it. They're talking about love, but really it's to do with ownership, possession, and sex, whatever.

And I have fallen for that, and that was because I fell in love. The lesson I learned from that was that it was a series of conceits. I was only feeling engaged because I had my ego supported by making love or being told what a beautiful person I am. Or all those other intrigues that go on in that sort of relationship — just having my ego boosted all the time. Even in disputes it would still have been. Because the very dispute was an extension of the same thing. And all of this precludes a broader symbiosis. I had to go through something that extreme to actually come out on the other side and understand it at last. And now I have that love universally. The universal love I always saw through the agency as an individual, is now removed.

Self-forgiveness   The ego really doesn't like self-love. The ego wants to hold the love and use the love. It doesn't want the deeper self to experience that because then it no longer has its control. And forgiveness, and self-forgiveness is the beginning of dealing with that. The self-love that arises as the result of self-forgiveness involves a TAKING BACK of what is our right from this imagined self who's stolen everything from us.

I think the key… is the idea that until we can accept that everything is at this moment EXACTLY and only, the ONLY way it can be, until we can accept that, we can't move. We have to accept that — because otherwise what are we building on? If we accept that then immediately we're put into the compassionate zone. It's only when I realised that, in relation to, for example, the gas chambers, suddenly I held a whip. And I was also the back that I was whipping. We were as one. Then the devastating past disappeared. It filtered away. All the time, people believe, I think, that by hanging on to the devastations of the past they, in someway, are manifesting a self. Well they are. They're manifesting an ego self. They're feeding the ego. All of that stuff about abuse and all those things it's ego feeding. It might have happened, it might not have happened. It makes no difference, it's ego feeding. As long as you feed the ego, there's no way of healing. The only way of healing is absolute compassion and compassion is as much for one's own folly. The first person to forgive is oneself.

We're all doing our best in the circumstances Sometimes I experience that old duality where I'll say, "I've done the best I can" and the other dualistic voice says, "Well, it was a fucking poor shot," and then I'll get into self-pity, which is pure dualism. It's dualism of an external being; two ideas of self — the good and the bad — which is a complete separation and is nothing but ego. The ego doesn't actually care whether it gets attention through being bad or good as long as it gets attention. Most people remain in that situation for a great deal of their lives. In a sense, it doesn't matter which one's best at the moment.

Everyone's doing his or her best. Adolf Hitler was doing his best. Ronald Reagan was doing his best. They do it in good heart, even if we can't understand that heart. Generally speaking, if one can be bothered to inform oneself away from commonly held prejudices, which are really only social mores, one can begin to understand. It's not difficult to understand Hitler's vile anti-Semitism. It doesn't mean one's sympathetic with it in any way whatsoever, but it's very understandable.

There is no blame. There can be no blame. We are all doing our best. Neither is there any better than that, there can be no better than that. We are all quite perfect entities at any given time, whatever horrible manifestation that might be taking. Because it is allowing this moment to happen.

Looking at this politically, I loathe socialism. It is a horrifically patronising position to be in. It's a conceit. It denies people their being in a strange way. They're being, whatever they are on the path to, wherever they're going, and I don't think anyone is qualified to be critical of that, unless invited of course.

I've got no gripe against any politicians. It's of no consequence. They're all doing their best and whether I do or don't happen to agree with them is irrelevant and inconsequential, and it lacks any compassion. If I'm going to talk about any of this, we have to acknowledge that there are wounds that exist, and that they're not going to be healed through more aggression, and they're certainly not going to be healed through violence as such, but only through compassion. I think that is common to all human kind. I think that people are inherently good and I don't mean that in the value sense, they're inherently kind and I do believe that. I've never met anyone that isn't, even if I detest their political views or their social behaviour, it doesn't remove their essential kindness. I mean Jack the Ripper thought he was being kind by killing whores. That's not my line, but it's part of the same point.

You don't need justice where there is forgiveness and kindness And on the question of whether that kindness leads to justice, my view is that you don't need justice where there's forgiveness and where there's acceptance. And one either lives in the world one believes, or one doesn't live in the world one believes, and I choose to live in the world I believe. So I am perfectly aware that there are horrific injustices, I'm perfectly aware of suffering, I'm perfectly aware of all of that, but I'm not about to act as compounder of those things. Whereas I was prepared to engage in some way 30 years ago, I'm not prepared to do so now; to do so simply empowers the opposition. It takes two to boogie. It is by removing opposition to the opposition that the opposition itself ceases.

I became pretty much dependent for a period of about a year. I had cancer and didn't want to have my eyes fixed (as there were some problems there too) because I couldn't deal with having so much going on at the same time, so I was dependent in a sense that I couldn't see for about a year. Everything else was just cloud. If I went out I had to either be with someone or just ask for help, which is very humbling, and then I had trouble with my back, so for three months I could not walk without one or two sticks, and even then I could only possibly manage five yards or so, and again I became dependent. But the kindness was unbelievable. And I enjoyed it; I'm not complaining about it, I was learning so much. Not once did I get in the train when someone wouldn't immediately stand up – people know, they recognise pain, they recognise real need and that's amazing. I thought in all probability I was going to die. And because of the decisions that I made when I was very young that I was not going to contribute to an extension of myself by having children, I've got nothing in that sense, my flesh ends here.

Ugly from the mind, beautiful from the heart   One of the things I find really stinks about academia is the way that an academic is required to quote supportive ideas, because you can find a supportive idea for any possible idea in the world. It's an absolutely pointless exercise. It has no value. Simply because Schopenhauer said something doesn't actually give you any weight in saying something similar. Unless you understand it in your own way, in relation to your own feelings, you don't understand it; you simply understand what Schopenhauer is saying. I mean I find it insulting when people say, "Oh, well yeah that's what Freud said." Or, "Oh yeah, that's what I'm saying." Because I don't give a fuck what Freud said. I care about what I feel and what I have to offer and my understandings and what I can show to someone. Which is not going to be supported by the fact that I might have read a book about Freud.

These two things are very different and that's why academics remain forever behind the screen. God bless them, they're trying their very best, but they're incapable of breaking the glass. They're not prepared to walk through the looking glass.

If it doesn't come from the heart it comes from the mind and then it can be poisonous. From the mind it's ugly, from the heart it's intimacy. And knowing the difference between the heart and the mind is the beginning of one's own self-intimacy.

Making a synaptic leap of faith   I want to end on some broader thoughts. I think in Greek times they thought the mind was located in the heart. The more modern idea that there's a central part to the brain as well, went out of the window a long time ago. The idea was that the left and right were independent aspects and there wasn't a convenient middle station in between things.

The suggestion now seems to be that there aren't even locations as such. The pieces of 'it', are located all over the place. My own feeling is that pieces of it are located over every atom of our body – every molecule of our body, particularly within the water flow. And also outside of it – that's the auric body and the auric body extends across the cosmos that is beyond the universe. This is what's suggested in quantum terms. All of that stuff about the butterfly flapping its wings and this having an effect in the Amazon is absolutely 100% right.

Neurologists aren't able to say categorically that neurological patterns can escape, that they DO drift. But they do fly; they are actually being reflected across the universe. Neurologists can't say that until they can actually prove it. But the suggestion is that this is probably what's happening.

I've talked about this before in terms of the synaptic leap. And I've come to the view that the synaptic leap is actually the governance of form. It's the governance of form because actually at the point in which infinity is touched, form cannot be created outside of, or separate from, the infinitive nature of being; of 'itness.' The only time we connect with that in a profound sense is possibly at the point in which the atom is in drift.

This is it — get used to it

Conditional peace is war. Conditional love is psychic violence. Conditional freedom is slavery. Slavery is the de facto condition of the Cartesian mind. In its efforts to circumvent this condition, and despite being a profoundly useful road map for manoeuvring the day to day vexations of the material world, Existential freedom (to choose or otherwise) is a materialist deceit and, for however long it is that we choose to cling to those vexations, will remain nothing but delusion. Quite regardless of our singular philosophies, freedom simply is. It cannot be created because it already exists absolute, and thus also cannot be recreated. Equally, it cannot be found because it was never lost. If we choose not to see it, then, in an act of denial, we have chosen not to see it. However, should we choose to see it, we will not, because in choosing to see it and, indeed, to be able to see it, we must abandon everything that we imagine ourselves to be. Thus, paradoxically, in seeing it we must cease to be the seeing I (at last collapsing Cartesian conceits).

A manufactured freedom must by nature be a personal idea of freedom which, equally by nature, must be conditional in that it ignores the impersonal, unconditional and absolute nature of freedom. In short, through dividing ourselves from freedom we perpetuate the duality which in the first place created the sense of non-freedom.

In reworking *Yes, Sir, I Will* for performance at the Rebellion Festival of 2014, I became crucially aware of the fundamental dualism within the Existential thought that had driven the original script of 1983. Quite naturally, I became concerned that in my attempts to affect the material world I might very well have been doing little more than adding to its vexations. It was a predicament, one which for some time appeared insoluble. I was committed to perform the piece, but was unable to find the key wherein I could rework it to reflect what I knew must take a more compassionate overview. Eventually, this came to me from two different directions.

One particularly beautiful summer's day, I was lying half asleep in a London park and found myself (as I often do) humming a John Lennon song. In this case it was *All You Need Is Love*, and that, I felt in a rather dozy, dreamy fashion, was enough — *There's nothing you can make that can't be made, no one you can save that can't be saved, nothing you can do, but you can learn to be you in time, it's easy...* However, on returning to the *Yes, Sir* rework, I found that it wasn't easy at all. John had handed me the key, but I now needed to find the door upon which to use it.

As part of my endeavours to *learn to be* [me] *in time*, I practice daily meditation, sitting in front of a blank wall attempting to get out of the way of myself: this is it – get used to it. Often whilst meditating, thoughts (or possibly even insights) pop up out of the blankness, some of them sticking with me, others returning to it. Following my daydreams in the park, one in particular that did stick with me, and appeared to have a deep resonance with Lennon's *All You Need*, was *between left and right there is a universe*. I soon realised that this was my door. From then on, if not entirely easy, the rework was certainly easier.

Through replacing vicious anger with love, and *grey robots* with *people* (albeit sometimes as puppeteers), I was largely able to satisfy my wish to change the passionate outcries of *Yes, Sir* into ones which expressed and promoted compassion and love (albeit the hugely demanding realm of love in its unconditional form).

It is not for me to judge the success of this project, but I am able to say that, although I could and might have taken it further, I am happy enough with the outcome.

WHEREAS PASSION IS THE LOVE OF FORCE,

COMPASSION IS THE FORCE OF LOVE.

Penny Rimbaud.
Summer 2014.

YES, SIR, I WILL

- the truth of revolution -

In memory of John Ono Lennon

People try to put us down just because we've stuck around, / well I'd be happy / to cause a big sensation just talking about our generation, / our generation, our generation…

When you woke this morning you looked so rocky-eyed, / blue and white normally, but strange ringed like that in black. / It doesn't get much better, / your voice can get just ripped out shouting in vain. / Maybe someone hears what you say, but you're still on your own at night. / You've got to make such a noise to understand the silence, / screaming like a jackass, ringing ears so you can't hear the silence, / even when it's there like the wind seen from the window, / seeing it, but not being touched by it, seeing it, but not being touched by it.

We are poets, armed with the cobblestones of language, / and if sometimes our words don't seem to mean too much, / that's fine, for the moment it's the best we can give: / feelings from the heart, expressions of our love, / a blessing on the lives we chose to live.

We are poets, armed with the cobblestones of word. / Words are the stream, flowing from the ocean of consciousness, / and while stones perish, words will remain. / Sometimes what we have to say might seem a little frail / against those who try to put us down, / but their efforts to silence us will always fail / because we know that our life is our own.

We are poets, armed with the cobblestones of imagination. / We are fluid, washing over the rock of vanities, / wearing it away with warmth and love, / juggling realities with the absurd, trying to make it clear / that we have the right to be free, you and I together.

We are poets, armed with the cobblestones of love, / unconditional, uncompromising, beyond need of proof. / Yet in attempts to moderate our righteous anger, / people ask why we don't write love songs. / But what is it we write about if it is not love? / Our love of life is total. / Everything we do is in expression of that. / Everything we write is a love song. / Yes, we are poets of love.

Yet how easily we can be seduced / by tawdry billboards, the pulse of neon, / flashing screen and ugly tabloid: / the braying voices of Mammon's minions. / Yet away from the looking-glass windows of consumerism / we create cascading waterfalls of glee: / a tumbling rush to other landscapes / where dancing summer winds lift our spirits / to colour distant futures.

For all our efforts to create a better world, / people still see us as outsiders, but outside of what? / Surely they can see how much we care, / or feel the force of the love that we share? / Standing together as the crowd, / standing together tall and proud, / it is we who are the many, they who are the few, / so who's on the outside? Not me and you. / And no, we won't conform to the standards of others / when ours often seem so much higher. / For all their criticism, doubt and deceit / they'll never douse our fire. / So, *what in the world are they thinking of, / laughing in the face of love.* / What on Earth are they trying to do / when surely it's up to us, yeah, me and you.

Lennon also said *they hate you if you're clever and they despise a fool,* / he was right, it's just the same old game of deride and rule, / but our life-confirming intelligence cannot be dismissed / simply because it doesn't conform to mainstream values. / Oh yes, the State demands our agreement and compromise, / but in exchange for what? / Oh yes, the boundaries seem to get tighter as the / State becomes more paranoid, / but boundaries to what? / Cowering in our temples of self, / there'd be little chance of change, / and the State is aware of that. / But what is the State / if not a state of fear held in thrall by a state of mind? / If victims we are, victims we be: / it's only through cracking that state of mind that ever we'll be free. / The choice is ours, the voice is ours – why wait? / Under the pressure of fool's rule, / fear is the message, fear is the tool, / fear of self and other, fear of heart and soul: / fear, the savage weapon of mass control / wherein the crippling dictates of social conformity / offer no more than a pretence of security. / But we have our love and in that we can be, / the you that is you and the me that is me. / With all the force of life on our side, / we've got everything to give and nothing to hide. / Bad-mouthing us with labels and definitions, / cynics say that we're just naïve dreamers, / but throughout history dreamers have been condemned / only to be later celebrated as heroes. / Mahatma Ghandi had a dream, / Martin Luther King had a dream, / John Lennon had a dream: / Shot dead, but their dreams live on in heart and mind, / in the power of love they left behind.

But why is it that the kind and gentle / are subjected to ridicule and abuse? / What is this perversion that allows fools to rule / like puppeteers pulling the strings? / But rule who, I ask you, rule who? / Isn't unconditional love an ungovernable force / and the betterment of the world its only natural course?

Sometimes the terrible inequalities amongst the peoples of this earth / seem to undermine ideas of freedom, / but that inequality is only added to / through our inability to see ourselves as one. / Whereas each death is in part our death, / each birth bears new possibility. / Each moment is fresh and new, / its outcome is solely up to you. / There are so many things that can be done, / if we could but learn to see outside the problem. / It's only beyond the suffering of our world / that the true blossom of life might at last be unfurled. / Only you, only me, only we, together that we might see.

Making the compromises, / what did you know, what did you care? / Brave fronts, deceitful disguises, / what did you know, what did you care? / Turning a blind eye to the lies just to keep it all together, / but at times when we are gathered like this / I truly feel it was worth it. / So what do you know and why should you care? / What do you know, why should you care?

Oh then, borrow my tiredness, young girl, young boy, / and wrap it in your hair like garlands, / take it as a kiss and feel it upon your lips.

Oh, borrow these aches, young girl, young boy, / and make them into the spring of your lithe bodies, / the laughter of heart and the chuckle of soul. / We who are the children, eternal and free, / the unborn, beyond false grace, / who claim back an immortality / beyond the burnt offerings of time and space.

Oh take my love, young girl, young boy, / and use it as your own, / take my poetry, take my song, / that we might be as one / beyond division, beyond all pain, / that to heavenly heights / we might fly again.

Then share my joy, / young girl, young boy, / and we will sing a love supreme, / that we might dance the dance of life / and feel the promise of our dreams, / feel the promise of our dreams.

But yes, even our dreams can become institutionalised, / becoming a poor parody of themselves, contained by themselves. / There's no point in just mouthing the words: / the token tantrums just aren't enough, / and nor is speed or weed or acting tough. / We don't need exclusive little tribes and their back-slapping, / nor their stand-off vibes all a'bull-crapping. / Punk spawned another rock'n'roll elite, / another bunch of hypocrites out to knock us off our feet, / mouthing platitudes just like X Factor trash, / talking revolution whilst pocketing the cash. / Just another cheap product for the consumers' head; / is it any wonder I once wrote *Punk is Dead?* / Who's a pretty boy, then? / Yes, ladies and gentlemen, boys and girls, / it's *The Feeding of the Five Knuckle Shuffle.*

If there was no government, wouldn't there be chaos, / everybody running round setting petrol bombs off? / And if there was no police force, tell me what you'd do / if thirty thousand rioters came running after you. / And who would clean the sewers? Who'd mend my television? / Wouldn't people lay around without some supervision? / Who'd drive the fire engine? Who'd fix my video? / If there were no prisons, where would robbers go? / Well, what if I just said **fuck off?**

What if there's no army to stop a big invasion? / Who'd clean the bogs and sweep the floors? / We'd have all immigration. / Who'd pull the pint at the local pub? / Where'd I get my fags? / Who'd empty out the dustbins? / Would I still get plastic bags? / If there were no hospitals and no doctors too, / if I'd broken both my legs, where would I run to? / If there was no medication, if there were no nurses, / wouldn't people die a lot, and who would drive the hearses? / Well, what if I just said **fuck off?**

And if there were no butchers' shops, what would people eat? / You'd have everybody starving if they didn't have their meat. / If there was no water, what would people drink? / Who'd flush away the you-know-what? / But of course mine never stink. / What about the children, / who'd teach them in the schools? / Who'd make the beggars keep in line, / who'd learn them all the rules? / Who'd tell us to whitewash windows, / or when to take down doors, / tell us to make a flask of tea to survive the holocaust? / Well, what if / I was to say, what if you were to say, / what if we were to say…**1, 2, 3, 4, FUCK OFF?**

Oh yea, the media pundits were always ready to rip us off, / happy to use our messages of peace and love / to make profit in a world of hate and war, / to undermine everything we were striving for. / Describing futures whilst nailed to the spot? / So where's the free individual in that? / Where's the hope and aspiration / in identities stolen by the mega-corporations / to be sold back as vanities shaped in media moulds / of Botox babes with tucks and folds / and, if by chance you're a really Big Man, / a six-pack of Tennents and a Tango tan. / But let me ask you this; just who do they think they're fooling? / What silken hand was ever cut away in the battlefield / or emperor's boot ever rotted in squalid trenches? / We don't accept servility in exchange for dignity. / We don't accept death as a bargain for life. / We don't accept this psychic pillage / like we're no more than some kind of toxic spillage. / We take up our beds and walk the walk, / open our mouths and talk the talk. / The rights of the individual / are dependent upon us claiming our individual rights, loud and clear, / beyond the delusions of political choice / where the voice that speaks is not your voice, / but the gutless voice of the passive observer.

Passive observers do nothing but passively observe, / passively soak up creativity and say *Wow, that was me,* / passively soak up destruction and say *Oh no, not us, not me.* / Turning a blind eye to unpalatable fact, / they prefer to put down those who act. / Then, bemoaning the loss of what might have been, / spend their days glued to the screen, / confirming the life they've already missed / by buying into the Judas kiss. / While three quarters of the world struggles to exist, / the other quarter is tapping tittle tattle texts, / mobilising mobiles with chatter that never ends, / or sending selfies to ever-absent friends.

Hello, hello, where are you? Where are you? / *Hello, where are you? Where are you?*

Space Invaders, / and hidden persuaders, / dot, dot, dot, dot, dot, dot, coms, / information networks, media extensions, / where, being no more than ad-mens' schemes, / nothing's really quite what it seems. / Where you buy out the now and pay as you go / and, minding the gaps, just join in the show. / Hollywood? Bollywood? Jolly good. / Celebrity culture feeds the greed / for a nonsense life that none of us need. / The TV serves to keep us hanging on / to a worn-out reality to which none of us belong. / The media puppeteers pull the strings / trusting we'll take flight on broken wings: / tired old clichés for cul de sac minds / where everyone's looking, but no one finds, / where words are banded about, strictly PC, / but are always headed with a *me, me, me.* / But sorry, sorry, no need to worry: / those who suffer the inevitable headache / from too much digital or cathode intake / can drop a pharmaceutical fix-it-all / or take a trip to the local and piss it up the wall.

Fancy another? Oh go on then, you only die once.

True enough, but when the real killing gets going, / Palestine, Syria, Libya, Iraq, Afghanistan, / government censors attempt to block us from knowing even a half of it. / Yes, the Internet could redress the imbalance, / but against porn and gambling what's the chance?

In terms of *national security*, / nine-eleven was a second heaven: / the matter of three-thousand deaths / seems to mean nothing against the formidable aftermath:

For or against, against or for? / was declaration of a lifetime's war / against the peoples of the world, one and all, / and where fools fear to tread, angels are bound to fall. / The fearsome *War Against Terror* was born / and the *them and us* line was conclusively drawn. / Terrorism became defined as any form of political dissent, / and suddenly everyone's a terrorist, guilty until proven innocent. / That's you, babe, that's me, / up against a wall of political illiteracy. / War on terror? / One small error and we'll be doing time. / One small error and we're on the firing line.

Oh, but no, not the gentle goat-herd in those wildernesses of desert and hill, / nor his milk-mouthed, dark-eyed child / tugging on the rag of her mother's coarse cloth skirts. / In their timeless innocence they understand nothing of war.

Not those tormented souls driven to the shelter / that the whining shells of Mammon might defile compassion, / destroy grace and erase love. / They were neither for nor against, yet in their multitude / it is they who were mown down…always they, always they.

Yet it is I, I who knows the fearsome intellect of war, / born of it, torn by it, I the politic, resolutely against. / It is I then, I alone, who must stand against the ignorance of might / and the cool sophistication of collateral revenge. / My name is known, my address given. / I am the enemy if enemy must be sought, / so let them unleash their wretched bombs on me.

Fight war, not wars, fight war, not wars, / fight war, not wars, I know you've heard it before. / And yes, it's said that truth is the first casualty of war, / but war is also a casualty of truth, / just another nail in the coffin of love.

From birth we're teased into submission / by family, school, church and State, / who, whilst claiming to protect our innocence, / will keep at it until we capitulate. / From then on, we're easy game: / *do this, do that... thou shalt not,* / Pavlovian dogs chained to the spot. / But if our true nature finds a way out, / we can bark'n'bite just as much as shout. / For this reason, we are dissuaded at all costs from realising our true potential. / Then, most surely, we have been conditioned to be passive observers. / If the puppeteers want war, / we have been conditioned to accept it. / After all, war only exists through passive acceptance. / But if the puppeteers were to offer peace, / surely, we will have been conditioned to accept that too? / But whereas war simply requires the masses as cannon-fodder, / peace requires individuals to realise their own strength. / No wonder, then, that the puppeteers' sights / are always set on fracture and division, / while for the beauties of peace there'll be no provision.

Freed from sedation, released from bondage, / the ordinary peoples of the world / could realise their own strength, / but how well the puppeteers know of this: / the strings are pulled, the names are called, / and another generation marches out to another war to end all war, / or are tied to the production line / which has no end but the production line, / which has no end but the production line, which has no end...

But within this, a voice, always a voice crying, / *we have the choice, we have the choice.* / It is precisely here that the puppeteers will always lose / against our fundamental right to choose: / this is our life, let's make it, / this is our chance, let's take it.

Che said that revolution without love was no revolution at all, / but neither is a thousand angels with their backs against the wall. / It's impossible to measure the power of love / or to give it its rightful place, / yet only love and love alone / can define the true nature of peace. / For so long, people have been saying no more this, no more that, / only to be handed pithy concessions to accommodate their grievances. / The puppeteers juggle on the boundaries of our tolerance / attempting to ensure our placation, / determined never to give peace a chance / against their program of devastation. / And yes, they have tabs on those they regard as subversives: / recorded, digitised, and backed-up on hard-drive: / ones and zeroes for ever. / What's more, it's too easy to be forced back into tokenism, / making hollow gestures beneath the shadow of the juggernaut, / and, with this in mind, it's now or never. / Yes, now is the moment, now is the place / to take on love and to carry its grace.

The line is delicate: / Mammon blinks, and his acolytes pay homage. / Murdoch burps, and the fetid clouds of deception / fill unwatched azure skies. / Bland, blind corporate security guards lurk as shadow, / batons at the ready to beat the head, crack open the skull. / But even under threat of bullies and egotists, / the spaces have always been inhabited by the gentle and caring, / ordinary folk existing on the power of love. / Gandhi called it *Ahimsa*. / The Greenham women called it *The Politics of Whimsy*, / but the common name is *common decency*.

The love that creates peace is a deep state of heart. / The hate that creates war is a distorted state of mind. / Then once and for all we should leave behind / these contortions that so cruelly tear us apart. / There is peace if we make it: / *War is over if you want it.*

Poverty is a double-edged sword. / Throughout the world, / underprivileged people are employed making armaments / to kill underprivileged people like themselves. / And this is the truth of the dignity of labour; / feed thyself, kill thy neighbour. / The puppeteers exploit our natural kindness, / distorting it into slavery, / yet we have the fundamental right to break those chains / as long as we have the bravery.

The puppeteers have their laws and those who impose it: / we have ourselves and each other. / The puppeteers have their order, a New World Order, and those who impose it: / we have ourselves and each other. / It's easy for them to dismiss as dreamers those who seek peace, / but isn't our whole culture built on past dreams? / We have ourselves and each other, and that is enough, / through our continued existence we prove the power of love. / For all its horrors pushing people to their limit, / histories have never broken the human spirit. / However much violence might persist, / together we do and can exist / dancing the dance of life, / life lifeing life in individual frames. / The line is delicate, the lines are drawn, / but each and every moment a new future is born.

Harrods boasts that it can satisfy any whim of its clients: / tacky trinkets, gewgaws and trash: the cluster bombs of consumerism. / But let them supply me with a starving, war-torn child / and I'll demonstrate the politics of defiance. / Equality doesn't enter the equation, / there's either love, or there's devastation.

There are those who applaud the carnage from the grandstand / as if they were at Ascot, laying their bets: / five to one on the Four Horsemen. / It's a gamble, / but no amount of money can ever buy us out of our responsibility to life. / Yes, we all do our best, we're all as one, / some of us suffer as others have fun, / but until we realise the true nature of our unity, / we'll continue to add to the pains of duality.

The puppeteers dance about on the bodies of the millions of dead / that they have sacrificed to maintain control. / But control of what? / For all the palaces, cabbages and kings / the golden wings of spirit has never been controlled. / There's never been proof that violence pays. / Yes, the puppeteers are no less than murderers and thieves, / shadows in the darkness of night, / but we are so much more than that. / Love is the power. Love is the hour. This is the time to act. / We can give it, we can live it, beyond the shadows. / We're given life, so why court death? / Why prostrate before crucifixes of cold stone? / Why bargain our lives for this? Will we ever learn? / Military acts are bathed in this holy unwholesome tale: / He gave his only begotten that the killing might prevail. / Ill-begotten squaddies are blessed to shock and awe, / blessed in His name to unleash the horror. / Pious virgins prostrate before the Lord, / awaiting his coming, awaiting his word: / consummatum est, that they too may be blessed.

Sweet Jesus, have mercy on them, / share not your agony, abandon your misery, / divorce yourself from piety. / Down from the cross, Jesus, that the light might shine.

Oh bless the lowly, the destitute, / the deprived and the poor. / Blessed, ah, blessed, bless them the more. / And this is beauty, the day of creation. / We are the angels of distant heavens / come to lie down with our seduction. / Our spirits rise in flame, for we are the fire of life. / This is the dialogue, the apple fallen from the tree, / but still the warplanes arrive and are disgorged, / and carrion is cast into those leaden skies. / And sunsets, what of them? / That red glow that silhouettes the smoke-clouds / casting black wings like hoods upon our memories. / As if the truth was already written, / as if we were perhaps engrossed in its scripture, / we journey to infinite bombed-out cities, / Babelic and driven. / But who the broker? Who the warmonger?

Over three-quarters of the world's population is starving, / crucified by the greed of corporate capitalism. / In the name of progress, / every minute of every day, / billions upon billions of dollars / are spent on the machinery of oppression; / natural resources both mineral and human / are ruthlessly exploited; / native people are slaughtered in their homelands; / pride and dignity is bombed into extinction. / American Express? You bet.

At the wave of a silk-gloved hand, / young men are sent to their deaths, / but not before others have fallen from their bayonets and guns. / Such armies were once called *peace keeping forces,* / but today they're *liberators* - horses for courses. / Every military victory is a defeat for humanity.

While across the planet millions upon millions die of starvation, / Western democracies wage the war that will last a lifetime. / Oh yes, we can satirise the obscenity, / inwardly laugh at the absurdity, / but the hysteria soon wears thin / and tears are a cold cosmetic. / Yet even against this background of fear, / we can find our deeper, inner-selves, / through which to realise our own authority. / We bite into the heresy, / become gestures of a better life, / singing with such strange a voice. / We wait upon islands of soul / in defiance of the tides / and then know for sure there is better; / not even the thunder could break us from that knowledge. / Against a backdrop of devastation, we seek a sanity / to negate the fools' vanities. / The glib rationalisations of the puppeteers offers no solution. / I'm tired of politicians, / tired of political experts, / tired of their *if onlys.* / They've always been the same people: / blind to love, they would have us all share in their death. / History is simply a justification for oppression, / written by those who practice it: / a tempest of convenience / blasting across the blistered bodies of the dead. / I'm tired of the dull rationalisations of politicians and generals, / weighed down with their pale rhetoric and intellectual paucity. / How can peace be achieved through the tools of violence? / What kind of hope is there in that straightjacket? / We look through one eye trusting the other won't see, / that way we only have to deal with a half of it. / Then is it that we can see through the lies / but are too afraid to admit it? / It must be so much easier to be the passive observer.

All the indications are there. / The super-powers seek daily / to capitalise on the global population: / their fire-power is massive, their cynicism absolute. / As innocents die in their thousands, / so the puppeteers chant their tawdry mantra: / *it is with deepest regrets we have to inform you* / *that we are at war,* / *at war in the killing fields,* / *at war in the workplace.* / *We regret to inform you, regret to inform you* / *that today the sweet angels of mercy* / *were shot through the back of the head.* / *We regret to inform you, regret to inform you* / *that today another Christ, not yet ten years old,* / *was burnt to death by our liberating forces.* / *We regret to inform you:* / *tactical response.* / *We regret to inform you:* / *executive action.* / *We regret to inform you:* / *collateral damage.* / *Terrorist threats, weapons of mass destruction:* / *in the fog of war, accidents will of course happen.*

Mirrors in our pockets, / guns upon the bathroom wall. / Even here the bombardment can be heard, / even here the lanterns spit / and the worn steps groan beneath the weight of terror. / But love is both the answer and the question, beyond the wind. / Is this not the serpent devouring its own tail? / How then can we look away? / Isn't everything a reflection? / Not a voice that is not a warning. / Not a slumber that is not a death.

The puppeteers dispute the information that we offer, / claiming that it has no basis in fact, / but where are the facts where there is no truth? / These weavers of sorrow cast their net / of violence, falsity, lies and deceit, / blind to everything that is worthwhile and good, / unable to see the trees from the wood.

As if the truth was already written. / As if we were perhaps engrossed in its scripture.

And yes, fed from birth on American propaganda and Hollywood trash, / our resistance level can run pitifully low. / Maybe the missiles and warheads are too much. / Maybe the challenge of *the war that will last a lifetime* / is too great to contemplate. / Maybe the *New World Order* is the nightmare we've grown to accept. / But is this really all we can hope for as life? / Is this really all we can hope for as death? / Maybe our lives don't matter that much, / but why allow this madness be imposed on those as yet unborn? / It is only through passive acceptance that a holocaust can happen. / We regret to inform you, regret to inform you.

But what is there to lose where nothing has been gained? / Beyond the darkness there are reflections and echoes, / towering chasms in which we might realise ourselves. / Is it not the greatest warmth that the blood has flowed? / Each season is a lost memory even before it has existed. / Is that not enough? / Yet in our failure to act against the hideous dangers / of unbridled imperialism, / are we not guilty of being gutless passive observers, / helpless bystanders waving flags in mute acceptance? / Are we so divorced from humanity that we can let this happen?

The culture of protest is the core of the individual soul. / One clear voice in the wilderness / is better heard than all the muddled gabble of Babel. / Protest cannot be judged by numbers, / but through the inner feelings of those who practice it.

War and oppression are the logical and inevitable / consequence of gross capitalism. / Until its roots are torn from the soil, / the terrible toll will remain a daily reality. / It's as if those narrow streets were treasure troves, / as if Solomon had cast his riches on those sands. / Each huddled, dismembered body was a gem, / a perfect moment, a treasured pearl of existence, / but they are not forgotten.

If the puppeteers lack compassion, / then we shall double our own. / They can be stopped. / If the puppeteers show no love, / then we shall show our own. / They can be stopped.

They talk about their revolution, well that's fine, / but the revolution is already won: / an imperative, a state of mind that daily, / hourly must be nurtured against any delusions of a dominant culture. / Between left and right there is a universe / unmoved by the conflicts of the *them and us*. / It is we who make the world around us, / it is our victory, / and it's up to us to open our hearts and sing, / open our eyes and see, / open our ears and hear, / open our minds and think, / open up our lives and act.

We are poets, armed with the cobblestones of love. / Hear this then, the carnival: / the charnel houses are no more. / Nothing but beauty, nothing but grace. / No need to settle the score. / No more cruelty, no more greed. / The doors of Mammon are shut. / No more loss, no more need, / no more maybe, no more but.

As responsible citizens of planet Earth / it's up to us to defy the power of the puppeteers. / Their rule has created untold suffering. / Their insanity precludes all reason and compassion. / We must overcome our fear of the puppeteers. / We must understand that the strength they have / is the strength that we allow them.

Then tell me this, what kindly fairies might ignite / the paper devils of doubt / that the flames of resistance may dance again in defiance? / Oh, let us dance and let us sing, / tear off the chains that we be free again.

We must learn to live with our own conscience, / to have faith in love, to trust / our own morality, / our own determination, our own self.

The material world is a manifestation of our own ideas, / a graphic reflection of all our hopes and fears.

Love is all or love is not at all. / We alone can do it. / You alone can do it. / I alone can do it. / There is love if we make it.

THERE IS NO AUTHORITY BUT OURSELVES.

THERE IS NO LOVE WITHOUT YOUR OWN.

Penny Rimbaud
Essex.
Summer 2014.
Words to *The Feeding of the Five Knuckle Shuffle* by Steve Ignorant.

Distraction

Many of the messages in punk, particularly the anarcho-punk genre, are about participating in your own life with engagement and authenticity. They are about living each moment with a sense of the consequences of your actions. While this philosophical imperative may be compelling, it takes a great deal of self-awareness and discipline to live in this way. There are many distractions that can capture our attention and take us away from the task, and there are hooks that can pull us in all manner of directions.

The people we spoke to are well aware of the barriers that lie in the way of leading an authentic life and have struggled with this themselves. They understand how people can become caught up in the stresses and demands of everyday, mainstream living – the expectations of others, the pressure to 'succeed', paying the mortgage, getting a good job, landing the right partner, holidays in the sun and so on. The pressures and the temptations that we meet in the prevailing culture can be hard to resist and, because we exist within that culture, we may not always be aware of them. However, instead of the hard-line attitude that some might have expected from the architects of punk, there is compassion and an understanding that we are all doing the best we can at any one time.

The first step to making different choices is having an awareness of all the drivers that act upon us. These are some of the distractions that our interviewees identified from their own experiences.

The distraction of attachment   In Zen the 'Second Noble Truth' states that the origin of suffering is both the attachment to transient things, and being in ignorance of that attachment. Suffering comes when we lose the thing to which we are attached and, as a consequence, we find ourselves craving more of that thing. We can become trapped in cycles of desire and loss that are ultimately harmful.

Not only can we become attached to material objects, but also to ideas and attitudes. In this way, we can be as attached to a new car as we can to our sense of ourselves as beautiful or successful or as an outsider. We can become attached to political ideologies and these can all serve to condition, or even predetermine, the choices that we make. And as we do this, we move further and further away from a truly authentic response to our own experiences. Our thinking becomes 'unthinking'. Our ideas become cages.

Many of the people that we spoke to made specific attempts to not engage with consumerism, and typically had little interest in the accumulation of material things.

"I don't particularly have an attachment to the stuff. There are things that I do love but they're things that are virtually worthless. Like a crushed bottle that I found in the road. A crushed plastic bottle that's got a face in it. That's the stuff that I really like... I'm not that bothered about possessions." **Mark Wilson**

Some attachments are so ingrained within our idea of 'ourselves' and our culture that they are almost impossible to perceive, although our interviewees were optimistic about our ability to break free from them.

"Obviously you are born of people so you are attached to people whether you like it or not. But practically everyone has a problem with the family that they grew up with and coming to terms with that is, I think, a major part of one's growth." **Gee Vaucher**

In a sense, attachment is the basis of many of our fears and inauthenticity in our behaviour, and so it is useful to look at how this manifests itself in everyday life.

The distraction of the spectacle Returning to Situationist ideas, many of the interviewees are intensely aware of the distracting effects of the Internet and mass media. They spoke about the anaesthetising escapism offered, for example, by television and how it eats up the mental capacity and time that could be used in effecting change, or enjoying more engaging experiences.

"The basic premise is to be aware of what's being fired at you. I mean watch this rubbish if you want to be marginally entertained, but realise the stereotypes being shoved in your face non-stop ARE stereotypes. They are not true. They have been written down as fiction by people getting paid to write that sort of fiction... It's distraction from the misery of actual life. It's distraction from the weather; it's distraction from having a shitty, repetitive, underpaying job... You can take yourself out of the world and into the world that is put in front of you. I'm not surprised people go for it." **Dick Lucas**

Many people counselled against the dangers of information overload as another form of distraction. We all have so many interfaces with the Internet through a plethora of devices that we can be pulled out of the moment into a passive consumption of information for consumption's sake. No subject is too horrifying to be consumed as material for our entertainment, and as passive consumers, we are removed from the reality of the events and fail to truly engage with them.

"I was watching Baghdad being BOMBED on the TV. And I was thinking, 'Fucking hell! There are bombs being dropped on this place and people are dying.' And the other thing I was thinking was, 'And there are all these pretty colours and things.' And I wondered, what is this? It's just like entertainment. We spoke earlier about Situationism, and I thought: this is the ultimate spectacle." **Steve Lake**

Most people acknowledged the Internet and social media as powerful means of getting information and making connections, but were very wary of devoting too much time to it for a number of reasons. These ranged from suspicions about the provenance of the content, to issues with surveillance, to the sheer waste of time.

The distraction of fear and regret Unsurprisingly, for a group of people committed to living life in the moment, there was little support for the idea of planning firm life goals. At best it was seen as a futile attempt to exert control over an imagined set of circumstances taking place in the future. At worse it was a trap, conditioning the way we act in the present as a way to allay our fear of the unknown. A rigid life plan can only give the illusion of guaranteeing success in an uncertain world, as we cannot know all of the circumstances that we may be faced with. Conversely it also sets us up for failure when our plan cannot be executed. For most people that we spoke to, dealing with the here and now was much more meaningful than the fantasy world of the future. They were also keenly aware of how our fears can be manipulated for the gain of others.

"I think there are industries built up around the idea of planning for the future. And I think they're often malicious industries because they prey upon people's fears. 'What am I going to be doing? I'd better go to college and get a degree!' And meanwhile all these companies have worked out that you HAVE to get a degree to work for them, that guarantees their income, right?" **Ian MacKaye**

In the same way that rigid planning gives the illusion of control, so regret belongs to the same misplaced idea. When we regret, we believe that we made the wrong choice, when in fact we most likely made the choice that looked the most reasonable at the time, with the information that was available to us. By driving our attention into the past and dwelling on failure, regret is an equally corrosive distraction.

"Regrets are pointless and negative. But I don't think I've got any regrets. The best thing to do is not have too many plans, and that leads to not having so many regrets, because if you plan too much then things go wrong, and you think, 'Ooh, I should have done that differently.'" **Dick Lucas**

"Regret is a bit of a waste of time. Isn't it? You can only deal with what you have got now, what cards you have got to play with today and I don't see any point in looking back and saying, 'I should have done this or I should have done that'. I'm very happy with where I am now. Perhaps I'm lucky to be so." **Mark Wilson**

"Right at this point, right now, even though I've got two types of cancer that they claim are going to kill me, and I've got ulcers on my feet that make walking so difficult, I've never been so happy in my entire fucking life. I feel contented that I've done something that I wanted to do." **Sid Truelove**

A fear that everyone must face and come to terms with is the inevitability of our death. This can also drive our thoughts away from the present and into the future, preventing us from engaging in the moment.

"I don't think there's any point in getting maudlin about death. It's something that everyone knows is coming and you should get on with your life, really and don't waste time. I think all you can do is live the best life that you can in the moment from day to day... And thinking about death is something that distracts you from what you are doing now. We know about the inevitability of death but it has nothing to do with your dissatisfaction now with your life. That is something that you can work on now." **Tim Smith**

The distraction of prerequisites   One of the most liberating elements of punk for many was the way in which the Do-It-Yourself ethic swept away ideas of certain necessary prerequisites to any meaningful endeavour. In punk it was no longer necessary to train for years as a musician before forming a band, or to have studied at university before you had something interesting to say, or to have formal authority before you could be heard. However the idea that you have to earn the right to do something can still linger in people's lives, often in areas like the workplace or the family. These ideas of deference are a constraining force on living a self-determining life and are often excuses for inaction to cover a fear of failure. **Jeffrey Lewis** has made it part of his artistic purpose to challenge preconceptions about the necessity of material things and conducts his career with the barest minimum of requirements.

"I've always kept my overheads low and from that I've made a living in ways that people would not think possible. Everybody in the industry when I was starting out was always saying, 'You can't do this unless you have x or y.' I never even had an amplifier for like the first 10 years that I did this. I have never owned an amplifier in my life. I mean every club has something to plug into."

The distraction of status and success   In a related set of ideas, while punk challenges the need for certain prerequisites to success, it also challenges the power and importance of status and success. Some of our interviewees have experienced a conventional version of success, but found that there was an unwelcome price to pay. The expectations placed upon them as a result of elevation and privilege had curtailed their freedom. Some encountered this in the music industry.

"I got the glamour but I never got the power. I was with a major label for all of ten minutes and I had the power not to sign the contract unless my mother got sent the long stem roses or my father got the bottle of brandy. This was me being a despot, y'know? Then I figured out about acting lessons and I wanted them to pay for theatre school and they would send cars. Suddenly I had my own apartment and stuff, but I was totally at the mercy of these motherfuckers because they could take it all away again. And you've actually got less power because you have to worry about everything because you can lose it and now you have something to lose. I've had to get it, to realise that." **Little Annie**

Others experienced this in their working life. "There's a myth that as you rise up through the ranks in work you have more power to make a difference, but I've actually found that I can make more of a difference with what I am doing now. If I was a manager within the organisation that I'm working in, I wouldn't be able to do permaculture projects because I'd be sifting paperwork. It wouldn't have happened. I can actually make a difference where I am. And even though there's a financial implication to that, I rather like my sanity." **Graham Burnett**

Where there is the opportunity for success, there is also competitiveness and this can be a damaging force acting upon people. If the philosophical ideas in punk call for building communities of mutual support, learning from each other, and breaking down the barriers that separate us, competitiveness tears us apart from one another. Competition needs winners and losers and conflict, and promotes the happiness of a few people at the expense of others.

"Unfortunately the key word in society is 'competition'. I think competition is the wrong way of approaching it because it becomes the war of all against all." **Steve Lake**

The distraction of expectations   The final word in this section goes to **Gavin McInnes**, who brings his contrarian approach to make a good point about the expectations that we feel are placed upon us. The punk movement has accomplished a great deal in demonstrating the value of being different and encouraging people to make unconventional choices. He argues that the freedom to be whatever we want must support, as equally valid choices, the mundane as much as the unusual. We need to release ourselves from the idea that it is a failure to want something that is commonplace, as this becomes another form of tyranny that goes against the principle of self-determinism. This is an important consideration when thinking about the quality of freedom of choice and one that is often overlooked.

"If you want to be something that's unusual you should embrace that. If you're born to be a ballerina and you're an accountant, its just as bad as if you're born to be an accountant and you're a ballerina. Pursuing that strange ideal is what true happiness is. Now what a lot of old punks have done is the opposite and they've said, 'I need to be creative. And I need to NEVER settle down' and that was a dismantling of traditions without anything to replace them. So I feel like part of my role, at least with my friends, and to the people around me is to say, 'yes, you can be whatever you want to be, but if you want to be something shitty and boring, like a housewife, that's cool.' We've almost been so determined not to sell out that anyone who does have a normal life now feels like they're letting down Penny [*Rimbaud*] and Gee [*Vaucher*] and we need to get over that. [*laughs*]"

Gavin McInnes

Born in the UK in 1970, Gavin McInnes moved to Canada when he was four. As a teenager he played in Ottawa punk band Anal Chinook. In 1994, in Montreal, Quebec, Gavin and two partners founded Vice, *an international magazine focused on arts, culture and news. NBC described him as 'the Godfather of hipsterdom'. His controversial comments and Situationist stunts often put him in the media spotlight.*

In later years, the company expanded into Vice Media, incorporating the magazine, a website, a film production company, a record label and a publishing imprint. Editorial staff championed the 'immersionist' school of journalism – a kind of DIY antithesis to the working practices of mainstream news outlets.

Gavin left Vice *in 2007 due to 'creative difference' and built a country home in New York's Sullivan County. Amongst other creative contributions he has since published a book of memoirs entitled* How to Piss in Public *and in 2013 he co-wrote and starred in the movie* How to Be A Man.

What I think is interesting about punk, as far as the mentality and ethos of it goes, is that people assume it was a unified thing. But it was at least two disparate groups, and they were based on class. One group was the Exploited's 'Just fucking PUNK!'. They wanted a riot, and they wanted anarchy just to watch cars burn [*laughs*]. And then there were the anarcho-punk, middle-class intellectuals. And of course there were crossovers, with poor kids being smart and rich kids being dumb, but there were these anarcho-punks that had a plan. And that was Crass and a lot of the British bands, and they wanted an anarchist, socialist commune that was dismantling the state and self-sufficient gardens and all of this stuff that had nothing to do with cars burning. And you'd go to these anarchist gatherings and it was these two groups. I was even at events where there would be a sort of a semi riot. Like I was in Berlin staying at this squat and there was a riot with these skinheads, these Nazi skinheads, and half the group were just going "FUCKING RIOT!!" and the other half were going "DISMANTLE THIS AGGRESSION AND LET'S, ERR, HAVE A TALK" [*laughs*]. Almost with opposite goals because socialist intellectuals don't want cars to burn because it gives them a bad name [*laughs*], so it's funny seeing those two worlds collide.

I was definitely part of the latter group, the nerdy punks, yes, punks with books. That's who Crass were for, Crass were for smart punks. And it's funny because it was Penny Rimbaud's upper-class intellect sung by a yob, with a blue-collar accent [*laughs*], which was part of the appeal. But anyway, I still have these ideals. And I'm on Fox News every week and people go, "Oh, you're a Republican now?"

"No!" "Oh, are you a Conservative?" "No, not really", "A libertarian?" "Well, sort of." But I've just got the same anti-government stuff that's always been punk. I get caught shitting on Islam or shitting on socialism or shitting on basically a lot of things that Conservatives are for.

But I'm still a 14 year-old liberal, punk rock, anarchist; it's just that America has swung so far to the left that to say "I'm not into multiculturalism when it includes genitally mutilating women" is somehow wrong. Occupy Wall Street this year was all about government regulation and I thought what happened to all these anarchists? Where were you in the 80s when it was about getting government out of our back yard? And the modern movement, the modern left or the modern anarchists even, sound more like socialists to me.

Fuck the government! There was actually an interesting incident when I was with Gee Vaucher of Crass at Occupy Wall Street this last year, and there was a guy with a Crass T-shirt and he had a big table in front of him and he had *The Communist Manifesto* and Gee said, "What's that? What are you on about?" The guy did that thing that I did when I was his age, the guy was all college commie and said, "Well actually it's more metaphorical, it's more about the concept of equality and blah, blah, blah." And she goes, "No! This is all about oppression. I'm not with this! What are you doing with that shirt and this book?" And he goes, "Well Communism, you know, it was really good for a lot of people, you are just taking some bad examples…" And then some dude, some 70 year-old guy from Czechoslovakia says, "Excuse me, I grew up under communism. I know of Stalin sleep depriving people until they wish for their own death sentence in a court of law, representing themselves. I'm aware of this fascism." So it was Gee now, and this old Czechoslovakian, two white-haired people hammering on this poor guy. But he deserved to be hammered; I mean this is what's happened with youth rebellion.

This is an incredibly roundabout way of saying that what I appreciated about punk and about anarcho-punk was the "fuck the government" perspective; fuck a bunch of ruthless morons, because that's what politicians are. They're not Machiavellian geniuses planning out the fate of the world, they are ruthless people with low IQs, who would be in marketing or acting if they weren't so ugly. Let's stop bequeathing them all this authority.

DIY, entrepreneurship and the death of deference DIY is a great way to be an entrepreneur because being an entrepreneur is saying, "I can do this myself, I don't need your help, and by the way, I don't think you're very special. I'm just as special as you are, I can do it. I'm not taking orders from you." I've always said entrepreneurs aren't people who can't take orders, they're people who can't

take stupid orders. They just don't want to be led by the blind. If you have a good plan, by all means, let's do it, but when you don't it takes a certain type of person to say, "Why are we listening to this guy?" I heard that the Native Americans – it's probably a bullshit story by the way, they are probably being glorified – but I heard that, in a lot of tribes, when somebody had a bad idea they would just cease to be the boss, so it was like the opposite of the military where you just do as you're told. And I think that's what an entrepreneur is and that's what an anarchist is and that's what we got out of punk. There are so many facets to punk and it's a global movement now. But if you had to boil it down, put it in the pot for three days, I think you would end up with this, "Don't be scared, just fucking do it"… For the most part punk was a way of saying, if you are weird, then go be weird.

A man of constant rage   I'm in a constant state of rage. It might be my Glaswegian upbringing but I'm mad every day. And what really outrages me in America is the lack of outrage. I think Americans have been lulled into a state of media bliss where we can talk about a plane in Malaysia that has disappeared or the news item of the day, but we've lost the days of the Watergate guy with the notebook saying "I've got a scoop boss!" Maybe that's because the supply of journalists is not meeting demand so they are all getting paid nothing, whereas back in Watergate they would get five bucks a word. So now they just check out Google or they go check someone's Twitter feed and they create a nice narrative and it's just story time, at the end of the day. I was on Fox News recently and we were talking about this surfer, who was on food stamps, he's in a band and he's abusing food stamps and buying lobster and having a gay old time on welfare. And everyone is using it as a thing, and it's just a great story because you have this guy with sunglasses and a surfboard and he's on welfare. He doesn't represent the people who are abusing welfare, and food stamp abuse is a fraction of a percent of welfare abuse. There's all this tax credit fraud that is going on involving billions of dollars and all clear fraud, but it is just too expensive to pursue them all so the government continues to haemorrhage billions, but no-one talks about that. And that's what makes me fucking insane.

Tofu stunted my growth   I got into Crass when I was 14 and became a vegetarian because of them and I blame them for my diminutive size too. I was eating tofu when my bones were trying to grow. My brother and my dad are giants and I'm a little fucking tiny punk munchkin [*laughs*]. No, I got into them because they had so much to say and I was so enthusiastic about punk. I wasn't satisfied with The Exploited saying "sex and violence, sex and violence, sex and violence, SEX AND VIOLENCE" for an entire song. And they influenced me a lot too. As Penny Rimbaud himself says, weirdos tend to congregate.

No love of rules   I was always trying to avoid 'isms' and just about a week ago I said, "Fuck it, I'm a libertarian" and it feels un-punk to adhere to a group like that, but it is just so convenient, and it felt kind of cathartic too just to say that. I don't like their love of open borders. They've always said that the only reason why you need borders is to make the map more colourful, but I don't think that's good for anyone, especially the poor. If they open borders with Mexico it will just make the rich richer on both sides and the poor poorer, on both sides. But besides that I like their ideals. Their ideals are, "This might be good or this might be bad, but I don't know because I'm not making a rule about it. Go ahead and do your thing, I'm not trying to force anything." Whereas the modern American left says, "If every single thing in the world does not perfectly represent a pie chart of the population then it's wrong and I have to fix it." And so short, fat, bald, Jewish men have to be in the NBA doing their terrible shots and getting jumped over by giant black guys [*laughs*]. No, we don't need that; some people are good at things. And the beauty of libertarians is that they say, "Maybe they're not, maybe short, fat, Jewish bald guys would kill in the NBA. I'm not holding them back, go ahead chaps!"

Stop speaking on behalf of other people   Regarding political correctness, it's become more than policing. When you don't know if you are supposed to say 'African American', 'person of colour' or 'black', you just go, "I'm just gonna avoid them. Entirely. I don't wanna say the wrong thing." So you put them on a pedestal until you can't reach them, and that's the way with a lot of young people. And they change the rules everyday. Did you know that 'tranny' is now a hate word? And no one even told THEM! And now there is a big campaign to ban the word 'bossy' because 'bossy' is used to keep young girls down and not be ambitious and you go, "What?" My wife calls me bossy every fucking day and now you're telling me it's gender-specific and it's ageist? I didn't know that!

I went through so much with Crass and with anarcho-punk, and I went so far to the left, to the communist left, that I created this world where… Look, let me give you an example. I remember I created this stencil which in French said, "We're sick of being your fucking secretaries," because I noticed that all of the secretaries were women so, on their behalf, I wanted to say that, "We want to be CEOs not secretaries". So I spray-painted this all over peoples' corporate property. But the problem was the women were perfectly happy being secretaries there. Many of them were there to meet rich CEOs and they were having a great life. And the companies would have been happy to hire a woman if she was qualified and was busting balls and wanted to stay working all night to work on the proposal. So who the fuck am I to go spray-painting all over the place? Which is actually sexist anyway me thinking they're too stupid so that I will do their thinking for them now. Plus when I was stencilling I was so nervous that when I did the stencil it was totally illegible with just some French swear words. And I guess one of my motives is to say to other people, "Don't go speaking for secretaries OK, they have it under control." You worry about your thing, and if secretaries are being oppressed by law then by all means do something, but otherwise let them be. And that's really my agenda. Just to stop people from wasting time.

A different take on feminism   I sort of drifted from anarchy into communism and at that point I thought, "I know what equality is and now I'm going to enforce it" just like that pie chart I was talking about before. If that Alpine ski club is not one of each, like an Island of Misfit Toys, then its WRONG! But now, I'm sorting of screaming against this 18 year-old me and saying, "You have the right ideal, and the freedom thing is great, but stop telling people what to do." And one thing I've been saying about housewives is that's an incredible job, you're shaping lives, but so many of these women who look down on them are doing seating charts for fashion shows. This woman is at home is not keeping a stranger's house. She's keeping her own house that her children are raised in. And the pictures on the wall on the stairway, the kids will remember those pictures on the stairways. Everything she is doing is incredibly consequential and men call me a sexist pig for saying that, and stay at home mums say "thank you, finally!" So I guess in one sense we're still speaking on behalf of women [*laughs*].

Gee Vaucher

Gee Vaucher was born in Dagenham, East London, one month after the bombing of Hiroshima and Nagasaki, and three weeks after the end of the Second World War. At 15 she left school and went to art college. Between the years 1968 to 1972 Gee worked with an avant-garde performance group called EXIT, which included Penny Rimbaud, who she had met at art college. Amongst other projects associated with EXIT, Gee helped to organise an International Carnival of Experimental Sound at The Roundhouse in London. The festival brought together individuals from around the world including John Cage and the composer David Bedford.

The body of Gee's work built considerably in the period that followed, aided by collaborations with Penny Rimbaud and others. In the mid 1970s Gee worked in New York City as an illustrator for titles that included Rolling Stone, New York *magazine,* Ebony *and* The New York Times.

During this period she published a newspaper International Anthem *- a nihilist newspaper for the living. It was a platform not only for her own work but for other invited artists and writers, and was the project where she began to develop the graphic collage effect that became so synonymous with the band Crass. As a core member of the group, and at times going by the name G Sus, Gee crafted the iconic album covers, posters, inserts and visual onslaughts that, in many ways, came to represent the anarcho-punk movement.*

As a long time resident of Dial House, Gee has inspired many artists in the international contemporary art movement, undertaking scores of collaborations. Her always uncompromising and visually arresting work is perhaps illustrated best in the book Crass Art and Other Pre Post Modernist Monsters. *Gee's artistic endeavours continue to evolve and take on new form. Recent outputs include a filmed piece entitled* Angel *and* A Week of Knots *a volume of seven books still in the making, which offers an interpretation of the original novel* Une Semaine de Bonté *by Max Ernst, and uses the inspiring words of* Knots *by R.D. Laing.*

The school I went to didn't have any exams (well that's not quite true, you could do RSA typing if you wanted, but that didn't exactly inspire me at the time). It was considered a place to prepare you for work, either at Ford cars in Dagenham or the Yardley cosmetics factory in Stratford. The boys went to Ford's and the girls went to Yardley's. That was it. I seem to remember it was the only school outing we had, visiting the factories to prepare us for our future. But, factory or not, we were all excited to be out of school and on an outing, where I certainly wasn't expecting much from looking at the workings of the factory floor. On arrival we were led into Yardley's, young lads wolf-whistling, and out onto a high walkway, a bit like a prison, where you could look down on the factory floor and see how things worked. I was absolutely gob-smacked. We were looking down on these massive vats of colour, every shade of red lipstick, the blues and green of eye shadow etc, and it was, "Wow, look at all this colour!" [*laughs*] I was mesmerised; it was an amazing sight. And I thought, "Wow, yes definitely. That's where I'm going! ART!" [*laughs*]

Imagery was always my first language. I have never really thought that anyone can learn to be an artist especially by being at art school, because to me, being an artist is a deep, internal drive and commitment that can never be taught, only experienced. What art school can offer though is the space and time to explore, and, when I went to art school in the 60s, all the materials you needed.

I didn't express myself in words well when I was young. As you can imagine the school I went to was pretty limited when it came to the teaching of vocabulary, and speaking in public was certainly beyond me, I even found it hard to eat in front of strangers because I'd never done it.

Meeting Penny at art school led me into a world of words and debate which was fascinating, but I just couldn't keep up with the conversation, there were so many words I couldn't understand, and by the time I had figured out what everyone was talking about, the subject had moved on. I had to learn really quickly, didn't want to be left out! But when it came to drawing and imagery, it was the other way around [*laughs*].

It wasn't until the Aberfan disaster that I found my political voice [*the collapse of a colliery slag heap onto a school in the Welsh village of Aberfan in 1966 killed 116 children and 28 adults*]. Penny was dealing with the news in a way I could not understand and I thought cruel at the time, I was really angry at him and suddenly the words all poured out. That was a real awakening for me, like having the cork pulled out.

The space inside the cup   I don't know where the creative work comes from and I don't want to know. All I do know is that it can come anytime, anywhere from anything. When I do a work, I let the understanding of it take its time once I've finished a piece, it comes from somewhere within and it's a different language. The pictures I make are for me, it's a sorting out of my own head, not therapeutically, but I see something and it triggers something else and then I wonder where it's leading and the excitement of the chase can lead you to a new understanding. It makes me laugh.

Whilst I was at art school I got into Zen. I loved Zen. I was in a second-hand bookshop in London and I picked up a book as it had an interesting cover. I opened

it and there were photos, even better, then it had some riddles, kōans, short lines of not many words and I remember reading, 'clay is moulded into vessels, yet the hollow parts are essential to the usefulness of the vessels'. Obvious really, but I just thought, "Bloody hell!" It was like an epiphany. [*laughs*] It lit up my brain and my whole thinking turned around. I've still got that book and dip into it now and then. Funny how it can take just one line, or one image, or a shadow on the floor, and for some reason it opens a door in one's thinking. I still find it's the same process for me. I'm aware that could be the same for others so I try to be careful, especially when I'm with kids, you just never know what they might pick up on, be inspired by, or damaged by. At school they're already faced with too many demands and rules that so often lead into a dead-ends.

Life should be an adventure. Kids visit Dial House and talk about what they have been doing, especially at school, how they are being asked to choose what they want to work at and specialise in for their future. "But you don't know what you want to do yet do you?" "No." "How can you choose then?" "But we have to." Mmmh! Well I suppose the best way to handle it is to remember that nothing lasts forever, all doors are still open when you are ready.

But children get afraid of authority, of bending the rules, of being different, as if being different is weird, or they won't be accepted into the gang or something, but each child has a rite of passage, their own rite of passage that if left alone will take its own path, it's so little trusted and acknowledged. As I come from the old school where kids were left to run in the open air, build from their imagination and play together, I try and understand why so many young people seem so happy to spend most of their time inside either on the phone or the computer, it drives me mad when there is such an exciting world out there! Yet they seem happy and bright enough, I must be missing something?

Did we ruin a generation of kids? With regard to Crass, at first the band was chaotic and everyone was just having a laugh. As time went on and the audience actually started to take an interest, a structure was put in place so that information and experiences could be shared more clearly. For instance, Crass didn't allow people on stage if possible, we felt we were trying to say something and to say it in a particular way using music, words, film and imagery, and anything else would have distracted. It was an hour-long onslaught really, visually troubling and confrontational. For the audience, especially for the really young, it could be pretty scary, and along with all the leaflets, handouts and fanzines that people brought to each gig, a total overload. It's why we always got off the front of the stage when the gig finished and didn't disappear out the back. It was understood that it would have been irresponsible to not be available having exposed the audience to so much. There were always a lot of people wanting to ask questions afterwards. One we were often asked was how to become a vegetarian? I'd ask them where they were living. "I live with my mum and dad." "Well take it easy, quite likely they are not going to understand your decision, especially when they have made you a meal and you say you don't want it. Take some time to think about it, and make sure it's not a knee-jerk reaction, it's not a big deal, you need to get the timing right if you are determined."

Going back to your original question "Did we feel we had ruined a generation?" Well yes, at first when we had finally stopped playing, plus we were upset and confused by how Crass had ended and I felt very numb, really wasted and run-down from everything. But since then, over the years, people keep coming and keep talking and you realise how positive it was. So many say that what they got from Crass was the strength to say, "No, I'm going to choose my life." We have many friends and visitors from those days that now work in local councils, the police force, in hospitals etc, working inside the system to try to make changes, taking their punk philosophy and applying it now, brilliant! I couldn't do it that way, that's for sure.

Don't believe in government   I think the ideas underpinning punk, were to 'do it yourself, give it a try, do what you feel is right, but not at the cost of anybody or the earth you live in'. For me that's the philosophy which concerned the second wave of punk that Crass was a part of. Crass was an extension of Dial House where we all live, of trying to work together, solve problems, be creative together and choosing to get out there and do it, whatever 'it' was. We were doing our best, having a laugh and finding out about life, but it wasn't all easy. It got very serious towards the end, but then so did the whole country under Thatcherism.

Information and sharing of ideas are just as relevant today as they were then. I'm not keen to go on marches anymore or take on the world in the same way but it seemed worthwhile at the time, certainly at Greenham Common. I get too frustrated at marches now, and I get bored of the whole rhetoric. They're great as an occasion for people to come together and share information and ideas, but they do fuck all as far as governments are concerned. That was very clearly proven by Blair, when over two million marched against the Iraqi war. I'm more interested in the things that place themselves in front of me. I have enough information now on how people are torn apart in war etc, it's the same pain, the same shit, corruption, arrogant governments that treat life as nothing and I find it gets harder to take. But I think that there are things that one can have an effect on that are staring you in the face and could help future generations.

If asked about a local problem that could be easily solved for the community I usually advise them to just get on with it. And people up and down the country are doing just that. In some of the poorest areas people are clearing the crap away from their communities that they have been asking their local council to do for years, and replacing the crap with new orchards, playgrounds and gardens with food and flowers for the community. The council isn't going to complain about it, that's for sure, something like that is not on their agenda, but you can do it. A great example of that is a project that Eve Libertine worked on with her community. To get into the local park you had to run the gauntlet of a drug alley of long grass and the usual rubbish. This time, negotiating with the council they finally cleared the area of syringes etc and planted an orchard, it's beautiful and since the trees have matured they hold an apple festival every year, a new tradition has been born in that area!

Guerilla gardening is another great example of taking control. I don't think things are really going to change for the betterment of all until people get together to share and organise themselves. It's not easy, it's hard frustrating work but the value of trying is incalculable. Until people can knock on each other's doors and say, "let's talk about the problem we have in our area, enough is enough, let's try and work together", then things won't change. That's how it was before. I'm not saying let's go backwards, but we have to go forwards by creating smaller communities that aid each other. There are other fine examples up and down the country where people are creating small businesses and employing local people. Not having to waste petrol and hours on commuting and hopefully working at a job which you find satisfying is surely going to be more conducive to the family and good health? Food obviously is essential to everyone and feeding the community a priority. But people need to look at how much meat they eat. When you realise an acre of land could feed the whole village in vegetables, whereas it takes what, approximately one acre to graze one cow? Cattle are eating their way through mountains and mountains of vegetables that could keep hundreds of people healthy and alive. I'm tired of people saying there's not enough food to feed the world. I think, give land back to people, re-access the system of how you produce food for the masses. Since the recession a lot of people have turned to having an allotment, they have had to learn to grow what they need and then how to cook it. I think that's great, that's undermining a system that tells us to go to your local multinational and buy 'fresh' food that has been picked a week ago and flown around the world. I'm much more interested in quietly undermining a system if we want change. I'm an optimist in that respect, or is it romantic?

Getting closure with family members   On the subject of family, I don't think a family should or could operate one way. What does the word 'family' mean anyway? It's a huge word that means different things to different people. It can be hell, it can be heaven. Obviously you are born of people so you are attached to people whether you like it or not. But practically everyone has a problem with the family that they grew up with and coming to terms with that is, I think, a major part of one's growth. Talking with 'grown ups', I'm aware of how much they are still affected by childhood family experiences, whether extreme or 'normal'. I think everyone needs, in varying degrees, to come to terms with their parents before it's too late. It's almost impossible to find real peace when they are long gone. If asked, my advice to anybody who still suffers from their past is to hold out your hand, because maybe your parents can't, they are often in such an entrenched position. Complaining that you were never hugged as a child but still wanting to be, is painful. If you want to touch, then it's you that has to act. If you need to hug your mum or dad then do it, but don't expect one back, don't expect anything back. Love at best is unconditional.

Somehow, even when very young, you need to make friends of your children so it's not just, my mum, my dad, my daughter, my son. As parents, I don't think children are yours to own, you are their guardian and guide and eventually, hopefully, their best friends.

I didn't have kids. I chose not to because I didn't want to be forced by powers beyond my control into directions I didn't agree with. Plus I wouldn't have made a good mother, I'm sure I would have ended up resenting the sharing of my time, when all I wanted to be was on my own in the studio. I think if you choose to have children it's all or nothing.

Children have intrinsic knowledge to share, the trouble is they have no experience with which to understand. Most children are very inquisitive, it's something we could all nurture in each other as we grow instead of hearing 'don't, 'stop' 'quiet' 'you can't' etc, who would want to stop the joy of inquisitiveness whether you are young or old? Sadly school and families close too many doors that are hard to open again.

Doing it for ourselves   I'm often labelled a feminist but it's not a title I'd give myself, I don't feel like a feminist, not that I really know what that feeling might be. If I feel like anything it's a humanist, but mostly I feel myself. Everyone has the right to make their voice heard, whether male or female, young or old, after all we have all been exposed to powerful repression. I had trouble fully understanding the feminist movement when I was younger, not that I didn't feel that it was time for women's voices to be heard and recorded, but I had trouble understanding where it was coming from, especially in the 70s, the "all men are rapists"statement left me feeling very outside. Attending various feminist meetings in London during that time, I heard the tragic experiences that so many women had experienced, but the venom and the cutting out of half of the population of this earth to achieve

I might be getting on a bit, but I still climb trees because I enjoy it, so why would I want to give it up?

What's the problem?

'liberation' didn't ring right with me, I could see no way forward unless everybody was in this awakening together.

I've never had the tragic experiences which so many women clearly have had, all my men friends were good friends and remain so. Continuing to recognise and celebrate women of this world is surely crucial if we are to move into a calmer world where everyone can feel safe and valued, but you don't have to go to war to achieve the deep peace that I think we all would choose for each other.

It's funny, I've heard people say that women are much more liberated now, (true in some areas), and that they can now work their way up in finance, the office, go to war, climb the corridors of power, and I think, "What?, No I don't think that's liberation, that's just joining the enemy." [*laughs*] That's not liberation to me at all. I think what's more liberating is something like the 'Incredible Edible' project in Todmorden where the women just thought, "Enough! We're going to make every bit of unused land here in the town useful by growing vegetables for the community and let them help themselves." And it's worked beautifully and inspired similar projects throughout the world. I remember the bravery that women displayed in Northern Ireland, and on the Lower East Side in New York City there were drug dealers on one particular street who were causing the deaths of so many young people, and it was the women who forced the ceasefire and cleared the street of dealers, enough was enough. For me that's 'liberation', women truly realising their power to make change.

Grown-ups that climb trees   If I think about happiness and meaning in life, for me it's about sustaining and revealing the child within. Seems that so many people lose sight of the sense of adventure, joy and inquisitiveness. More often than not society tells us that at a certain age you leave all 'that' behind, grow up. For example you are told that beyond a certain age you don't climb trees any more, and I think, "Why not, I do". I might be getting on a bit, but I still climb trees because I enjoy it, so why would I want to give it up? What's the problem?

Of course one is growing all the time in some way, even if it's only to grow old, but along the way, new experiences are gained that take different reasoning to solve different conundrums. Hopefully you become a better person day by day if you can be true to yourself and not pretend. It takes a lot more strength and courage to admit one might be wrong than to strut and think you know it all. There really is nothing to lose by admitting one's vulnerability.

My biggest problem to admit to myself, which definitely came from my childhood, and I carried this with me for 40 years, was that I hated the feeling of being left out. And I've had to come to terms with it. It was a pain in the arse. Now I have to deal with the thought that I might have missed something [*laughs*].

All this talk of the past is a story, one that is a part of the now, an illustration. I dislike nostalgia. My journey is just one of so many and I'm trusting that the main theme of this book shows how our experiences, the philosophy, actions etc. learnt especially during punk, have influenced and continue to play a part in the way we live our lives now.

My feelings about this beautiful world we live in are no different now from what they were then, more informed and better formed I hope, but different in how I might express them. Now that we have brought Exitstencil Press back to life, we have opened another avenue of communication, for without communication in some way, we are alone.

As always, I'm just happy to wake up in the morning and have another chance, even if I know that it might be a gruelling day ahead. I'm happy I made it through the night and, "here we go again, who knows what could happen today?"

Ian MacKaye

Ian MacKaye is a legend of the Washington DC punk scene. In 1979, he formed hardcore band Minor Threat, who rapidly built a fearsome reputation on the local live circuit, insisting on low ticket prices wherever they played. In a bid to promote local talent, Ian also co-founded Dischord Records in 1980, on which all Minor Threat's recorded output was released, including one studio album, Out of Step, in 1983. The band broke up in the same year.

Straight Edge, a song from Minor Threat's first EP, helped to inspire the still influential Straight Edge philosophy, which encourages those on the punk scene to abstain from drugs, alcohol and tobacco – a lifestyle that Ian adheres to himself.

Following a number of short-term projects, Ian formed post-hardcore group Fugazi in 1987, and they went on to release six studio albums on Dischord. They played more than 1,000 gigs worldwide over the next six years, but continued to turn down many offers – including a headline slot at Lollapalooza – on the grounds of inflated ticket prices. Fugazi went on an "indefinite hiatus" in 2002.

Ian currently sings and plays guitar with the Evens, who often play live at unconventional venues such as community centres and bookshops. He is also a well-respected producer and has worked with bands such as Nation of Ulysses, the Rollins Band and Lungfish. A strong supporter of the Riot Grrrl movement, he produced Bikini Kill's self-titled EP in 1992.

When questioned about his political stance once, Ian replied, "My rule of thumb is to vote for the person who is electable and is least likely to engage in war."

I feel that punk has marshalled some very important ideas. I think those ideas have always been present. My idea of punk is it's a free space, a space where ideas can be presented. And without that being dictated by a profit motive. But it is not a new concept to have this kind of space; it's always been present. I'd actually argue that jazz and folk and blues and rock'n'roll in all of their nascent eras – they were the same thing. There were people getting together and making something for the purpose of making it, and finding new forms of expression. And punk in some ways was broader because it involved a lot of philosophical stuff.

What I saw was an area where people could challenge conventional thinking across the board. And so when I first got involved with it I thought, "Oh! These people are talking about sexuality, and these people are talking about politics, and these people are talking about music, and these people are talking about fashion." But everyone had these different ideas that were challenging these very conventional notions about it all. It was the underground. It was the counter-culture. And it was something that I was DESPERATE to find in my life. Because I was born and raised in Washington DC and I grew up in an environment when the 60s underground — the anti-war movement, the civil rights movement, the women's lib movement, the gay rights stuff — all that stuff was happening. That was very normal for me. That was progressive thinking. Then the 70s came along and that just sort of froze up in a sea of cocaine and terrible music. And I was a teenager and I looked around and thought, "Where is the counter-culture?" And punk was where I found it.

So I don't think that punk invented those ideas. They inherited them, they took care of them and they marshalled them. I see these things as gifts, and like a lot of gifts some people polish them up and sell them. Whereas other people realise that if you keep them, and share them, then they just keep on giving... there was an enormous emphasis in the 70s of people being happy. Just don't cause a problem. The reaction of someone who is trying to effect change is to try and cause a problem for those people that would rather have a quiet life. I think that the anger found in punk was demonstrative of that in the sense that it got people's attention. But the people who seemed extremely angry were really the sweetest people. I think in history, in storytelling for example, people use exaggeration for effect, to get across their point. I think seeing somebody really lay it on the line whether they're angry or frustrated or being passionate, in fact just being vulnerable and putting it out there. That felt like a way for people on the margins to collect, to come together.

Money stinks   The real financial crisis in this world is that there are some people in this world who are making a billion dollars a year. That's a real crisis. And they're making a billion dollars a year by doing virtually nothing other than making deals. That's a crisis. If you think that in the 70s the highest paid CEO made, say, 200 times more than the lowest paid person, but by '95, the highest paid CEO in this country made something like 2,500 times the lowest paid person. That's a financial crisis. Where is the money? It's either here [*takes out dollar and put's it on table*] or it's there [*moves it across the table*]. That's all we need to fucking know. Where is the dollar? And I know where the dollar is. With those houses during the sub-prime crisis somebody made money. I was talking about this thing the other day about Colorado where they've just legalised marijuana. Good. About time! But they have a real problem because their jails, their state prisons are filled, with mostly, young, black, men for possession of marijuana which is now legal! So what do you do? Do you keep them in, or do you let them out because it's not a crime anymore? Can you imagine being jailed for something that's not a crime? And still having to do your time? But the real issue is that the jail industry is ENORMOUS. And there are people who sell water, toilet paper, the phone service, laundry services to the jail... everything...

and the jail industry is HUGE. And those particular hotels need to have those beds filled. That's why those bizarre drug laws are in place. And it's always about money. And money stinks.

Revealing the ugliness of the dominant culture   One thing about being a punk is that you emblazon yourself with the mark of the enemy. By becoming a punk, even cutting your hair was a political statement. You put yourself in a position where you suddenly reveal the bias, the bigotry, and the ugliness of the dominant culture. And that's a really shocking thing to learn about.

Think about us as high school kids: perfectly nice kids; we cut our hair and maybe someone is wearing some green pants, a leather jacket, or sunglasses or something like that and suddenly people just want to beat your ass. It was a real education. That probably was really disruptive. It's like painting a target on your back. And then realising that there are actually people who would shoot you. And that's startling. And we weren't even doing anything wrong. In fact, we were totally honest. We didn't do graffiti. We didn't do vandalism. We didn't steal. That was our whole thing. We looked tough, and we WERE tough, but we didn't do drink, we didn't do drugs. We were totally nice kids. And yet, we felt like people hated us.

But it was a really great place to be because it gave you a sense that you were on to something good because you're getting such an honest reaction. And you think, "I get it. This society is sick." Individually, I think people are good. But as a culture, it's fucking problematic here...You realise how unfriendly our society is. And if you look at the way media treated punk it was always really derisive, saying repugnant kinds of things. I think it dismissed creative freethinking as a joke, because it threatened them. But also, it fired up the bigotry even more because it made people say "Let's beat their asses because they like to eat vomit". And then worse of all, the people who eat vomit say, "Oh good, I like to eat vomit, so I'm a punk". So the nihilistic, the self-destructive, the violent people go "Oh! I'm a punk". So suddenly the punk scene is filled with nihilistic, self-destructive, violent people because they've inferred from the media that's their thing.

Be present   I never thought about the future. I never did and I still don't. I just live right where I am. People always ask me about where I see myself in five years. I just don't. It seems irrelevant to me. And that hasn't changed as a result of having a child. I mean, aside from the fact that it's not lost on me that people usually live to about 75 or 80 years old. So for example I know that my son is six now. I'm 52. So I'm probably not going to know him when he's 40. So to that degree, then sure, but I don't think about the future. It's irrelevant. So I don't know if it was conceivable for you a year or even two years ago that you would be sitting at this

DUKE · WILLIAM

LA DUKE · WILLIAM

ERNEST M SKINN

RICKE · ERNEST M SKINN

RREDONDO · EDDIE P

S · JEFFERY D BOUTON ·

JAMES E CAREY · R

WARD TEGAN Jr · SAMN

TEMADGE C STEVENS

III · WILLIAM

THOMAS A M

CE J O'CAL

H · DEN

Indefinite hiatus

table interviewing me [*laughter – no*]. Was it conceivable that you would have been walking by the Vietnam War Memorial in the snow? Of course not. The thing about the future is that it's always at the point around the corner.

I have this concept that you're on a road and you're driving up a cliff and you have the mountain on one side and the ocean on the other. The future is always at that point just around that corner and you'll never see it until it is the present. So you don't know what's there. It could be sunny skies; it could be an ice storm. The road could be out altogether. There could be a truck across it, you just don't know. All you know is what's right in front of you. So the most important thing to do is to take care of the vehicle and to pay attention. Be present. If you're driving along that road and you can see a boulder half a mile up shaking then you might think, "Oh shit! That thing's going to tumble down and fall. I'd better think what I'm going to do about that." Well, while you're looking at that you've just driven off the road in front of you.

There are industries built up around the idea of planning for the future. And I think they're often malicious industries because they prey upon people's fears. "What am I going to be doing? I'd better go to college and get a degree!" And meanwhile all these companies have worked out that you HAVE to get a degree to work for them, that guarantees their income, right? It's all business and, just to be clear, I'm not judgmental of people who want to plan things out and "do the do". I respect that everyone has to live their life the way that they want to live it. But for me, I just couldn't imagine living that way.

When I was 15, I was in high school. I was walking through a parking lot and I suddenly heard the screeching of car tyres, a car skidding, and it seemed like it was right behind me, and I braced myself to be hit because it sounded so close. And it turned out that there was no car at all. There was a weird audio illusion. There was a car in the street and the sound bounced off a wall. I don't know. And I just thought, "God, if I was just killed then I would have spent the majority of my conscious life in school. That is not living, so I am NOT going to college!" At that moment I decided not to volunteer to go to college. And it was really reinforced, because the moment I decided that I was relieved of so much pressure because I didn't really care about the various tests and I wasn't really worried about getting into a college. My friends were really FREAKING OUT about it.

And then I went to visit friends who went to college and I thought, "This is just a day care for kids who want to smoke pot. Is this all there is?" It just seemed insane to me to be wasting so much time, plus you had to go into debt. They aren't free, these colleges. People have to take loans and you are essentially signing up to indentured slavery. The moment you come out of school you have to pay off the loans and you have to get a job. It's too sorted out, but I decided that I wasn't going to do that and once I had decided that it gave me a different point of view.

Like I spent a lot of time thinking about the source of light – how things looked depending on where the light is. And I never drank coffee, not because I think that coffee is evil, I just didn't drink coffee. Because of that it gives me a really peculiar vision of what the coffee cult is all about. Or I just didn't drink. I just never drink alcohol; it's not interesting to me. Like I never use drugs. And that gave me a perspective that is extremely weird. It just didn't occur to me, it's not on my radar… If you live your life the way that you believe, and think that you just don't want to do these things, then you create a perspective on it and it gives you a sense of what's going on in the world.

Our hours are not ours   I think with many people, they choose to engage with things primarily because that's just what people do. And that's just a slippery slope… I always feel that people must wake up and think, "What have I done with my life?" I've never really had a full-time gig. I don't have a full-time job, I have an all-time job, which is different, you know, my work is never done. But sometimes I think of the way that people have their work set up. For example, in England, like Leeds or somewhere, you work this 40-hour thing then on Thursday nights you see all these kids with their white shirts and their black pants and the partying starts, and it's just that cycle: "Go to work, go to the pub, go home, go to work, go to the pub, go home." I can't really imagine doing that. I don't feel like my life is so incredibly perfect, I work my ass off, but I can stop and take a break. I think that it is important for people to have some proprietary control over their time. And the whole point about the way that the system works is that our hours are not ours. People's submission to things, "Well, that's what people do!", ends up with them being locked in schedules that are not their own.

There are plenty of people who work all the time and are totally broke. In fact, the people who live like that are in debt up to their fucking eyeballs. Because they think, "That's what one does. One goes on a cruise and puts it on a credit card." So, one has credit and the credit card companies charge them 30% interest, and they don't even get it. My thing was always, "Never owe money." I just don't owe money. Obviously there's been a few times when we are pressing records and we've borrowed from X's brother, but I don't owe money. If I don't have the money to buy something then I don't buy it. There's four fundamentals in life, right? Air, water, food and fucking… That's pretty much it. If you break it down, that's it. Everything else is accoutrement.

Bob Dylan said something like "You have to be honest to live outside the law," and that's my kind of thing. I do everything I need to do. That's why I pay taxes. A lot of punks said "We ain't here to fucking pay taxes" but they're tourists because they're going to be gone right? I'm a long distance runner. Don't give them any reason to shut you down.

Creation

In talking to artists of all hues (musicians, painters, poets, etc.) it is no surprise that creation and creativity are of paramount importance. Interestingly, for a great many of the people interviewed for this book, it was apparent that rather than being a choice, the practice of artistic creativity has been more of a compulsion. Or put in another, more dramatic, way, creation and creativity have been a calling. For some people it is absolutely clear that they simply HAVE to express their ideas, instincts and feelings in a creative form, and the medium that they take has not been rigid in any way. Jeffrey Lewis, for example, is just as at home with playing an acoustic guitar as he is with meticulously drawing cartoons, or for that matter giving slide show lectures on the Vietnam War accompanied by music on stage. Penny Rimbaud moves seamlessly between art and poetry, and in music can be heard as part of a jazz ensemble one day, and then found performing with the dubstep and electro-house band the Bloody Beetroots the next. Arguably, Steve Albini finds as much self-expression and creativity in his sound engineering as he does when he is at the poker table as one the World Series poker champions.

And it can be an immersive experience, and a spiritual one for many people.

"If I see a building that excites me, then I'm going to paint buildings, or sing buildings or talk about buildings. I can't rein myself in, and that's probably a good thing, that's probably why I'm still working. But it didn't make life easy for me or anybody around me." **Little Annie**

"In Bristol, I was in love with reggae. Reggae, and fun, was as important as punk. Going and seeing U-Roy, and Tappa Zukie that mystical sense of 'upliftedness', of feeling like a human being when you were 14 or 15, and being with a lot of complete strangers... There's a mystical place where you need to belong as well as a political place. Bass lines and stuff, I was just drawn in." **Mark Stewart**

Punk changed my life   It is in no way an exaggeration to say that punk changed the lives of very many people, from the performers to the audience and all those in between. And variations on this theme of the transformative power of punk extend to instances of punk having saved lives too. If we were talking about an ambulance crew, a lifeboat or even a particular drug treatment, this might be easier to understand, but there really is no shortage of instances where people have claimed that punk has altered the course of their life for the better.

"When we were doing the *Last Supper* tour in America, we had a gig in Baltimore... and this guy from Chicago turned up with this six-pack of beer and said, 'I haven't got a lot, but this is for you.' Anyway, after the gig he came up to the band and said, 'I just want to say that I appreciate you coming tonight because Crass has helped me through a really bad time'. And he suddenly burst into tears. And I said, 'Fucking hell mate. Are you alright?' And he said,

'Yes, its just that I saw my dad shoot himself with a cattle gun in front of me, and I've been suicidal myself.' Another time, in New Zealand, a girl said to me 'Are you Steve Ignorant?' And she burst into tears. 'Crass's music helped me, I was abused as a kid.' So you won't find me stuck in the dressing room at gigs saying, 'I'm not signing any autographs, I'm not talking to anyone', I'm always out talking to people, that's the job you do." **Steve Ignorant**

"What is so deeply emotional for me about Crass, in particular, is that when I was sent to the correctional boarding school I was completely alone, and I was SO afraid that I carried a knife... I felt so alone, and there was nobody to tell me right from wrong, there weren't even teachers at the place, so at a VERY difficult time in my life, Crass was there for me." **Jón Gnarr**

"Punk was a creative and productive avenue, I'm sure the other route would have been criminal. A lot of criminals are very clever, just bored. I've been quite lucky and I'm thankful that punk was there for me at the right time." **Tony Drayton**

A question that might be posed is: "What is it about punk that has had this effect?" And part of the answer must relate to punk's artistic and creative manifestations, (alongside the ideas conveyed by them). And these carry a different significance for different people. In the case of Jón Gnarr, for example, he explains that his oversensitivity to music in general, led him in part to be inspired more by the graphic, and often shocking, artistic work of Gee Vaucher and the particular styling used in the way Crass lyrics were presented. The trigger for people might be anything but it is the alchemy of these different creative elements that gives rise to the profound effects experienced by people.

The power of creativity as conveyed through artistic endeavours is felt in many ways. For Jeffrey Lewis this is partly about a battle between different creative forces. For Steve Lake it might be a lens through which we can view society, and for Einar Örn Benediktsson it can be a key to self-understanding.

"If you had two billion dollars and you created a whole ad campaign, with posters all over the world that said... 'the Sex Pistols are crap'... then somebody had to design the poster; somebody had to decide what the font was... How are we going to print this? What colour is the poster going to be? What colour are the words going to be? And so on. So if the billionaire, who is trying to convince the world that the Sex Pistols stink, put... billions of dollars into a worldwide blanketing ad campaign, it would still be a battle of artistic power." **Jeffrey Lewis**

"I sometimes do these experiments on myself and I did this experiment about 18 months ago where I was only going to listen to music by women for a week. And once you do that... suddenly you realise how little music there is that is just made by women. If you say that you are only going to listen to music made by men, you'll find there's this record that was written by a bloke, it's performed by a bloke, it was produced by a bloke, there was a bloke who was the engineer and so on. So I had to broaden it to just listen to music where women play a central role in it." **Steve Lake**

"With punk, I found the key to be creative because there were no barriers. There was nothing that was predefined in terms of how I should be writing things. I was writing about my reality in the city of Reykjavík, seeing a peeping Tom or later more abstract ideas like standing on top of a lamp post and asking should I jump? Should I jump? Punk was the key to unlock my heart... Punk opened for me the way to express myself, to write and to work, and to carry on. But also I developed the ability to work with other people, to listen to other people, and to be in cooperation... I took on the ethos of punk, which was about expressing yourself, publishing what you want, publishing the way you want it and connecting punk and surrealism in a way that created art." **Einar Örn**

Matching artistic expression to philosophical stance   We see that punk artists have articulated their ideas in ways that mirror many of the features of the punk ethos. For example, it is important to many performers that there isn't a perceived divide between fans and band members. Particular care is taken to remove the effects of celebrity so often found outside the genre, and attempts are made to collapse the categories of 'them' and 'us.' This can have the effect of opening up the creative process so audience members at gigs, for example, might find themselves singing or performing with the band (and to a much greater degree than simply singing along).

"Live experiences can be empowering and bands can make a statement by the way they play, the way the treat the audience. I mean there are some people who refuse ever to play on a stage. They like to get really, really close with the band." **Deek Allen**

"For the audience, especially for the really young, it could be pretty scary, and along with all the leaflets, handouts and fanzines that people brought to each gig, a total overload. It's why we always got off the front of the stage when the gig finished and didn't disappear out the back." **Gee Vaucher**

There are ways in which artistic expression is reflective of deeper philosophical underpinnings, for example the existentialist and more Zen-leaning idea of being and creating in the moment. Penny Rimbaud, formerly of Crass, has performed for many years in an improvisational style that illustrates this.

In the improvisational realm you can do nothing but be fully engaged. And, in this self-authoring way, you are constructing your own script moment to moment. But this too has a situational quality to it, in that the truly live and ultimately unpredictable nature of it, for both artist and audience, presents a situation that has to be dealt with. A different example of this is the dramatic and performative way in which Einar Örn and Jón Gnarr, while in government in Reykjavík, offered surreal provocations to inspire action.

"We said that we wanted polar bears to come here, which also sounds like a silly slogan. The issue though is climate change – we are getting polar bears on the icebergs drifting away from Greenland and when they land ashore here in Iceland, we don't have a method of capturing them or a means of trying to send them back or anything like that. We just shoot them. And so we're highlighting climate change. This is happening. It's about opening up, in a different way, and speaking about the situation." **Einar Örn Benediktsson**

Creativity as a weapon Creative expression, particularly in punk, can have a cogent effect, and there are many examples that can be found of this. One is the Crass symbol which has the dual quality of being both visually arresting, and also being highly reproducible. It operated simultaneously as if it were a shield AND a weapon, behind which the second wave of punk gathered. It was a force to be reckoned with and over time various attempts to appropriate it have been made by companies such as the London Fashion House Hardware, as well as Hollywood celebrities such as Angelina Jolie.

"Regarding the Crass symbol, you can't get more powerful in Western society than a cross and a snake... It's hard to find anything that is as culturally resonant and the only other thing you might mention would be the swastika and there were accusations that resided deliberately or not in the symbol. It immediately got people's attention. It was carefully wrought... Each component was separate and concise because it was designed to be used as stencil, and that gave it this solidity." **David King**

As a means of political power, the music of punk has clearly made its mark. It has helped to mobilise a generation of kids into engagement and action on issues of racism, nuclear deterrence, capitalism and so on. But importantly it is not the message or the lyrics alone that have done this. Rather it is the creative rendering itself that has helped bridge the gap between punk shaman and any potential audience.

"A lot of people's reaction to anything you say in a song or any political comment you might make as a musician is, 'Well, what would you do about it?' Well this is what I am doing about it. This is what I do in my area. This is how I operate." **Tim Smith**

"The Pop Group absolutely blew my mind. Absolutely! They, more than any punk band, completely blew my mind. I'd gone to see Patti Smith at Newcastle City Hall and the Pop Group were supporting. What they did was just the most sonically amazing thing I had ever heard... I thought, 'What are they doing with those instruments? I've never heard anything like it!' Then you buy a Pop Group record and you read the lyrics and they are the heaviest, most dense political tracts that I'd read... They'd be singing about torture in Indonesia or somewhere and you'd think, 'How can you put those words into a song? How can that be a song?' There was one B-side that was just a list of human rights violations around the world. That was the moment when I thought that this has got a more political and philosophical slant than what had gone before" **Dunstan Bruce**

So, creativity and artistic ingenuity enabled punk to become what it was. Some of this was born out of a scarcity of resources, and the photocopied fanzines of the time are testament to this. Some of this was possible through a reinterpretation of pre-existing art forms like jazz, folk, surrealism and agitprop. And some of this innovation was the result of experimentation and, at times, unadulterated courage.

But, it is no coincidence that we see the philosophical roots of punk finding expression in the medium. The existentialist mode, for example, explains the self-authoring spirit of Do It Yourself, which in turn inspires a kind of instrumental eclecticism – where the tools of surrealism and agitprop, for example, are borrowed for the job. The libertarian underpinnings of punk facilitate a diversity of artistic styles that collide together in an explosion of colour, noise and inventiveness. And the anarchist sentiment of not bowing to authority releases punk artists from travelling within the tramlines of conventional creative method. "No Gods, no masters" applies as much to the creative orthodoxy as it does to the instruments of the state.

Mike Watt

Bass player Mike Watt co-founded seminal US punk band The Minutemen in 1980, in San Pedro, California. They released four acclaimed studio albums on SST Records, but disbanded following the death of Watt's close friend and band-mate D Boon in a car crash in 1985. Watt was distraught and initially intended to stop making music altogether, but an invite from Sonic Youth to hang out in New York reignited his passion.

He went on to form punk free-jazz trio fIREHOSE, who released five studio albums over the next eight years. Since then, Watt has undertaken various musical and literary projects, releasing four solo albums in the process, and has collaborated with the likes of Henry Rollins, J Mascis, Nirvana and Beastie Boys. His innovative playing style, coupled with the massive respect of his peers, saw him receive the 'Bass Player Magazine' lifetime achievement award in 2008. Most recently, he has been touring with his band the Missingmen. In his spare time, Watt plays bass with an up-and-coming band called the Stooges.

I wasn't really a musician. I got into music to be with D Boon, my buddy, and it was his mama who put me on bass. She said, "You've gotta have a band and you're gonna be the bass!" I didn't even know what bass guitar was. I'm 13 years old in 1970 and all I know is arena rock. So D Boon and myself go to our first gig, which was T-Rex, and it was actually pretty neat. After some time, we graduated up to bands like the Who, Blue Öyster Cult and so on, and we were trying to copy these, of course getting half of the shit wrong. But we never thought of music as an expression, it was really just a way of hanging out.

And then we graduated high school in '76, and there's this cat named Nicky B, he'd joined a Hollywood band named Weirdos and he was wearing a Cotex [*sanitary towel*] around his neck. And he told us there was a scene up in Hollywood where people write their own songs. And we saw some pictures in *Creem* magazine, which is how we found out about the Stooges. And boy! It was a big mistake to tell people in high school you liked the Stooges, because everyone HATED you.

And I remember that I said to D Boon "We can do this." I just FELT it. And hanging around at the clubs where bands performed was an incredible experience. You didn't know any of these dudes, and most of them had fake names, but they were really deep in the music. And they were weirdos and you could tell they didn't fit in. But you'd get to talk to lots of different dudes and I'd never been in something like this. And then you'd meet people like Raymond Pettibone, who would play me some John Coltrane material for the first time. I thought John Coltrane was punk too – just a little older. And then he taught me about Dada and this stuff that was going on 78 years ago.

Autonomous connections   But punk to us was NOT a style of music. It was a state of mind. A big part of our scene were the fanzines, they were the fabric, and that's how you knew what was happening in your home place and other areas too. Punk was all about the people, and it still is. And it's about making connections, what I call autonomous connections, where they're not about hierarchy. They're not power plays. For us, in punk we were going to have associations between us that were different. D Boon and myself were boys in the 60s so we were seeing people take things into the streets – Civil Rights, the war issues, all kinds of stuff, and the 70s came and we were all getting ready for it but it was all wilting. And they even lost the humour. One good thing about the hippies was there was some funny stuff. But autonomous things are trippy things. For me it's the only genuine, honest way to do it, the other ways are just military units of organising society to like fight a fire, with a bucket brigade. Making autonomous connections for me is a process – and the honest fabric for me is the artistic expression. In my book you should allow no coercion. Humanity has to be at the bottom of it. In some ways it's part of tradition, and I think that punk is the next shift.

My pop's grandfather was a Klansman, can you believe that shit? I tell you; it's about dealing with that stuff and doing that with integrity. And I think that means autonomy. It doesn't mean better-than-thou, looking down from a gated community – it means being in the thick of it. Not letting the jive prevail. John Coltrane said that all music people are engaged in a noble endeavour; it's not about servicing lifestyles. We're all different, but yet there's so much common ground. That's the dangling duality. So there are so many quirks that we all have, but there is so much common ground.

Punk is whatever we made it to be   Thinking about the artist Banksy, I think he's pretty intense. There was this guy saying in New York City that he's too obvious, but I don't think so. I like it. I think you need people to design toothpaste tubes I guess, but then you need truth tellers like Banksy. And the creativity problem should never be solved I think. It should always be a problem. What I'm looking for is some easier way for people to connect without having to have these hierarchies and someone having to get stomped down. The creative process in relation to this is always going to be difficult. Because it's about imagination, and putting it all together. But it can also be transcendent. I'm only saying this because it's why D Boon wanted that name Minutemen, because there were some people appropriating patriotic symbols, and we wanted to confuse the issue.

What is punk about? Write your own poem, paint your own picture! Start your own band like D Boon said. D Boon had this quote, and this skater made a sticker out of it, and it said, "Punk is whatever we made it to be". The idea is that you fall down, you can't really talk your way out, you gotta get back up on the board, and you get a thing going. It's like Walt Whitman. He writes 12 poems to try and stop the Civil War, and put it out himself. This is in 1855 — DIY a long time ago!

A world of possibility   The Stooges. I'm very aware that I don't want to ruin their legacy. I have this nightmare that on my gravestone it just says, "Fucked up a Stooges gig". Believe me, I feel the weight there. But Iggy Pop is a great teacher. What a work ethic that guy's got. I really like touring and I like playing for people. I like the possibilities when you get down with other people, you don't know what's going to come, and that's a trip. That's a world of possibility again. You think you've seen everything, you think you know it all. But you gotta fight that tendency. Everybody's got something to teach you. So I really think it's classroom all the way. Sometimes you're gonna get asked to teach something, but a lot of times you're here to learn. And the knowing is in the doing. It's gotta have a heart, man, it's gotta have a heart.

Jeffrey Lewis

Born and raised in New York City by beatnik parents who didn't own a television, Jeffrey Lewis is a singer/songwriter and comic book artist. In 2000, he spent time living in Austin, Texas, playing open mic nights and distributing his autobiographical comics to local coffee shops. Then in 2001 he signed to Rough Trade Records, with whom he has made a number of LPs, including The Last Time I Did Acid I Went Insane *and* A Turn In The Dream-Songs.

In 2007, Jeffrey released 12 Crass Songs, *an LP consisting entirely of songs written by Crass – the songs were reworked in his unique 'anti-folk' style, but retained the political power of the originals. "I wanted to see what the substance could do if it was removed from the style," he said.*

Live Jeffrey mixes 60s acoustic psychedelia, experimental art-punk and urban lyricism, with songs ranging from folk narratives to full-blown garage rock. Most often as a trio, although occasionally just solo, he has toured the globe extensively, playing with the likes of Thurston Moore, the Fall and the Television Personalities along the way. Live shows are often embellished by low-budget videos and illustrations.

He has been self-publishing a comic book series called Fuff *since 2004, and has lectured around the world on topics such as the limited comic book series* Watchmen *by Alan Moore and artist Dave Gibbons, and independently produced music.*

I'm coming at all of this from what I guess you would call a working-class perspective. I have never had a safety net and none of my stuff has ever been funded by anybody. When I started out if I ever had a couple of bucks to buy blank tapes I would record my songs onto the tapes and then I would sell them at the open mic for $3. So I'd make a few dollars profit so I could buy some more tapes, and literally it has been like this, moving from one step to another and building up like that more than 15 years now. And at any time along the way there have been opportunities to advance to realms of higher money stakes or bring in managers or promoters and so on. And if I thought one of them would be a good business decision or would benefit me, or the fans that are interested in me, or the music or the art I make, then there wouldn't be a reason not to do it. But I think "how is it good if the ticket prices go up?" That's not good. "How is it good to be on a bigger label or have a bigger advance if that means that you have to spend $20,000 to make a record and then you have to sell x amount to recoup the $20,000 before you make any money?" None of that ever made any sense to me.

I've always kept my overheads low and from that I've made a living in ways that people would not think possible. Everybody in the industry when I was starting out was always saying, "You can't do this unless you have x or y." I never even had an amplifier for the first 10 years that I did this. I had never owned an amplifier in my life. I mean every club has something to plug into. You don't need to pay to carry one on an airplane. You just show up — they're a club! They either have an amplifier or a DI box or the opening act says, "You can use my amp." The general point is that while I can make some moral statement about not selling out and this reflects the fact that I have come from a socialist, activist background; this bohemian, political, New York City background, there's also general mathematics.

Our band could be your life   Most people would not think that I could make a living doing this while remaining totally unknown as I have remained. I am not even a drop in the bucket of the public eye of the music industry. I'm smaller than, say, Giant Sand or the Tindersticks who aren't huge bands. You know they're not as big as Sufjan Stevens for example, and even Sufjan Stevens is not as huge as Vampire Weekend. So, from the layers of known bands, there is nobody as unknown as me. You can't possibly get as unknown as me [*laughs*]. For me, a huge inspiration was the book *Our Band Could Be Your Life* by Michael Azerrad that came out in 2001, the first year that I started touring. Although I'd been making music for a few years before that, I had just started doing tours and everybody in the record label told me "You can't do it that way! How can you go and play a show if you don't have a hotel booked?" All of this stuff being said that it was impossible to do that. I was like "Isn't it possible? What if I just show up? If we're only getting paid $150 and a hotel's going to cost like a hundred bucks then we're not going to make any money, so why can't I ask the audience if we could sleep on somebody's floor?" Like, "Shouldn't that be able to work?" When that book came out it justified all of my imaginings about ways in which it could be possible. Not only is it possible but also this is about all the bands I love. This IS how they did it — from the Minutemen, of course, to Sonic Youth and Beat Happening. Logically, I knew that it seemed that there should be this other way to do it than everybody was telling me.

How serious was punk?   Punk is a fashionising of a risky impulse, because until you are willing to get punched in the face for something it is merely fashion. The freedom riders in the 60s, who went to the South to register black voters, went on these buses and there was no question. The bus would arrive, there would be people with baseball bats waiting and everybody that stepped off the bus gets smashed in the head and sent to the hospital. It's like Pussy Riot. Everybody can talk about Pussy Riot, but until you're willing to go out there to Russia and get smashed in the face by a cop, it's just talk — it's just fashion. It's just exciting music. Some people even say that the music is a diffuser of the social tensions, so the music is to blame for eliminating real action or political change. Music is an important safety valve, like punk or gangster rap or psychedelic music. It's like, I don't need to be on acid for 12 hours because I can put on a 40-minute record by so-and-so and I can experience this really interesting facet of creativity that is now in this harmless form. Even though it has all the excitement and it speaks of all these things, I don't have to take the physical risk or even take the time. So whether it's dressing punk or owning punk records or even if it speaks of that anger, the 'incendiaryness', and this taking responsibility and saying "Fuck you" to culture, it is still essentially taking physically life-threatening ideas and turning them into something that is different from getting punched in the face, when it really comes down to it.

Outrage at a lack of outrage   Lou Reed's *Walk on the Wild Side* was meant to be an outrageous culture-changing single, but what was outrageous about *Walk on the Wild Side* is not that he is talking about transgender people, it's that he takes it for granted as part of reality. It's like that's just the way it is, and even though it was taken as outrageousness, the outrage was not his outrage. The outrageousness is his lack of outrage, which is the same for Crass, the Fall, and the same as Jonathan Richman. What outrages other people is just, like, who they are, which is also a really good artistic lesson because when you realise who you are, that is where your artistic power is. It shows other people that it is possible to live a life where certain things are taken for granted as reality, which for those people are beyond the pale of acceptability.

And Crass's outrage at all the things we take for granted, and where all of that anger comes from, is still amazing to hear. They take for granted that you should be FEROCIOUSLY outraged at things that we assume are normal, like we go to the supermarket and so on. And you say, "Oh! Perhaps I should be really angry. THEY are REALLY angry about this, so maybe there is something to get angry about." Maybe you should be screamingly outraged like "NO FUCKING WAY!" So there is a lot of artistic power in both what these people take for granted as normal and what they take for granted as abnormal that you should be outraged about.

Art from another dimension   I think of art as like another dimension. If your fingers were to dip into the surface of water then from a two-dimensional perspective, you would have this flat surface and you would see these four circles. But from a two-dimensional perspective you wouldn't know that those four circles are actually part of this three dimensional hand. And I think of art in the same way.

An making a good song?

And as I try and grasp onto it, And myself thinking

of it that is coming through here.

And maybe there is some weird string

the dark. For this thing that's in another dimension:

Great art, when it hits you,

is part of this thing in,

another dimension. And everybody who

Great art, when it hits you, is part of this thing in another dimension [*waves hands in circle to illustrate enormity of it*]. And everybody who is an artist is like grasping around in the dark for this thing that's in another dimension. And maybe there is some weird string of it that is coming through here. And as I try and grasp onto it I find myself thinking "Is this going to work? Am I making a good song? Am I making a good comic?" And then somehow, unbeknownst to me I grab onto this thing that's part of the big shape… that connects to everybody else because we are connected in this other dimension that we can't see. It may sound hokey, and yet we feel it unquestionably, somehow. And we share that with certain other people that also feel that. So I feel like the dimensional explanation makes sense in a philosophical way. There is something that rings true about that. Like why do Bob Dylan songs affect people? What does it mean? It's just a string of images and sounds. He probably couldn't even tell you what it meant. But somehow it means something to millions of people – why? To me it's like this collective unconscious thing.

Crude music by the sharp people   Punk is crude music that is actually made by people who are smarter than the people making the supposedly smarter music. So when you have that polarised combination of music with this purposefully de-intellectualised exterior made by sharp people you have something quite special. If anything is worthy of a definition of punk in the 1977 punk sense that's what it is. It's like the Ramones, they weren't idiots. Lou Reed, he was a really smart poetic guy, he's not like this degenerate scumbag – or maybe he was – but he's also really smart. And the ground zero of all of that is the first Fugs album. To this day you cannot find a record in the 45 years since this came out that has this combination of the level of intellect, at such a high level, and the crudity of the music.

Steve Albini

Steve Albini's expansive career in music began in 1982 when he formed Big Black while a student at Northwestern University in Chicago, playing most of the instruments himself on debut EP Lungs. *With a full band soon assembled, Big Black fast gained a reputation on the US underground scene for their brutal live performances, releasing debut album* Atomizer *in 1986. But just a year later, Steve put an end to the group shortly before the release of their second LP,* Songs About Fucking.*

Post Big Black, Steve wasn't short of sound engineering work for other bands, soon becoming known for his trademark huge guitars and raw percussion. In 1988, never one to make life easy for himself, he called his second band Rapeman. They released just one album, Two Nuns and a Pack Mule, *and faced constant flak for their controversial name. In 1992 Steve launched his "minimalist rock trio" Shellac, who continue to play to this day, and have released six studio albums, including 2014's* Dude Incredible.*

In 1997 in Chicago, Steve opened his Electrical Audio recording studio, choosing to go against the industry grain and use analog technology only. A key influence on his methods was the work of producer and Southern Records founder John Loder, who had close connections with Crass many years earlier. Steve doesn't like to be referred to as a 'producer' on the music he works on, preferring the title 'recording engineer'. He accepts no royalties, just a flat fee, believing that his role is technical rather than creative.

Steve's view that you should "make only music you are passionate about, work only with people you like and trust, and don't sign anything" has served him well over the years and he has clocked up an impressive CV that includes Nirvana, Pixies, the Stooges, Mogwai and Cheap Trick. He is also a keen poker player and was ranked 12th at the 2013 World Series of Poker Seniors Championship.

When I was a teenager and I first heard the Ramones, my friends and I thought they were hilarious. We thought they were inept and we listened to them as a talisman of my little group of friends. We listened to them because we thought they were absurd. Gradually over time there was something magnetic about that first Ramones album that made me play it again and again and again and somewhere around the 10th or 12th play I realised that it was actually the greatest record that was ever made and that actually that's how I wanted to live my life – being a goofball with a bunch of my friends and writing offensive and absurd music.

What punk rock meant to me was that the parts of culture that had previously been dismissible, i.e. young people, crazy people, people on the fringes of society, people of abnormal behaviour, abnormal tastes, abnormal standards – those people had to be taken seriously now because they could do amazing stuff.

And punk was the first time where I thought that people who thought like me, people who had the same sort of background as me, the same sort of world view as me, were taking themselves and these preposterous notions of theirs seriously and they were expressing it.

During punk rock all of the anti-social, morbid and indulgent and borderline insane ideas were given vent... the effect that it had on me, very personally, was that it made me less judgmental of other people, it made me more willing to consider ideas that were not mine. Rather than disregarding ideas because of the source I had to consider an idea on its merits because, well, it turns out crazy people can do really clever and intelligent things.

It was a great moment for me of feeling I was valid, like the ideas that were in the back of my head, however goofy or morbid or weird or inappropriate, maybe I should take those seriously... this just became the framework through which I saw the world... I just assumed that everyone has moments where they imagine cutting the throat of a neighbour.

Just as good as everyone else   The thing about punk shows in Chicago was that you would see completely different people of all types; you would see a lot of recent immigrants at punk shows in Chicago. One of the people who were regulars on the punk scene in Chicago was a guy named Alan Jones. He started a band called End Result, a totally amazing band that I loved, and for a while he was living in a mission, a men's shelter... You would see people selling pills, you would see girls that you knew were occasional prostitutes, you would see all manner of freaks and weirdos at the punk show because that was the place where it didn't matter how weird you were; you weren't going to be singled out and it wasn't going to be uncomfortable and I took to it like a fish to water. Rubbing elbows with all these different kinds of people that I would never have met under any other circumstances.

There was a very close symbiosis between the punk scene in Chicago and the gay underground because gay culture in Chicago was still officially oppressed. There were gay bars and there was a gay neighbourhood, but it wasn't nearly as open as it is now. It certainly wasn't celebrated. Now there are pride flags on the street, but there was nothing in Chicago in 1980. That parallel experience of the outsiders of all different things like drug addicts and criminals and people in the gay community who weren't comfortable being out, all of these outsider people agglomerated into the punk scene. I think that it was good for everybody, everybody learned to get along with everybody else. The Chicago punk scene was not this safe, white, male haven that punk scenes in other places have been described as being.

You were in the company of all these people and you can either choose to be afraid of them or you can see them as comrades. And I saw them as comrades and

I realised that we were all in this thing together. You wouldn't find out where the next show was unless you screwed up the courage to ask someone, and then once you had asked somebody then, all of a sudden, OK – you've met your first homosexual then he introduces you to your first prostitute and she introduces you to your first drug dealer, he introduces you to your first painter. Suddenly you have a peer group and a circle of friends that includes criminals, prostitutes, drug dealers, painters and musicians and that would never had happened if I had just gone to baseball games, done academic stuff or been in the same cultural stratum that I showed up in. I would never had met those people, I would never have been forced to take them seriously, I would never had broadened my world view to include the concept that those people are just as good as everyone else and they have ideas and aspirations and creativity like everyone else.

The inspiration of self-reliance From a practical standpoint, what I admired about the punks was the self-reliance and creativity and the making-do aspect, and that's been embodied in everything that I have ever done. My band books its own shows, organises its own business, records its own records. My studio was built by the people who work here. We taught ourselves how and we built the studio. I feel that that sort of self-reliance and making do with the materials available, making do with what you have at hand – that doesn't need to be a limiting factor, that actually can kind of be the spark of inspiration.

Music was never an option for a career for me and I still don't consider it an option for a career. I run a recording studio as a business and I make records every day and that's my job, but up to that point it had never crossed my mind that I would be doing it professionally. It was always a passion of mine, something that I did. My friends and I were in bands and if ever they wanted to make a record I would help them make a recording. And you do that a few times and then somebody that you've never even met calls you and says, "I understand that you do recordings, can you record my band?" And then, "Sure, yeah, that sounds great. Let's do that." Then over time you realise that this seems like something that I can do professionally. But it wasn't an aspiration of mine to be a professional musician. I'm in a band now and I still don't consider myself to be a professional musician. It's a thing that I do.

If you see something as your career and you think, "This is how I provide for myself" and that something is subject to other people liking it and wanting to buy it then you put yourself in a very precarious situation: you might start pandering to that audience or trying to compromise what it is that you are doing for the sake of making more money out of it. And I like music too much to do that to it.

I've heard the idea expressed that if you're not trying to make a go of your band as a full-time thing, as a career, then it doesn't mean that much to you. I see it in the opposite perspective. I feel that music means so much to me that it would be indulgent for me to expect it to also pay my way.

I'm willing to work a job to support my involvement in music in the same way I would a wife and family. That just seems normal to me and almost all of my peers and friends in music in the US saw it that way. That music was something that you did, like you might be in the bowling league or paint watercolour landscapes, or do ballroom dancing. Things that were certainly very satisfying but you wouldn't expect them to be your career.

In Utero and ethical business   If they had offered me half a million dollars for [*Nirvana's*] *In Utero* I would have taken it, but the specific thing about my work as a recording engineer is that I don't take royalties because I consider that a parasitic means of compensation. If I want to be paid for something then I should set a price, and say, "I think that this is what it is worth so pay me." If they agree they will pay me, if they don't, they won't. I think that this is a perfectly reasonable way to go through life. What I don't think is reasonable is for me to attach myself to your enterprise so that every time you are successful I steal a little bit of your success. Every time that they sell a record, I don't need to get paid any more. Any more than every time that my toilet flushes I shouldn't have to pay the plumber another nickel.

In the 80s I had a straight job that paid the freight for me to spend all of my leisure time working on bands and being involved in music, and now my straight job is keeping the studio running and that requires much more of my attention. In a lot of ways, in the 80s when I was more active in the band scene and a lot of my friends were in bands, people would complain about having to have a job. They would complain that they couldn't just work on music all of the time.

Having a job was such a fucking luxury; regularly I pine for the days that I had a job. I could show up at eight in the morning, leave at five in the evening and never think about it a-fucking-gain. It's done! Five in the evening I walk out of the place where I was working and it's over, I don't have to think about it for a second until I get back there the next day. I had weekends, the whole fucking weekend when you didn't have to do anything. And then paid vacations, oh my god what a joy! That's when you go on tours, on your paid vacation. So it doesn't matter if you go bust on the tour. It doesn't matter, yeah it's nice to turn a profit on a tour and I'm kind of proud of the fact that every tour I've been on has turned a profit, but if you don't it doesn't matter, you've got a pay cheque waiting when you come home. Having a job was so fucking great — I loved it.

I worked as a photograph re-toucher, like I worked on images that were used in advertising... reprehensible behaviour on my part, really. I can't defend the fact that

Every time that they sell a record, I don't need to get paid any more. Any more than every time that my toilet flushes I shouldn't have to pay the plumber.

I was trying to induce people to smoke this brand of cigarettes rather than that brand, I really can't defend it. I feel like that is what a job is. You are doing something horrible for money. And so I don't fault people who do horrible things for money. If a band finds itself in a desperate situation like selling a song for a beer commercial for money, they did it for money and I understand. I knew people that got by doing criminal stuff like sucking dicks or whatever. I can't judge somebody who needs money and does something horrible for money, that's fine. But it does change the relationship with all the things they are doing. If somebody is doing something purely for money then that changes my respect for what they are doing in the interim, because I know that's why they are doing it. I would not want to be judged based on the quality of the colour yellow in the Marlboro man's rain slipper or whatever the fuck it is, which was my responsibility at the time... I really don't think that defines me as a person.

The tyranny of goals   There is a very specific perspective that I have maintained for a very long time that has enabled me to be satisfied with the moment, which is that I have essentially refused to have goals. If you have a goal or an aspiration then the motivating factor is that you are frustrated that you have not achieved this goal. You have this tension or this anguish that you have not achieved something. You're trying to get to this specific thing and that goal may very well be unattainable, you might never actually get there, so you spend your entire life frustrated and in tension and anguish because you are not achieving this thing that you desire. As a corollary to that, if you achieve your goal then you are kind of lost. Like, OK, I did that, now I guess that I have to pick another spot to get to. I think that that's a very crude way to get through life. It's sort of a methodical approach where you are tunnelling towards this thing and it prevents you from experiencing what's happening at the time, it prevents you from diverting yourself or makes you feel guilty about diverting yourself, if you are not tunnelling toward the thing.

So I've always tried to see everything I do as a process, and evaluate it on that basis. Like, is this a reasonable way for someone to behave? Is this adding to the general decency of the world? Is this satisfying in its own regard? And if it is, then I continue doing it. It also allows you to take tangents. Like, "That looks interesting as hell, would that be an interesting thing for me to be doing? Would that be an interesting project?"

Punk changed everything   Punk changed the whole world for me. Punk changed all of my friends. Everything that I do with my life. This studio. All of this that I am doing for a living. Everyone I know. Every significant friend I've ever had. Every significant life experience that I have had, I owe that to the Ramones. Without any question whatsoever, all of those things that I got to experience, all of my moments in my love life, all of my creative moments, all of my professional accomplishments, every single thing that I did in my life has to do one way or another with me hearing the Ramones and deciding they were great.

All of those people that abandoned those core principles that all of us identified with when we were deeply involved with punk at the time, even people who have totally abandoned those principles, they know they're there. And while they were still cognisant of them and acting on those ideals, they accomplished things and those things have survived. There is any number of people that put out great records and then later on turned into Republicans or those born-agains or whatever; those records are still kicking around and those records are still awesome, and are still inspirational. There's any number of people who misread punk as a thing and they got lost on a tangent of ideology. Because of punk, that tangent of ideology or politics or whatever they are proselytising, now has a spokesman for it that it wouldn't have had before.

A friend of mine described punk as a brilliant flash of light. Very few people were there at the spot where that flash of light happened, but it illuminated everything and cast really long shadows. For people like me that were dazzled by that light it really did change everything about the way you saw the world... punk rock still has the effect of clearing the table of all the bullshit.

Just don't give a fuck what other people think   Punk was evidence that people outside of your immediate peer group, or friends, don't matter. If they have an opinion on you and your peer group and your circle of friends, you are your own barometer. You and your friends know what's cool and what isn't cool, or what is and what isn't fun, what's an asshole move and what isn't an asshole move. You have to trust your instincts about that stuff and not worry about external yardsticks, because you are the one that's living this life experience from which you derive this philosophy that you want to be consistent with. Other people that have an opinion about it from the outside – fuck all those people! They're not in the room at the time.

If you're following a train of thought, that train of thought will guide you in a lot of different places and give you ammunition or give you a structure for how to live your life. And if you want to live a life consistent with that structure because you are enjoying this train of thought or this mania that you're riding then you shouldn't worry about what other people outside have to say about it. Say like you have an unconventional relationship with someone you love, it's like – fuck off! Or you have an unconventional approach to money. They don't get to have an opinion on it.

The dark side of punk

There is a darker side to punk, or at least there are features of punk that generate important questions about its contribution and its legacy. There is rightly little space for romanticism in the movement, and the accounts offered by the main players in the scene make no bones about its shortcomings. It is clear to us that the architects of punk are under no illusions and they see the disappointments as much as they see the power and merits of punk.

There is an argument too that as soon as punk was named as such, and effectively captured by the media as a reportable phenomenon, it had in fact disappeared; in much the same way that a desert mirage evaporates the closer you get to it. In this sense it might be seen, at least after the initial explosion, as a construct rather than a naturally occurring movement – no more real than any other fashion, and no more significant. This is not our view but one that is offered. And at the level of the bands and the personalities, punk was no different from the bands and personalities found in the rock'n'roll tradition. There has been in-fighting and break-ups and tensions and grudges that are still held to this day. But to be honest, who really cares? Take any grouping from the family to the village to the organisation, and you will find exactly the same. We acknowledge this, but are much less concerned with these frailties.

But we DO want to look at some of the less constructive aspects, if only for completeness, and at the level of the efficacy of punk as a generator of ideas and thinking. The question being – in what ways does the shadier side of punk help us to better understand or learn from the philosophical contribution it makes?

'Punkier' Than Thou   The idea of being 'punkier', or holier, than thou, refers to a kind of informal hierarchy of 'punkness' within the movement. It is, of course, strange that within the doctrine of punk – to the extent that there is one, which so vehemently challenges hierarchy and rules – that this should occur at all, but in many instances, it does. This can be seen, for example, in the division between the political and the non-political sides of punk, embodied by bands such as Siouxsie and the Banshees as contrasted with bands like Crass. It is manifest in the views expressed by some that regard the first wave of punk (Sex Pistols, the Damned, the Clash etc.) as more 'punk' than ensuing waves (Discharge, Chumbawamba, Big Black, etc.) Particularly in the UK, it is exhibited in a punk hierarchy that suggests that working-class punks have a greater right to claim punk than middle-class punks. It is exhibited in subdivisions between meat-eating punks and vegetarian punks, and then again between vegetarian and vegan punks.

It finds expression too in the notion of 'selling out'. The famous 'Pay No More Than' moniker first used on Crass label records and elsewhere afterwards, including the likes of post-punk artists such as Billy Bragg, becomes both a liberating device and simultaneously a stick to beat people with. Voices within the punk movement are often very quick to call 'rip off' and to offer sometimes vitriolic attacks against other parts of the punk scene for stepping outside of a narrow frame of acceptability. This frame of acceptability can relate to a dazzlingly broad spectrum of issues, including the pricing of merchandise, the clothes people wear, the shops people spend their money in, the provenance of the food people eat, the extent to which they have, in fact, done it themselves, and so on.

"If you take vegetarianism, there are people I've heard that are vegans and they won't go to the cinema because gelatin is used in film stock. Gelatin comes from cows, and so they would boycott movies in their own personal lives. And other people would never go in vehicles that have rubber tyres for the same reason. Of course one wants to try and live somewhat consciously but it's a great danger that you draw lines between these things. Are you not going, for example, to be friends with someone that eats meat if you're vegetarian?"
David King

"I was writing songs with my friends and it was unheard of that we would ever have a record. And at that time putting out a record was considered selling out. Because as a punk band you were there to do shows. It was like, 'Fuck art, let's dance.' And so if you were to make a record then all of a sudden you've made a product. You would be monetising something that was not supposed to be monetised." **Ian MacKaye**

"The funny thing about punk and a lot of anarchists back then is there were SO MANY RULES – what boots you could wear, what clothes you could wear, and your credibility. We're all against hierarchy and yet the first question is how long have you been on the scene, and who do you know?" **Gavin McInnes**

And so one of the consequences of the 'punkier than thou' mind-set is that a movement based on freedom, self-determinism and personal responsibility, at times sails dangerously close to being an authoritarian, hierarchical and prescriptive ideology. And in this ideology we can switch the state, or the institutions of the state, for a number of regulating forces explicitly invoked by punk such as social class, age, ideological 'purity' and so on. And the practical risk of this is that rather than breaking people out of social regulations and state control, punk creates a straightjacket of its own.

Anti, Anti, Anti   The beliefs associated with punk, ranging from views about state intervention to capitalism, were never, and perhaps should never, be ordered or formalised as a single thesis or design for life. The movement is diverse and as such reflects differing opinion. It is a cultural phenomenon much like hippy, folk or the beatniks and not a political or philosophical treatise. However, what has characterised much of the genre, at least politically, is an 'anti' stance, such as anti-capitalism, anti-racism, anti-fascism, anti-war, anti-religion, anti-government, anti-sexism, anti-authority, anti-vivisection, anti-corporatism and so on. Punk philosophy is often defined by opposition, and by a rejection of many prevailing conventions, and other less widespread dogmas such as fascism.

"I think the emphasis in punk was on protest culture. There was the Anti-Nazi League, then the Campaign for Nuclear Disarmament and that led into Anti-Apartheid. And I suddenly became aware that this was all 'anti', and I wondered what was I FOR?" **Graham Burnett**

Graham raises a powerful point which, placed in a wider frame, is about what punk stood for, and not what it stood against – which is crystal clear. For example, was punk about personal freedom and liberation? And if so, at what point might it draw a line? If it is supportive, as it seems to be, of the idea of freedom of expression and the right to protest, what happens then when people express views that might be felt to be unpalatable, such as racism or sexism? And how might conflicting ideas under the umbrella of personal freedom be resolved? If punk is actually about personal freedom matched by personal responsibility, what should happen when people don't step up and take that responsibility? Should they be obliged or forced to do so? Should they be conscripted into being accountable for their actions?

And so a criticism that might be levelled at punk is that it didn't complete the analysis; it didn't finish the job. In the Nietzschean paradigm of having to destroy and sweep away conventional thinking, punk scores highly. But in the second and third phases of constructing new ideals, and then living by them, the work seems incomplete. At its worst, we might accuse punk thinking as being too assured of its own rightness.

That said, there are a number of voices in this book that have engaged with questions of what next? Graham Burnett and his work with permaculture is one example. Another is the Dial House living experiment. A third is the rigorous and often jarring political philosophy offered by Gavin McInnes. And a fourth is Steve Albini's humble approach to responsible business. Fortunately, the list goes on, although not as long as it might.

Not Enough Ambition   It is odd, in some ways, to seek to draw attention to the possibility that punk is not ambitious enough. Thinking back to the late 70s and early 80s when punk was at its most active, there was almost no issue that punk wouldn't confront – from nuclear weapons to the monarchy to police brutality to the American dream. It was almost the hallmark of a good punk tune that it would step toe-to-toe with the biggest Goliath that it could start a fight with.

"If you had heard those early Chumbawamba demos we fulfilled all of those criteria, we would have an anti-war song, an anti-nuclear war song, a feminist song which only the women would sing, we would have a song promoting vegetarianism. It was almost as though we had a tick list and we'd almost being asking ourselves 'What haven't we got a song about? Oh, I've written a song about Tierra del Fuego, should we include that?'" **Dunstan Bruce**

But, a few decades on, the narrative offered by many of the people interviewed for this book centres much more on the mantra of 'act local, and do what you can', which in some ways is a contraction of the reach and scale of the initial ambition. And the reasons for this will vary. One may be that the lead actors in the punk field have done their tour of duty on the front line for quite some time and can understandably be let off the hook. A second reason is beautifully captured by the Chumbawamba lyric for the song *Isolation*:

Ireland, El Salvador, battles to win, but the real revolution starts within.

What this refers to of course is a shift away from external to internal battles. A third reason may relate to the sheer complexity and enormity of the larger task that is now faced in tackling governments or the mass media which many recognise have become much more organised and streetwise than they were a few decades ago.

"I think that the trouble is there is an overdose of information and it has somehow become devalued. So what that there are bad bankers? So what there are feeble politicians? So what if they're all liars? Why has the spark gone out of it? Where is the shock? Or maybe we're all just desensitised by so much horror over the last generation or two, including the Second World War." **Vi Subversa**

And while much has changed with regard to the operating environment and our appetite for, or skill in, influencing it, many of the obstacles that punk thought that it had removed seem to stubbornly persist.

"In many ways, the old orthodoxies have changed, but to think that we are still being ruled by a kind of Eton, public school, Oxbridge, old money, elite, it's incredible. I don't think that you would have thought that a few years ago. It seemed archaic and on the way out when I was growing up in the 70s and 80s. That was all dying out. OK, we didn't know what was going to replace it, it might have been some other thing, a different sort of elite that might have been just as unpleasant, but to think that it is still those people is stunning." **Steve Lake**

"One issue I have is with religion. If people are going to decide that women have to cover up, or women have to do this, or women have to do that then that has an effect. People are asking 'Why are you wearing that mini skirt, why have you got a low top on? That's why you're getting raped'. No! That was changed in the 60s, and we'd been changing things since then, but it's going backwards. So yes, we became more angry." **Zillah Minx**

So this is not a complaint, nor is it necessarily an illustration of a dark side to punk, but it is a puzzle, and a question for interested members of the punk community to reflect on, should they wish. Perhaps it is less about ambition and more about the means by which action might successfully be taken. And this highlights at least two dominant approaches that in themselves have a philosophical underpinning. The first strategy involves engaging with the system in order to influence it. This may, for example, entail being a regular employee, say in the public service, or alternatively may involve working for a corporate body maybe even those that are not natural homes to punks, such as oil companies, advertisers and so on. In these roles, opportunities arise to influence the behaviour of such institutions and here the punk ethos and ethics will guide action and perhaps introduce a conscience that might otherwise not be there. Mark Stewart refers to such individuals as 'sleeper agents'. On the other hand, another approach is to remove oneself from such positions and instead take opportunities to challenge, undermine, agitate and disrupt from the outside, from a place that is relatively free from the constraints found within the system.

Both represent viable strategies, although interestingly within the punk movement there is often animosity between the two factions, the first regarding the second as potentially naïve, and in return those favouring an outside-the-system perspective regarding those within as tainted or captured by the system. Very often it would appear that never the twain shall meet. However, even within this construct alternatives are offered.

"There are people who are right on the fringes who'll have nothing to do with 'bastards', and there are people who are in there and engaged and I think there's value to both approaches really. In a way, I would draw a parallel with the animal rights scene where there were always those arguments. Do we smash the doors and take the rabbits out or do you engage and try to change the law? I think you can't have one without the other; you always need both ends of the continuum. They are kind of mutually necessary even though they may not necessarily want to have anything to do with each other." **Graham Burnett**

From DIY to DIO to DIB   We return to the one central design feature of punk, for which there would seem to be unanimous support, and that is Do It Yourself. This liberating attitude in many ways explains the existence of punk. It is like the procreative act that makes punk possible. Without it, only the big bands, managed by major labels, would survive. Only the artists with friends in high places would be heard. Only the filmmakers, the actors and the storytellers with money behind them would prosper. DIY is not just an important factor, it is an explanatory factor; it accounts for the existence of punk, as we know it.

Which brings us to the lesser-quoted practice of Do It Ourselves (DIO) which is really the engine beneath DIY. Behind every great punk (act, artist, filmmaker, poet, etc.) there has to be a great many other people; a community of individuals helping to make whatever it is happen. Success in this space depends therefore on the community of contributors around each individual.

But a slightly deeper look at DIY requires us to explore the terms on which you might Do It Yourself. For example, there are practical considerations about the hardships you are willing to endure, not only for yourself but for others too.

"We stayed once in a place in Cologne which was a squatted complex that I think had included a car showroom before. We met this bloke and he said, 'I'll show you around if you want.' He said, 'There are three kinds of people that live here. There are punks and they're great. There are political people and they're great. And there are the people with body lice.' And I said 'what?' 'Yes, the people with body lice.' I'm thinking that this doesn't sound good especially as this is the place where we're supposed to be sleeping. Anyway he starts showing us around and we go into this area that had obviously been the place where the cars were. It was just a huge space with just a few pillows and piles of fabrics and buckets. We went around the buckets, and the guy said, 'Don't go too close. This is where the people with body lice sleep.' It was the summer and we got a bit closer [and we saw that] the buckets were obviously the toilets containing faeces and urine and because it was a summer, lots of flies were attracted to the smell and drowned in the urine; layers of dead black flies, absolutely horrendous. The unacceptable side of the squatting culture." **Deek Allen**

The spirit of 'Pay No More Than...' that often accompanies the DIY production of commodities (music, writing, art, ideas, etc.), places a strong downward pressure on the costs of production, and this can have quality implications. And with this the DIY aspiration can turn into the reality of Do It Badly (DIB). Or if not DIB, then the model of production can become unsustainable based on the idea that: 'It was so difficult to do the first time that I won't attempt a second'.

"Maybe that's why punk fell apart, because everyone could do it. But maybe not everyone SHOULD do it [*laughs*]... The bar got really fucking low. We'd say, we're gonna do this ourselves so let's make it splendid, let's make it perfect, but it got so that was 'being elitist'. I watched that bar becoming sub-basement so that it became a tunnel. [*laughs*]" **Little Annie**

A final observation relating to the limitations of DIY is a risk that this, in turn, may limit the reach that artists, for example, might have. DIY can favour small models of operation, that reflect the reality of constrained resources and self-imposed (Pay No More Than) price caps. And if part of the agenda is to call for change or to influence others, then fewer people may be reached, or they may already be converted.

"Our ideas changed massively about how you communicate an idea and who you want to hear your idea. In those days... what you would hear over and over again is that you were preaching to the converted. And there was a huge grain of truth in that... To cut a very long story short... we had produced this album, with *Tubthumping* on it, and it was rejected by our record company, One Little Indian. We were outraged, [*laughs*] so we left. These friends got involved who sort of started touting the album around and people started saying, 'That song! It's got to be the single'... One of the offers was from EMI. It was so ironic that we ended up signing to EMI Germany... because we'd even appeared on an album called *Fuck EMI* earlier and we just looked like absolute hypocrites [*laughs*]. We had become this successful band and anything we did, we would get press for. With [our protest at the Brits against British Deputy Prime Minister] Prescott for instance, that was all over the papers, and we would never have been able to get into that position if we hadn't had a hit single." **Dunstan Bruce**

Deek Allan

Although Oi Polloi has seen 50 members pass through its ranks since the band's formation, the only ever-present one has been founder member and vocalist Deek Allan. He put the band together in Edinburgh, Scotland, circa 1981, playing Exploited covers in a friend's garage. The band is variously associated with the anarcho-punk genre, Oi music and, at times, harder thrash metal. Oi Polloi's sound has been heavily influenced by bands such as Crass and Flux of Pink Indians and the band offers an uncompromising and clear political manifesto that is firmly anti-fascist, anti-sexist, anti-racist, anti-homophobic and pro-animal-rights.

The band has released numerous LPs including Unite and Win *and* In Defence Of Our Earth, *and has played gigs all over Europe, the USA and Canada.*

Deek is also well known for his contributions to the Scottish Gaelic punk subgenre. He started singing songs in Scottish Gaelic in 1996, and has been doing so more frequently in recent years in a bid to promote this endangered language. Still active, the band's most recent release was the 2012 LP Duisg! *— with other releases in the pipeline.*

I think we were always keen on there being a kind of anti-fascist alternative in the Oi music scene. Although, when you look at the roots of skinhead culture, anyone that knows anything about it knows that it had nothing to do with racism. I think there are a lot of bands that have been very important in making sure that there is a 'left' or 'anarchist' alternative within that kind of basically skinhead punk music.

We are in a slightly odd situation. Because we have always had this mixture of anti-fascist, political, Oi music that appeals to skinheads who like punk music, but who also like harder, more metal/explicit and hard core punk stuff, we get an interesting mixture at our concerts… Sometimes we play at gigs that are exclusively skinhead gigs despite the fact that we've got hair. Somehow we manage to get away with that; but, we also play gigs where everyone has got dreadlocks and so on and we haven't got enough hair for them.

It is always important not to pre-judge people; there ARE groups like RASH (Red and Anarchist Skinheads) who are involved in things like providing protective security for gay pride matches and things like that, and then you do get these SHARP (Skinheads against Racial Prejudice) groups. You get some people though who are still really homophobic. I remember playing in Canada one time. We were just chatting to some people at the end of the gig, a couple of skinhead guys and I'm like, "What do you do here in Edmonton?" or wherever it was and they said, "We hang around in the park, we drink, and so on, a bit of queer bashing and stuff." I do a double take, "WHAT DID YOU SAY?" "Yes, I drink, a bit of queer bashing." I said, "Do you not think that's a bit out of order, that's a bit stupid? You're outsiders just like they are…" and so on and on but you're not always preaching to the converted.

We have a gay rights song. Over the years it has to be one of the songs that's led to the most abuse being directed to us when we play it live… stuff being shouted at us and bottles and things being chucked. You would like to think that the punk scene would be relatively free from that, and to a great extent it is, but there are still people out there with a lot of these ideas that you want to challenge. Sometimes, at concerts, that rears its ugly head. And it's nice to see a lot of times that it's other people in the audience that challenge these people before we've even had a chance to say anything, which is great.

Punk as a great leveller   I think that's one of the things about punk; one of the most important things was the idea that everyone is on the same level and it's breaking down the barriers between the audience and the band. A lot of the time when you play concerts it is possible that the majority of people in the audience are in a band themselves. I know a lot of the time they go to your gigs, you go to theirs and that's great. Everyone is really on the same level. There isn't so much of this fawning adoration of people, "Uh please let's have your autograph." It's not like that, which is great. I think it's really, really healthy. Also, people aren't afraid to take you to task if you say something that they think you've got a bit wrong. That's great. Someone wrote to us the other day and said, "I really like your stuff. I really like the things you say. I've liked it for a long time; however, I was listening through your back catalogue the other day and I came across this song, 'Fuck everybody who voted Tory,' where you have described Mary Whitehouse as a 'fucking slag' or something like that. I really think if the best you can come up with is misogynistic insults like that then you're not trying hard enough." That's great because that's completely true. We wrote back and said, "Yes, you're quite right. We did that 20 years ago. I'd like to think if we were writing a similar song today we would try a little bit harder and come up with something better." That's great.

Occasionally people will write you a letter, or nowadays it will be an email, and they maybe say how your band and your music and your ideas has touched them, affected their life, maybe in a really, really important way. I remember one time someone writing to us and saying, "I just wanted to tell you I've been through some really bad periods in my life when I was really, really down but thanks to your music… your lyrics and the philosophy, that kept me from killing myself, kept me going." Other people write and say things like "I used to listen to White Power but I came across your music and the lyrics made me think about some of this stuff, and what a load of nonsense it is, so I've burned all my Nazi records.

I feel really stupid that I ever was into that stuff. I'd just like to say thanks for opening my eyes." This kind of thing.

Community and Doing It Ourselves   Lots of us from the punk scene have been involved in things like anti-fascist action or hunt sabotage or something like that – situations that can sometimes be quite dangerous. You want to be able to really rely on people and to be working with people that you really trust. A lot of that came out of the punk scene: people who you've known for a decade or something going to gigs and so on. I think it's really, really important… if there are people that you've known for years, you feel more comfortable about being involved in certain things. It doesn't necessarily have to be anything illegal but something where you want to be able to rely on people. I think stuff like that, building the community, does have a political benefit as well.

I think that's where this DIY idea and the idea that you have power to change things comes from; a lot of that came from punk or punk helped put those ideas out there for a lot of people. It's about empowering people. You don't have to petition others to change things, make things better. You can actually do it and have the power to do it. It's the idea that you're not going to send polite letters to the Houses of Parliament begging your MP to enact some law. We'll actually just go out and stop it ourselves. We have the power to do that.

Again with anti-fascism we're not going to write and beg people to change. We'll just go and stop them ourselves. We would say that if you've got the power to do something, you therefore have a responsibility to do something; however, we should not necessarily expect that everyone will share our viewpoint. I think this is an interesting thing actually; a lot of people in the punk scene are getting a bit older. Lots of us are now the parents of this dilemma. There is something happening that we don't really like. We're aware of what's going on. We know we have the power to do something about it; however, taking action could result in us being on the receiving end of some punishment from the state, possibly jail time or something. We've also got a responsibility to our children. You then start to think maybe we're not going to do that, but we can do something else.

There is a role for everyone   When we're playing songs about the battle of Cable Street or something, we think it's very positive that people are/were prepared to go out and physically prevent fascists from marching. Adolf Hitler said that the only thing that could have stopped Nazism was if people had stood up to it in its infancy when they still had the chance. Nowadays, that could mean someone getting arrested and getting jail time or something. We know that not everyone is comfortable with that. When we talk about stuff like this we say, "This is not about being macho. Look at us, none of us are particularly macho or anything." There is a role for everyone. There is something everyone can do. It's not just about macho street fighting. It's about the graphic artists who design the leaflets and the posters for fundraising events or for propaganda stuff. It's about the people who write letters to antifascist prisoners. It's about the people who organise fundraising things. It's about the people who do the intelligence-gathering work – all these things. There is a role for everyone.

We shouldn't tolerate in-fighting within the community I remember going to see the American band MDC in Glasgow, probably a scarily long time ago now, but anyway, one of them – I think it was the drummer – had their son on tour with them. He must have been about maybe eight or nine. I think he came on and did a song with them or something like that. Anyway after that he was hanging around near the edge of the stage. At one point this drunken fight broke out at the front between these guys who must have been in their early 20s or something. Someone spilled someone's pint or something like that and these two punk rockers with their mohicans started tussling with each other. The kid came on and took the microphone and just went over to them and was like, "Hey, don't fight each other, fight the cops." It was just one of the most punk things I'd ever seen. And of course they looked really stupid and they stopped.

I think for a lot of the kids that you meet whose parents are punks, a lot of the time they seemed to have grown up really, really well; really self-confident and with a healthy disrespect for authority – that attitude of questioning everything which is great. I mean that's something people can do if they've got kids. Obviously, hopefully their punk attitudes and philosophies will be passed onto them.

Our thanks to Crass I have a real respect for nature because I was very lucky to grow up in the countryside for the first eight years of my life. I was fascinated by just looking at little beetles, wandering around oak trees and stuff like that, and I could sit for hours looking in a pond at all these different water scorpions and water boatmen and all these amazing creatures. That imbued me with a respect for the planet and that led into environmentalism and so on.

I put my hand up and say "Thank you Crass!" I think a lot of people really had their lives changed by Crass. I don't think that their effect should be underestimated. People might not consciously acknowledge that. Initially in '76 and '77, the Pistols started shouting about anarchy, for shock value, but not because John Lydon was really into Bakunin. I think Crass took this and brought anarchism to it, re-popularised it for a lot of people. I've read some of the stuff that they've written that suggests they were getting tired of getting right-wingers and left-wingers at the gigs and thought, "oh we can stick this anarchy sign up." They might initially not have thought that much about it, but it brought these ideas to lots and lots of people. I think there are a lot of ideas that people wouldn't necessarily be thinking about, such as the specifics of anarcho-syndicalism, but also this idea that YOU CAN do it, you don't have to think "oh, if we want to change something it's up to us to ask our leaders to do it." You have the power to do it, empowering people to do this stuff. I think one of the things that punk showed was that you had all these different bands, a lot of whom weren't particularly musically good but they would get up there and do it. People said, "Wow, I can do this too."

Self-empowerment   When we started the band, our school had these charity rock concerts every term. With teenage kids you couldn't get into pubs, and there were not very many facilities so you would flock to something like that. We'd think, "Wow! A rock concert!" We were listening to punk music and we'd get there and we'd see the same bunch of sixth formers playing some Rolling Stones covers and stuff, and think, "God this is appalling. I wish there was a punk band." There'd be quite a lot of us who were into punk and we'd just have to listen to this Rolling Stones stuff. Eventually, it was like the only way we're going to get any punk music there is if WE do it. It looks like you can be in a band even if you can't sing or play very well. So we started this band. The drummer had a high hat and a snare drum and he got a couple of plastic buckets of fertiliser from his dad's garden shed. We thought, "Right, we'll do this." The band needed a singer. I said, "I can't sing." However, that didn't matter; in a punk band you don't need to be able to sing. Everyone can do it; also, you don't have to let any obstacles, like the fact that you can't play or you can't sing or whatever, get in the way.

In Edinburgh, it was really difficult sometimes to get places to play that weren't commercial venues. Quite often, they would only want you in so they could sell you high-priced, watered down booze and then chuck you out at 11pm so they could get the nightclub crowd in and make more money. You were pushed around by some bow-tied security and so on. It's the absolute opposite of empowerment. You're just being fleeced and you're being pushed around and so on. The punk ethos is: hey, we don't have to take this shit. We shouldn't have to take it. We can actually do something about it. We were like "right, there doesn't seem to be any other venues, what are we going to do?" Then we thought, "Why not just go and play on a place like Cramond Island? There is no one there. No one is going to push us around. We can bring our own booze or whatever. We'll be in charge; there'll be no nonsense." So the slight problem was that there wasn't a stage. But what happened over the course of several months? The punks got together: wheelbarrows, tools, buckets, bags of cement and stuff. All laboriously taken out over this 20-minute causeway walk out to the island. There is now a stage that you can see on Google Earth and so on, and there is a festival there every year. It's free and no age restrictions, no one is getting ripped off; it's got nothing to do with money. YOU CAN DO IT.

You can put out your music without using a commercially exploitative label, and without using middlemen promoters and managers; there are so many bands like ourselves who organise most of the tours themselves. We don't have a manager. We don't have publicists and so on. We make the records as cheap as possible. If we're making money from them, that money will be channelled to groups or organisations that hopefully do something good. I think, as well, that there are ways in which the live experience can be empowering as well. Bands can make a statement by the way they play, the way they treat the audience. I mean there are some people who refuse ever to play on a stage.

The other thing is that there are no pockets on a shroud. You can't take money with you. At the end of the day a lot of us will be fairly skint but have had a bloody good time. We will have had a very interesting existence.

Tim Smith

Tim Smith grew up in a small coastal town in Devon, UK, where he developed an interest in poetry and David Bowie. In 1976, he headed to London with Gaye Black hoping to turn his dreams of starting a punk band into reality. Thus, the Adverts were born and the aspiring punks assumed the names TV Smith and Gaye Advert. The band became regulars on the live circuit, often playing at London's punk-central, the Roxy Club, and they released their first single One Chord Wonders *on Stiff Records in 1977. Controversial single* Gary Gilmore's Eyes *reached No. 18 in the UK Singles Chart in September of the same year and the band appeared on* Top of the Pops. *The song is written from the point of view of a patient who, following an eye transplant, discovers that he has received the eyes of executed murderer Gary Gilmore.*

The acclaimed LP Crossing the Red Sea with the Adverts *followed in 1978. Second LP* Cast of Thousands *confused the critics with its prog rock influences and the band split in 1979.*

Next, in the early 80s, Tim formed post-punk pop-rock outfit TV Smith's Explorers and politically outspoken outfit Cheap later in the decade. To this day, TV Smith performs as a solo artist, often playing more than 100 gigs a year across the globe, each one different, and all played without a set list. He has also released numerous solo LPs and has had a series of his tour diaries published.

I like the idea that I'm a punk. I do like the idea that I can be considered a punk because I think these days that it's shorthand for saying that you're not part of the established music system... There are a lot of definitions of punk from '77 that still apply now like, for example, DIY, basically doing it yourself and using whatever resources you've got, ignoring what the conventional music business says you should be doing or how you should write songs or how you should present yourself, how old you are (or should be). Almost everything I do has got nothing to do with the conventional music business so in that context I definitely like to consider myself a punk.

I don't do engagement with the system. It's either/or really. I would never consider going into government because I feel I can change more hearts and minds through song writing than I ever could if I was swallowed up by the political system... and most people can't carry through their ideals when they get in that system... they change. They are surrounded by different values, and different people who are in it for other reasons and for me it's much more powerful to be here, in this area where I can express 100% what I want to do, even if it's to fewer people. But these things happen step by step and every single person who gets

switched on by a song lyric, or by seeing what I am doing on stage, is important. That's the way this stuff spreads around. And if musicians think they can change things by getting into government then good luck to them. Everyone has their own talent, and the circumstances are different. In Iceland, for example, it's probably a lot easier to get in there and change things on a local level than it is for most of the rest of the world. But it's certainly not something that I'm aiming for or aspiring to.

The dangers of philosophies and ideologies   I do try and avoid 'isms' or 'ists' because I like to have an open mind. Every time you get involved with a political movement you find you're dragged along with all their rules and beliefs... OK, perhaps then I'm individualist [*laughs*]... I think that you should always be wary of movements. The greatest political movements in the world have often created an opposite effect. You know like Communism, even Socialism... because people get involved with them unquestioningly they are also tied to them when they start to go wrong and get overtaken by people who are so idealistic or have a more cynical approach. So I would generally say don't get involved with any movement. I think it's very dangerous. And I think these days any mass movement is a lot easier to manipulate than it used to be... not just through the mass media of television... but also there are more subtle ways through the Internet which is reaching out to everyone. There are already subtle ways to manipulate people's ways of thinking through the Internet and I am sure it will become much more sophisticated in the future.

I don't want an animal to die for my food   I'm a vegetarian and I will never eat meat again. I also tend more toward vegan actually because there is so much exploitation and cruelty involved these days in even the simplest of dairy products. I don't want any animal to die for my food when I can live quite happily without it. I just don't see a question. I don't miss meat. I don't want meat. I wouldn't personally go out into a field and kill a cow so I can eat it. We're a civilised, developed country and it's not necessary anymore and it's causing a lot of damage to the world's economy and causing a lot of poverty in other countries, this kind of system of farming. It's not necessary so I don't do it.

You can't really think that these fast food chains are in it to spread health and happiness around the world. They're in it to make a huge profit. But it certainly doesn't appear like it from their advertising or packaging. It's hard for people. You grow up believing that this is what the world is about – you HAVE to eat this way. You HAVE to eat this takeaway stuff. Its cheap, and times are tough, so you do this obviously sensible thing and pay a small amount of money for bad food and it's very hard for people to break out of this mindset, so I understand why it's happening and it's a big jump. If you're going to be alternative and think alternatively in one area it will inevitably lead to you eventually thinking alternatively and independently in other areas as well. And people are scared of that. Because you're safe and cozy in the motherly love of the advertising campaigns telling you how your life should be without you having to worry about all that complicated stuff like free will... and it's very hard to break out and push away the hand that feeds you and say, "I'm going to look in my own way about what the world is about and what the possibilities are."

It never was about trying to be happy   I don't believe in a life that's all 'happy, happy, happy.' I just don't believe it. I think that as a concept it's false and you're taught to strive towards happiness as a child. There's as much melancholy in life as there is happiness. Happiness is just one of the many things that coalesce together to make a complete life. So I don't actually strive after happiness and I think it just makes you unhappy if you do. I think that what you strive for is a complete life with all of the emotions and feelings that belong to it; a lot of life is not about happiness: it's about struggle and if you are just looking for happiness then you just go for the easy way every time and you are not going to get anything out of life... For me, I wouldn't want to be any other way, that's all I can say... I'm striving to be honest and authentic and to be fair and not exploit anyone and to look on the world as it really is. What the emotional impact of all that really is, I don't really care. If that leaves me with a sense of despair or melancholy or contentment or satisfaction or joy then I think you go through all those emotions and it's the mix that makes life so fascinating. And if you get stuck in any one of those feelings... then you are being very one-sided.

Live the best life you can today   I don't think there's any point in getting maudlin about death. It is something that everyone knows is coming and you should get on with your life, really and don't waste time... I think all you can do is live the best life that you can in the moment from day to day. No one's got any proof about what death is or what happens afterwards so it's not worth worrying your pretty little heads about [*laughs*], just get on with it. If you're not feeling that your life is in a good place, that's got nothing to do with death, that's to do with life and you're the only one who can change it. What is the problem if you feel like that? If you don't feel resolved with your life? It's not because you haven't managed to attain what you are trying to attain. I could say that I am trying to attain a number one hit record and it's driving me mad and I'm not ready for death, I haven't got there. But the thing is it's not about what you are trying to attain, it's about what you are doing now in this moment. And that's what life is, it's about doing the right thing now and not projecting all of your worries about all the things you haven't got that you want, forward. Don't let fear of death distract you from what you are doing now. We know about the inevitability of death but it has nothing to do with your dissatisfaction now with your life. That is something that you can work on now.

Steve Lake

Steve Lake formed the band Zounds in 1977 in Reading, taking on lead vocal and guitar duties. The band wasted no time in immersing itself into the burgeoning anarcho-punk, free-festival scene, forming close associations with like-minded acts such as Crass and the Møb, the latter with whom Steve shared a squat with in Brougham Road, Hackney.

Zounds released their first EP Can't Cheat Karma *on the Crass Records label in 1981, and their debut album* The Curse of Zounds *on Rough Trade Records, in the same year. In 1982, disaffected with the way the anarcho scene was heading, Steve split the band.*

However, he continued to make music, releasing two albums as a solo artist, and also completing a degree in cultural studies in 1987, going on to teach in adult education in London for much of the next 20 years.

In 2007, exactly 30 years after the band first got together, Steve reformed Zounds and the band toured extensively across Europe. In 2011, Zounds released a new studio album titled The Redemption of Zounds.

My grandparents brought me up, so they'd had two fucking World Wars and the Depression. And so for people who had been through that shit, the idea of that kind of "Everything in order, a job for life, a pension, a nice little suburban house with a garden," was fine because they'd had as much excitement as they could stand [*laughs*]. And of course the generations that came after said, "Oh, this is boring and stultifying, and we want to have a bit of excitement." I think they found that difficult to accept because they'd had the excitement of being bombed and going to fight in fucking Burma and Malaysia against the fascists. They'd lived through the Depression and the General Strike, when Churchill set fucking troops with guns on the miners. And so your parents, and their generation, had that little window where there's no return to the 30s and that's gone.

I didn't really learn very much at school. I didn't like school, I felt it was a bit cruel and unfair in its treatment of people and particularly in its treatment of me, but then I got into music… I liked The Doors, then you'd hear, "Did they take their name from Aldous Huxley or was it William Blake?" And then you'd think, "Who is this Aldous Huxley? Who is this William Blake?" And so for me, my obsession with music and with the people who were making it was that gateway to my education. So I'd start to read underground newspapers and then got involved with people who were running underground newspapers… The thing that goes with education and curiosity is doing stuff and I always wanted to do stuff, and that's why I'm still absolutely wedded to the DIY ethic, and that's where my

anarchism comes from (if that's what I really am)... And when I say DIY I don't always mean in an individual way, but with your friends and compatriots and like-minded people... When I was a kid and I saw films, I didn't think that I wanted to watch more films, but I would think, "Oh God, how can I be in a film, or how can I make a film?"

Punk, an eternal moment   The strange thing about that period when Zounds were making records, when we first started... was that it wasn't a very long period of time. It seemed like it went on forever... I was thinking about going to Stonehenge in the summer of '75 and then thinking, God! In '76 you've got punk rock starting with that first Sex Pistols record. And it just seemed like I thought it had been YEARS between those events but it was very intense, and maybe that's the thing of youth where every experience is kind of a new experience and everything's hitting you hard.

Where we were living in Brougham Road it became a bit of a magnet for waifs and strays, not least of all the Møb [*laughs warmly*]. Together, the Møb were a very attractive bunch of personalities. When they moved in it seemed like the whole of the world wanted to move in. It was weird. I was talking to a friend of ours from those days and she had a young son that she was bringing up in that situation and I didn't really fancy it myself; it just all seemed a bit chaotic, because everybody was young, everybody was taking drugs, everybody was going out late and coming back later. Everybody was nice, but it was chaotic. It was a very different situation from the one that Crass were living in. When you went to Dial House it was almost like going to a religious temple where everybody there was Buddha and it was all quiet and pastoral and bucolic and Penny [*Rimbaud*] was like a Guru dispensing wisdom, and it was ordered and very nice. That was nothing like Brougham Road. It was chaos, people coming and going, noise, people playing music. It was in the middle of a building site so it was always dusty and it was a lot of fun, but after a while it can get to you, so when I had kids we moved out and we moved into a housing co-operative situation.

We moved from that squatting environment, which was really so important in London. There were loads of empty houses. One of the things we did was to squat, and the other thing was housing co-operatives. We moved from Hackney to Islington at that time. We did this kind of survey amongst the housing co-operatives and short-life use groups and Islington had something like 19,000 empty houses that the council owned. And they were real vandals in those days. The councils used to go around and take out the electricity and the toilets so people couldn't use them. So immediately after I left Brougham Road, around the early to mid 80s, we were quite involved in housing campaigns. We were still kind of living communally and then I had a couple of other kids. The cooperative movement was really important to us in those days and I was also involved in a workers' co-operative at the same time and did that for a few years.

There was a lot of organisation around housing... and the councils were really useless in those days and there were all of these empty houses. Sometimes you could get into long-term squats that became established but that was never going to last forever and it became a bit more organised into housing co-operatives. Myself, and couple of friends of mine, including Lawrence [*guitarist in Zounds*], formed a workers co-operative and a quite clever friend of ours managed to get some grant funding out of the Department of the Environment and we set up this co-operative to provide access to media recording equipment and video equipment, the sort of equipment that was coming in at that point. We were going to operate partly as a company making programmes to give access to members of the community, disenfranchised groups, etc. That makes it all sound quite grand, but we were still a bunch of freaks; however, we really lucked into this money and that got us into some dilapidated premises in Hackney and enabled us to buy a load of equipment. The irony was that we seemed to be the least political of the groups that had done this sort of thing.

The other people that applied for this money were people like Hackney Law Centre who at the time were heavily involved in things like the Colin Roach case. I don't know if people remember, but Colin Roach was from Hackney and died in Stoke Newington Police Station, as people used to in those days. So I think we were considered the least contentious of the organisations that were applying. And we were working with a number of community groups in Hackney – working-class groups, Black groups, Greek groups, Turkish groups and so on. So I did that for a few years.

Back to school to learn about what we'd been doing   And then I decided I would go back to school and I did a degree in cultural studies in 1987, the second Summer of Love. And it kind of passed me by because I had two or three kids... I was in the last year when they were still giving grants and I was a "normal person" with two kids and a wife. I won't say that the grants were generous, but they were fine. I did have to do some part-time work, and I worked in the holidays and I worked in factories, but I was still funded to go and do a degree. And that was so interesting for me... I'm not naturally an academic person, but I've always been a curious person, and I've always wanted to know why things are the way they are and know how the world works... What was interesting was I was mostly with a lot of younger people, but the ideas in the course – which was basically a Marxist, feminist slant on stuff – I lapped up. And a lot of the ideas and experiences that I had come into contact with, just through the people that I knew, kind of put me in good stead for the course... Suddenly I was seeing the things that we'd been doing in a slightly different perspective.

And then the other big effect it had on me was that I thought that these university lecturers are making loads of money and have loads of holidays for reading books that they would have read anyway; the working-class scammer within me thought that I would manipulate myself into that kind of situation but I never managed to... What did happen though was that, instead of working in a cosseted academic ivory tower, I ended up working in a load of inner-city further education colleges in London, which is a completely different experience to being in a university or polytechnic and reading about Situationism. Mainly, I was teaching black and Turkish working-class kids from the Hackney/Islington/Haringey area and that was really interesting and soul destroying in a way... I tended to work with kids with special educational needs... I saw the education system, which I wasn't that enamoured with in the first place, getting worse and worse and worse. I ended up doing that for 20 years. Then I packed it in but now I do support work at the University of Bristol for students with disabilities.

In many ways the old orthodoxies have changed, but to think that we are still being ruled by a kind of Eton, public-school, Oxbridge, old-money, elite, it's incredible. I don't think that you would have thought that a few years ago. It seemed archaic and on the way out when I was growing up in the 70s and 80s. That was all dying out. OK, we didn't know what was going to replace it; it might have been some other thing, a different sort of elite that might have been just as unpleasant, but to think that it is still those people.

My son volunteers for a charity that helps vulnerable people with complex social and psychological requirements. There's one person who's an ex sex-offender who's come out of prison and he's camping by a school and he came in and that has to be sorted out, you know with housing or shelter where he can be watched or whatever. You know all these sorts of complex things with very vulnerable people that have got a whole multiplicity of issues. So I said to him, "I suppose with a lot of those people you refer them onto Social Services then?" and he laughed and said, "No, Social Services refer them onto us!" So these people turn up at Social Services and are told to go to this charity. So you have people like my son dealing with these complex social, legal and medical issues for very vulnerable people and they're doing it as volunteers because [*Prime Minister*] Cameron and his fucking cronies are taking some of these Libertarian ideas — "Oh! It's the 'Big Society', we can all do it for ourselves." By that he means, "You just fucking have the shit and we'll go off to our houses in the Cotswolds and to our parties on Abramovich's yacht," where they'll mix in with people from the fucking Labour

Party. No wonder we are all so cynical about it.

Messed up values in society   I'm a support worker and I support people in education, for example, that aren't able to take notes for themselves. I help people who are doing business studies and also people studying health and social care courses. And so there's this lecture where people are learning about credit risk and hedge funds and derivatives, and these people are all going to be really rich, and they seem a bit smug and self-satisfied. And then there are these other courses where there are people who are going to be wiping shitty bums and seeing people die, and they're going to be working on barely more than minimum wage. Where's the fucking justice in that? And it just confirms to you that the values of society are still all wrong and that you still need to agitate for a fairer way of looking at things.

Do we want no government or better government?   A lot of the people that you have interviewed are very nice people and are very positive and quite community minded and just are really great people. Those kinds of anarchist, libertarian, anti-state ideas have also been taken up by a whole lot of other people… which in America can mean the extreme right or the Tea Party idea of no state regulation, totally free markets. Now this is very difficult. For example, my eldest daughter has been living in Congo and Rwanda for a great deal of time and she's involved with the law and international justice and she's dealing with women, particularly, who are rape victims in war. Everybody knows, I assume, the situation in Congo around mass rapes, not just of women but of men and boys as well. A lot of those people who become soldiers were victims themselves as boys… Why I'm saying this is because she's dealing with FAILED states. So here's me saying, "We don't need the state, we don't need Big Daddy, we can get it together amongst ourselves" and she's saying, "Yes, but I'm working in these places where the state has totally failed and it's a FUCKING MESS." Now there are all sorts of reasons for that because those people had to put up with some of the worst forms of colonial exploitation and still are doing so. That's the thing. It's still happening. Everything we've got in our phones, in our computers, you know, use these minerals and Congo's the main place for it. And it's always been like that. Congo has had rubber, etc, and now it's got this stuff in our phones… So I'm going on about how we don't need the state and she says that I sound like one of these Republican Tea Party people. And so those anarchist/libertarian ideas are really interesting, but can still go both ways.

[*Regarding anarchism*] This sounds so trite but are you a nice, caring person or not? And if the world is full of nice, caring people who are going to look after each other then I think anarchy is absolutely fantastic, but if the people are bastards then they won't look after each other… and with respect to what has happened in Iceland with Anarchists in government the danger is that you might become corrupted by it… But, you've got to work with the world the way it is. You do get these people that want to be off-grid, and in the old hippy days you'd want to be self-sufficient. You know, "Society's fucked up so I'm going to move away from it." And if they're happy doing that and they have a nice life that's fine. I'm really non-judgmental, which always makes everybody laugh because they think I'm THE most judgmental person [*laughs*]. I like being in society. And I like people (and that's another thing that's going to make my family laugh)… So it's a difficult one. In a way it's really about what YOU are and what YOUR motivation is that guides you whatever that system is that's imposed on you. And these people in Reykjavík sound amazing. And it's so great to hear that there are people who are able to put some of those ideas, which are more social and humanitarian, and human rights ideas into the melting pot.

Progress on feminism? Obviously there's still a long way to go, in terms of the position of women in society; it is better now than when I was a kid, believe me, but I know there is a long way to go. My wife works for a rape crisis centre so believe me I know about domestic violence… I do have a whole range of feelings about how the feminist agenda got co-opted by the equal opportunities agenda. It seems to me that when I first started encountering the ideas of feminism, there were many different strands to it. One of those strands was equal opportunity and no one would argue against that. And another strand of it was "men are violent and aggressive and have all the power and need to be changed." The stereotype is that women are the caring, nurturing ones and men are into war and power, yet I think there are some elements of truth in that. One of the big things is that it was men that needed to change, not women. Men needed to adopt more of those things that were seen as traditionally female qualities and that hasn't happened. Men seem pretty much the same.

The feminist agenda became all about the glass ceiling, about equal pay and stuff, and of course nobody's going to argue with that, but the whole idea of changing the nature of masculinity, I think, seems to have gone out the window. And what's more, you have the rise of that ladette culture with women becoming more like men. I think that is the wrong way round; men need to be more feminised, to use that old-fashioned language. There's a long way to go… What's interesting in the music business now is that a lot of the big sellers are women artists, but it's still men doing the business.

I sometimes do these experiments on myself and I did this experiment about 18 months ago where I was only going to listen to music by women for a week. And once you do that… suddenly you realise how little music there is that is just made by women. If you say that you are only going to listen to music made by men, OK, there's this record that was written by a bloke, it's performed by a bloke, it was produced by a bloke, there was a bloke who was the engineer. Of course, there are girls who work in the office and reception and there are women who work in the factory… but if you try and find music that's JUST made by women it's difficult. So I had to broaden it to just listen to music where women play a central role in it. And in those punk days you had these great, different strong women and now I don't see that… When you see women in music on the TV it's all highly sexualised, and very, very stereotypical ideas of what women should be like. Yeah, there's been quite a regression on that.

The inspirations of punk   That was the thing about punk. Actually you don't all have to look beautiful and pretty. And you don't have to be a man. You don't have to be young. You don't have to be able-bodied and you don't have to be straight. As long as you've got something to say. In fact even if you've got nothing to say, it's there for anybody – gay, straight, black, white, disabled, blah blah blah. It's there for EVERYBODY. And that was one of the inspiring things about it.

Dunstan Bruce

Born in Billingham, a small town in the north of England, Dunstan Bruce was one of the key members of the anarcho-punk band Chumbawamba – serving on vocals, bass, saxophone and percussion for over 20 years. The band, known for their agitprop styling, were stalwarts of the cassette tape culture, but in 1982 they first appeared on Crass's Bullshit Detector Vol II *with the song* Three Years Later. *In 1985 they released their first single* Revolution *and in the years that followed, Chumbawamba released some 20 albums including the, three-times-platinum album* Tubthumper.*

Chumbawamba frequently played benefit gigs in squats and small halls for causes such as animal rights, the anti-war movement, and community groups. The band's collective political views are often described as anarchist, and Dunstan has described them as "a kind of northern Crass."

Since Chumbawamba, Dunstan has been engaged in a number of creative projects and has been a film director and producer for films including The Man Whose Mind Exploded *and the acclaimed documentary* A Curious Life *about the Levellers, described by John Robb as "A brilliant and heart warming tale of a dysfunctional band." Dunstan is now performing with his new band Interrobang‽*

For me punk happened twice I suppose, or maybe three times. Growing up in a small industrial town in the North East of England, it was a total and complete moment of liberation. When punk came along it blew my mind and that has instructed my life ever since – that one explosion.

When you read Jon Savage's *England's Dreaming* and it's all about punk being over by the end of 1976, it's funny because punk was only just coming to Billingham at the end of 1976. The people in Chumbawamba were from places like Billingham, Burnley and Barnsley – all small towns. We weren't from London. We weren't part of that same scene. And so when punk came along it was a bombshell, it was like year zero. And from that point on my whole world and everything I did changed.

For me that first wave of punk bands wasn't necessarily anything to do with politics. It was more an idea about how things could be different. It was about blowing away the old and starting something new. It was about not having to carry on listening to Rush's *2112* and discussing with my mates whether Ritchie Blackmore was a better guitarist than Jimmy Page. There was something that was short and vital and real and it made you FEEL different. It felt as though it was something new and it was something that was ours.

That wave petered out quite quickly, but then there was a new wave of bands like the Pop Group and Gang of Four who along with the Fall and Wire were the bands that I was listening to and taking note of what they were saying. Then the third wave was that whole anarcho-punk thing with bands like Crass. And when I moved to Leeds and I met everybody there, Crass became a much bigger thing.

Punk didn't save my life, but I would say that it was when my life started. I was at that moment when I was thinking, "What am I going to do? What is there to do? What am I going to do with my life?" I was 15 in 1976 and all I knew was that I didn't want to just get a job. My first concern was getting out of Billingham. There was NOTHING there for me. I could name all the people on the punk scene there; it was such a small little thing. While it was a very bonding experience, I wanted to DO something. I formed a band even though I couldn't play an instrument and we played a few gigs and they were terrible. But that's what punk did. It gave you the balls to go out and form a band even though you couldn't sing, you couldn't play guitar and you couldn't play the drums.

The politics of the Pop Group   The Pop Group absolutely blew my mind. Absolutely! I'd gone to see Patti Smith at Newcastle City Hall in about 1978 and I went by myself. At the time I didn't even know who the Pop Group were, other than they were supporting Patti Smith. And so they came on stage and what they did was the most sonically amazing thing I had ever heard. I thought, "What are they doing with those instruments? I've never heard anything like it!" Then you buy a Pop Group record and you read the lyrics and they are the heaviest, most dense political tracts that I'd read. They were in some ways a precursor to some of the stuff that Crass were writing I suppose. They'd be singing about torture in Indonesia or somewhere and you'd think, "How can you put those words into a song? How can that be a song?" There was one B-side that was just a list of human rights violations around the world. I thought, "Those aren't lyrics. What is that? What is he doing?" That was the moment when I thought that this has got a more political and philosophical slant than what had gone before. And it was the same with Gang Of Four when you think about the shit that they got into for singing about H Block and what was going on in Ireland. I hadn't even considered having a political opinion on Ireland. I was still in 'they're all terrorists' mode. I hadn't even explored the whole situation. It was bands like the Au Pairs and Gang of Four who opened my eyes to that sort of thing.

The Falklands War as a political lightning rod   The Falklands War was the moment when we thought, if we are writing songs, then this is what we should be writing about. As I recall, when the Falklands War kicked off, there was not a mass movement against that war, even though people were aware that Thatcher was going to war to save her skin, which she obviously successfully did. At the time it was almost dangerous to speak against it and we started a graffiti campaign around Leeds where we lived, based on opposing the war.

In those very early days, after that war was over, they had a victory parade in Burnley for people coming back from the Falklands and we went as a group and did a counter-protest and it's one of the most terrifying things I've ever done. There were just about eight of us carrying a banner around protesting about war and saying that we shouldn't be glorifying this war. And it was terrifying and we had to bail quite quickly because we were in danger really.

Back then, the stuff that we were doing was about, "Don't be like your parents. Don't do what your parents did, do exactly what you want to do." But the Falklands War was the big political issue that came along that we tried to confront and really say something about. And it was quite an easy thing to do because you could take a pacifist stance on it. And say, "War is wrong, this war is unnecessary. Thatcher's gone to war to save her own skin. We shouldn't be wasting money on this. Why are we fighting over this little bit of land in the South Atlantic?" It was quite an easy stepping-stone to becoming an anti-war band. I think from that point on we started looking round for other issues and I think that's about the time that we started listening to Crass a lot and seeing what they were doing and going to Crass gigs and becoming aware of their potency and their power. And what appeared to be their wise words and their amazing way of presenting those ideas.

If you had heard those early demos, we fulfilled all of those criteria, we would have an anti-war song, an anti-nuclear war song, a feminist song that the women would sing, we would have a song promoting vegetarianism. It was almost as though we had a tick list and we'd almost be asking ourselves, "What haven't we got a song about? Oh, I've written a song about Tierra del Fuego, should we include that?" We combined all those single issues into a set of songs that almost sounds twee now, but it did feel different. Crass was our springboard and for a while we were definite Crass copyists. We thought that we'd be a 'Northern Crass' and we wouldn't put our records out on Crass records, we were going to set up our own thing. We weren't in competition with them, but we were saying that if you were in a band you didn't need to go all the way down to London to put out a record.

As time went on we reached a point where our ideas changed massively about how you communicate an idea and who you want to hear your idea. In those days between 1981 and 1985 what you would hear over and over again is that you were preaching to the converted. And there was more than a grain of truth in that. It was like a very big club. While there's nothing wrong with that and for me that was a lovely place to be, we got to a point where we thought that we weren't

We always thought that humour and a great melody was a far better tool than aggression as a way to get people to listen

reaching anybody. We wanted to confront people with these ideas and get them to question what they were doing, what they thought and what was wrong with the world, and how we can make the world a better place. We came to the view that you can't do that by screaming in someone's face. For us that would never ever work as a way to get somebody to change their opinion.

So that is why Chumbawamba, over the years, used humour as much as possible. We always thought that humour and a great melody was a far better tool than aggression as a way to get people to listen. A big, big thing for us was that we wanted to play for ordinary people. It might just be a class issue, I'm not sure. The majority of us had lower middle-class or working-class backgrounds. None of us had any privilege, none of us had any money, we'd all come from relatively poor families and culturally bereft places and we'd reached this point where the people we wanted to talk to were the people we'd grown up with.

Widening the net   When we first put out a records we never even saw it as selling out, we just saw it as a natural progression. It was ridiculous because it was a totally and utterly DIY thing we were doing. We paid for the recording ourselves. We paid for the printer and designed the sleeve ourselves and we'd be sat in the house where we lived, folding the singles and bagging them to send off to record shops and take to gigs to sell. It's just ridiculous, we weren't even signed to anyone at that point, and we were just DOING IT OURSELVES. So to be criticised for it made us realise that we definitely wanted to get away from this scene. This scene's poisonous and it isn't going anywhere. We felt like we had outgrown the scene. We had done that and we couldn't just tread water and remain the big fish in the little pond. We had to try to move out of that. At that time we weren't even listening to that music. We wanted to do something more considered and smarter.

We were obsessed with Brecht and Weil and we used cabaret elements on stage; there was always a visual element. We weren't afraid to dress up and make a fool of ourselves onstage because we thought that it was all part of the agitprop tradition. That was a massive thing for us, we wanted to present something in such a way that it engaged on more than one level. To me, a lot of what was going on in anarcho-punk only engaged on one level and we wanted to bring in a lot of different influences. To this day, I am still obsessed with Dada and Duchamp and stuff like that. We were stealing ideas and reinterpreting things all the time.

We brought out an album called *Slap!* and around that time we were thinking that all we ever do is criticise things and say how much we hate something, or how crap something is. It became a big thing so we thought, "Right, let's do an album that celebrates stuff." So that album in particular was all about small victories and someone putting their finger up to the state, or winning something. And we also decided to start messing about with how we present ideas as well. At that point Danbert and Alice in particular just shone on stage. They really got into dressing up and presenting stuff in creative ways on stage — they were just amazing! When we did the final Chumbawamba show a couple of years ago, Alice still came on dressed as a nun and you forget how powerful it used to be, a smoking, whiskey swilling nun doing a Lenny Bruce routine. What we were trying to do was present a political show in an entertaining way. And in a way I still think that everybody in the band, since the end of the band, is still trying to do that, trying to present ideas in such a way that it is entertaining, but it still has a political point.

Tubthumping   To cut a very long story short, we had all given up our jobs to work on Chumbawamba and we were all earning a small living, mainly from touring. We had produced this album, with *Tubthumping* on it, and it was rejected by our record company — One Little Indian. We were outraged [*laughs*] so we left. These friends got involved who started touting the album around and people started saying, "That song! It's got to be the single." We thought, "Maybe it should, eh?" but we still weren't signed to a record label. At that time, believe it or not, Jonathan King was an influential taste maker within the music industry [*laughs*] and he used to do this industry-only magazine every fortnight called *The Tip Sheet*. It had a CD on the front with about 20 songs on, and for about two or three issues he put *Tubthumping* on it as the first track because he absolutely loved it. He basically drummed up all the interest in Chumbawamba and we had a whole raft of offers; it was absolutely bizarre.

One of the offers was from EMI. It was so ironic that we ended up signing to EMI Germany. We sat round having this huge discussion about whether we should sign to a major or sign to a small label. We'd had a really unsatisfactory experience with an independent label so in the end we just thought, "Let's go for it and see what happens, otherwise we might just live to regret it and we might stagnate." We thought it might take us on some kind of an adventure that could be terrible or it could be amazing. So we signed with EMI Germany and obviously we were totally slated for it and everybody was up in arms, because we'd even appeared on an album called "Fuck EMI" earlier. We just looked like absolute hypocrites. [*laughs*] But it was an indication of how little we cared about what other people thought about us. We realised that everything we did was because we believed it was the right thing to do and not because we were bending to peer pressure or not doing something because we thought it would look bad. Of the offers we had, it's totally ironic, EMI Germany gave us the most artistic control. We carried on designing our own covers. We carried on choosing our own singles and producing our own albums and nobody else had given us that amount of freedom. It went absolutely bonkers and we rode that wave for about two years and went all over the world with that song. We came back and wrote an album that was totally critical about American culture and it completely bombed. They all wanted another *Tubthumping* and we did something completely different. That was it. It was all over.

Universal in America claimed that we had the record for the biggest percentage drop in sales between albums [*laughs*]. In a way we deliberately shot ourselves in the foot. I was talking to Alice about that successful period and she hated being shunted around from one place to another as a rent-a-gob not knowing what we would be confronted with. But obviously we made a lot of money. We always split everything eight ways and still do today. We gave a lot of money away. We are now in a position where we don't have to raise 50 quid at a benefit gig, we could just give them the money. We decided to donate a percentage of our money each year.

We had become this successful band and anything we did, we would get press for. With the Prescott incident [*when Danbert from Chumbawamba famously threw some iced water over the UK Deputy Prime Minister at the 1998 Brit Awards*], that was all over the papers. We were railing against that New Labour honeymoon period that they were enjoying. We had taken some striking dockers from Liverpool along to the awards in case we won and they were going to go up and collect the award with a platform to say whatever they wanted to say about their situation. When they realised that Prescott was there, they explained that he had been part of the union that they were part of, and when they had gone to him to ask for help in resolving the dispute, he had turned his back on them. So they were furious. That's why it [*Danbert throwing the water over Prescott*] happened. But we would never have been able to get into that position if we hadn't have had a hit single with *Tubthumping*.

David Quantick, a journalist at the time, said, "Why are they attacking the Labour Government when for 15 years of Thatcherism they never did anything significant about that?" Which still makes me laugh to this day because, it's obvious isn't it? We DID do loads of anti-Thatcher stuff, it just never got into the papers because we were just existing in this little world where you could rail against Thatcher and do stickers and posters and write a song about Thatcher. But nobody would listen to you. It was only that we had a hit single and were at that Brit Awards that we garnered all that press attention.

Life After *Tubthumping*   After a few years we went back to being a band playing 500-capacity venues still making a living and living off the money that we made from the *Tubthumper* album. But it did change our lives massively in that we all had enough money to buy a house. People started having kids. We'd all got to the age of 40 without really having anything other than the band. It was quite a shift and everybody did buy somewhere to live. We went back to what we had been doing although we'd lost a large section of our audience. A lot of people had accused us of selling out. We realised that we had to change and we carried on as an eight-piece band until 2005. Chumbawamba had always been about changing; we'd always tried to take a risk.

I find it hugely frustrating in that thanks to how I am now positioned politically I don't know how to have an influence again. When I left the band in 2005 I was thinking, "Shit what do I do about that now?" It made me realise how much I had used Chumbawamba to express how I felt about the world and my views on it. Suddenly being by myself again, I have found it really difficult to find a way to have an influence again. I've never been one who has wanted to live in a self-satisfied bubble. I'll still be angry and pissed off with stuff until I die. But where do you take it? I'm too cynical to join a political party and I feel that I should be part of a movement. I know there's a movement out there but I don't know where it is.

When I was a punk growing up in Billingham, it would have been unimaginable to me then that someone of 50 years of age would be doing something that had a point or was railing against something or that they were angry about something. I thought your life would be over by then, I never thought that was something that anybody of that age would do, and my parents certainly didn't. I don't care what people think any more. I've reached a stage in my life where I say, "Look, I'm a 50 year-old man, I don't need and I don't want to do that." It feels really good, really liberating. I went through a really self-conscious phase that lasted for quite a long time, where I would always be thinking, "How do I come over doing this? How do I look doing this? How is this going to impact on that? What are they going to think about this?" Now I just don't give a shit, if I'm angry or pissed off about something then I am going to say and not care that it might be unfashionable to upset people. It feels too late to worry about that. I think it is a good role model. It has a lot to do with wanting to influence my own children's outlook on the world and having a sense of what is right and having morals and ethics and a feeling of getting a head start. Because I felt that when I was growing up I had to find those things myself.

Vi Subversa

Vi Subversa was a 44-year-old mother of two when she entered the punk fray. Originally born in London, she and Richard Famous formed Poison Girls in Brighton in 1976, sharing vocal and guitar duties. They soon relocated to Burleigh House, a licensed squat just outside Epping in Essex, and close to Crass's Dial House. The two bands shared a close working relationship over the years, often playing live together, including a number of benefit gigs for organisations such as CND.

Poison Girls recorded three studio LPs between 1981 and 1985, with the first one HEX *being released on their own XNTRIX label. Later that year they released* Chappaquiddick Bridge *on Crass. Vi's hard-hitting lyrics often explored sexuality and gender roles viewed from a radical feminist perspective. Her two children inherited her punk genes – Pete Fender and Gem Stone were both members of Fatal Microbes and Rubella Ballet at various stages, while Fender also played with Omega Tribe. Poison Girls broke up in 1989 but six years later more than 1000 people turned up for a reunion gig to celebrate Vi's 60th birthday. Up until recently Vi lived in Spain. Now back living in Brighton, she has been known to deliver low-key performances of new material under the moniker Naughty Thoughts.*

Some personal reflections on punk philosophy, *by Vi Subversa*

Punk took me by surprise. I had already defined myself as an anarchist and feminist well before the advent of punk. The world was based in a permanent Cold War economy and was in the processes of industrial globalisation – I craved a world that put the values of peoples' needs before, and above, profit.

I was already fully grown (over 40!) and a mother before Poison Girls. The band first worked together as part of *The Body Show* theatre project in Brighton. By late 1976 we needed a place to practice and make our noise and eventually got access to a crypt, the legendary Vault, below a disused church. We set up and ran Brighton's only punk rehearsal and gig space, which we shared with other local bands. I was surprised and delighted that we were accepted and supported by the Brighton punks – although I could well have done without the gob!

Was there a discrete punk philosophy? For me it is a fusion of attitudes. The flotsam and jetsam gathered from my experiences over my lifetime. The beatniks, 60s mods and rockers, the hippy culture, all in their own ways kicking against 'the system'.

My personal influences include early Libertarians – A.S Neill in education, Ivan Illitch on deschooling, the Kibbutz movement in Israel, Alan Watts on *The Wisdom of Insecurity*. Mostly though, my friends have influenced me. People who dared to be different, to think for themselves, who took risks in whatever field they found themselves working in, and are still fun to be with!

The bands in the punk arena were not all of one mind. There was no defining politics, beyond the idea that 'you can do it'. We knew that we shared a desire to transcend the mean-minded limitations imposed by people of power, and people of privilege who protected the status quo and their own vested interests.

Punk gave us the desire and permission to make music, to make art, to communicate with others, to be creative and the feeling of a 'devil may care' freedom.

Punk was fundamentally a spontaneous expression of youth. It was a time for refreshing and reframing the parameters of rebellion and protest. It was a time of raw energy, which is the lifeblood of all creativity. Let's not intellectualise or philosophise. I feel very wary of philosophy. The mass religions and political movements all boast splendid ideas and ideals that are betrayed by their histories. So let's not go down that route.

As for politics, political activity is what you have to get into when your access to pleasure, creativity, life opportunities, and fun is blocked, denied, controlled cut off...

Adversity makes for strange bedfellows. As Joseph P [*the Mob*] has said, "We bunched up together because the rest was plastic." A disparate lot of bands, we worked together over many years and we − and our friends, fans and supporters − retain the best of it in our hearts and memories. The encircled A served as a symbol of recognition and identity, and as a sign that read, "Here dwell monsters!"

My personal motivation to be out there in among the lads was to be able to put my two pennies worth into the mix. The music scene was so very macho. The decibels were excessive and, because of National Front activity, the threat of violence was very real. My satisfactions were in the moments when a very studded and spiked-up lad would tell me that he loved the gentler, slower songs we played.

I know our presence on the scene made a difference to the anarcho-punk culture.
I know we encouraged more women to feel safe enough to come to the gigs.
I know we inspired women to take up making music.
I know we added another voice to the conversations that were going on.

Don't get me wrong. I also rejoiced in the noise and the thrash − and Poison Girls gave it out with the rest and the best!

Vi Subversa: As a preamble to the prose that follows below, I'll say I've been here [*back in the UK*] nearly a year and when I came back I didn't know very many people here at all, in fact only my daughter and my two grandchildren, who are very young. I spent a lot of time just sitting in the flat, quite lonely, quite bored, not wanting to make too many demands on my daughter and her family, and waiting for something to happen. What I did, I met a few people and I got in touch with the U3A organisation — University of the 3rd Age. It's not an official body as far as I can tell. I signed up for a singing for pleasure group, a writing for pleasure group, and a couple of physical Tai Chi, and fitness for the over 50s sort of things — just to get myself out of the house. I'm going to a singing group just to get my voice back, and I might do some more singing of old songs, but only in a very, very low-key, small way in people's houses of an afternoon. All right? It might be some of the old songs. But that's the background. But this I wrote because I was required to come up with something for the writing group. I had said that I was interested in writing for children. Then we all met up, and so I wrote this for it. It's called *Off the Hook*.

~

This is an obituary for the writer I was, the writer who tried too hard and too long to be grown up, to understand, to know how things are and how to change the world. I'm tired of the world of war, and war weariness, of disillusionment and child abuse. I do not choose to write as a cynic, although I am aware that cynicism is what I often feel, along with disappointment. I've tried to find knowledge as an adult, and to find meaning, to piece it all together, with hope as the glue. I chased after fragments of meaning, like trying to catch snowflakes, running after bits of torn up paper with the story of it all, but the bits blew away in the wind.

But I wanted to know, to have a story, a narrative to live by, to make sense, and to heal the pain of the powerlessness I had experienced, as a woman, as a citizen, as a worker, and as a mother. But I confused information with knowledge. Knowledge, they say, is power, and that's right. But now we have information overload, plenty of evidence of how it fits together — cheating bankers, fumbling politicians, corrupt media. On and on the stories break.

But we still know little of how to make change for a better world, fit to live in for people and our children, and I need to get off that hook. I'm sick of the information sold to us by those who profess to know. I applaud the whistle blowers. Sure, I am confused and dismayed by the continuing sense of powerlessness on behalf of the children born into this abusive world, and I believe the current epidemic of obesity and easting disorders is no more than a mass expression of hunger, a craving. But for what?

I can only answer for myself. For me, I crave release. I use that word instead of freedom, because freedom is a bit used up. I crave release from the futility of phony hunger, of compulsive consumption, from the disappointment of political posturing and manipulations, from promises of fraudulent progress. What I do want and pray for is the joy of making music, the magic and freedom of poetry, the beauty of flowers and fertility, and the miracle of growth. For the instant warmth and intimacy of kittens, and the glory of wildlife. So I will write for children. I will read, out loud, wearing a funny hat and glittery clothes. I will tell them about watching wasps suck sweetness from spotty foxgloves, about mischief and mystery and magic. I will call my first collection *Daisies are Fried Eggs for Teddy Bears*. I will write as a child, from the child in me, to the child in you.

~

Vi Subversa: I don't want to give out a message of tiredness, although I was very tired. I found the gigs horrible. Always sort of noisy, horrible gigs. I mean, I was 40 before I started. I didn't ever get used to sleeping in the back of a van. So the thought of anything nostalgic wouldn't work for me. Glad to get out of it. There was a good cause, a good reason for it.

The reason why I got involved with feminism was partly because I am a woman, of course. The anarchists that I got in touch with when I was 15, years and years ago, were mostly men and all quite macho, and slowly but surely I met a woman who mentioned feminism, and was doing something with her life and I got caught up in it. It became something to fight for. It has become very confused for me. Girls as young as 9 or 10; my grandchildren, they put makeup on and they play together, you know that's what they do. They want to dress up like little grown-ups, teenagers. I talk to my daughter about it a lot and we try to subvert them [*laughter*]. I think it's about presenting alternatives, isn't it? I mean it is difficult. Their mother and myself included, we put makeup on sometimes and the little girls say, "Well you do it." Is that liberation or is it the opposite? That's what I mean by the confusion. What does it mean? I don't know. And who is doing the scrutinising? Is it you?

Lisa Sofianos: Well I suppose it has to be to some extent. I've always been shocked by the extent to which women police other women. That has always surprised me, and maybe one of the issues — one of the fault lines — in feminism is that women are not a homogenous group of people.

Vi Subversa: That's right, I was always given a hard time by radical feminists for working in a band with men. What are you doing with your energy giving it to them and working with them?

Lisa Sofianos: That's right. We are not all actually going for the same goals, so it becomes difficult to organise.

Vi Subversa: No, or at the same rate, or on the same pathway.

Lisa Sofianos: I think feminism is one of those words. Everybody thinks they know what it means but it's something different for everybody, so it's hard to then organise in a way that's meaningful or even very powerful. I think once you've got the basics in place, most people can organise themselves around the right to vote or those sorts of things. But after that it all gets a bit complex.

Vi Subversa: Well there are things, like we can get abortions, and that was a big one.

Lisa Sofianos: Yes, that's a right that is being eroded.

Vi Subversa: Yes and we don't have to be virtuous all the time. So it's a mixed bag isn't it? It's swings and roundabout and that's the problem. If only it was all swings [*laughter*].

Robin Ryde: Do you feel as angry or as mobilised as you ever were?

Vi Subversa: No.

Robin Ryde: What's happening now that's different?

Vi Subversa: I think my anger, that general anger, is still there, but I don't have the physical energy that I used to have to formulate it and bang on about it.

Robin Ryde: I guess what we're interested in is that arc, that kind of movement over the last 30 years for the people that we are speaking to; if their views have changed on things at all. There is one thing about having the opportunity or the energy to do something, but then there is something different about whether or not we've actually changed our position. Is your position still the same?

Vi Subversa: I don't think I have changed my position, I really don't. I can remember way back when there was a project; what was it? "Stop the City." I was counselling people, young people, to be very cautious about getting into anger in the city. That came from the fact that in the late 60s, when I lived in Suffolk, my neighbours were sheltering young French people who had been beaten up after the 1968 Paris uprisings. These young men who were with my next-door neighbours had their testicles beaten up and were still bleeding. I didn't want this to happen in London to people that I knew. So, I was counselling, sort of, against it. But at the same time I wanted to recognise, support and even celebrate the anger, but fear takes over at some point; or prudence or whatever. We don't want martyrs do we?

Lisa Sofianos: I think there is something about when it's yourself; you can make your own choice, but when you are asked to counsel another person, then you become more cautious because you want to protect them.

Vi Subversa: Yes, well we were in a position as a band of disseminating information, encouraging people to do all these things. I found myself starting to pull away from that, and feeling a sense of betrayal of it and "am I turning into a wimp?"

Robin Ryde: [*laughter*] Wimp is not a word we would associate with you.

Vi Subversa: I think that just not joining the herd might be one way of somehow being who you want to be. Speaking up for the whistleblowers and Crass were whistleblowers in a way, and I applauded what they were doing. Although I never had quite the courage that they had.

Robin Ryde: The Poison Girls were very courageous though weren't they? They were extraordinarily bold in what they did I thought. [*laughter*] It was just, head on, not in an aggressive way but a very strong confrontational position.

Vi Subversa: Yes. That's right. I think of stuff like *The Statement* and this is the system that murders our children, that one. Well I stand by every word of that, to this very day.

Lisa Sofianos: That is powerful and confrontational. It's the kick in the pants that people might need to get up in front of people and say that; to take the consequences and go public with that. Isn't that courageous?

Vi Subversa: I fear that people don't want to hear it anymore. I fear that, "Oh God, not that old stuff again!" That's what I fear. I've heard it; I've heard it from people. I mean I did a few gigs in Spain supported by people there who hadn't even heard of Poison Girls. They were all expats. They weren't Spanish. We did some stuff out there in the wilderness and people didn't want to hear the bad news. Perhaps it was something to do with the people that escaped to go out there — that they did not want bad news anymore, they wanted to live now in a happy way. They didn't want to be reminded of where we had come from.

Charlie Waterhouse: I wonder whether that is something that's more widely true. We've come through a period where we're told that it's a repeat of 'you've never had it so good.' We're told that there is no class anymore and these are all things that we're told have been swept away. You're also reminded that in 1976 there were dead bodies in the streets and the bin bags were piled high in Leicester Square. We don't see that.

Vi Subversa: That was quite inspirational really, having rubbish burning in Leicester Square [*laughs*]. I enjoyed it.

Lisa Sofianos: Nothing like a bonfire is there? To get things going. [*laughter*]

Robin Ryde: That's an interesting point, because although we don't have rubbish in the streets now, as you were saying, we've got bankers doing atrocious things, and we've got the media being appalling in the way they conduct themselves. But it's just odd that there isn't the level or reaction, or maybe there is but we just can't see it.

Vi Subversa: I think that the trouble is there is an overdose of information and it has somehow become devalued. So what that there are bad bankers? So what that our politicians are feeble? So what if they're all liars? Why has the spark gone out of it? Where is the shock? Or maybe we're all just desensitised by so much horror over the last generation or two, including the Second World War. My sense of being a child in the Second World War was that a whole population was traumatised and a lot of the mistakes that have been made since then, perhaps with the best of intentions, are because we were all shocked out of our heads. The adults, my parents' generation, they made stupid decisions and went after crap. I think it's because they had been traumatised.

Robin Ryde: One of your reflections on this is if you can connect to children and share your observations in a way, then that is one opportunity I guess?

Vi Subversa: Yes, but I don't think they are waiting for me. If I'm honest I want to do it more for me. I need that immediate sense of peace and intimacy as a part of my healing as it does take it out of you all this stuff over the years. I'm not that old anymore because people are living longer, but I am 79 and I have put up with a hell of a lot of shit. I think that to be stuck with the negative experiences and disappointments is no way to live. That's what I've realised in the last year. I came back full of fear and trepidation about what I was going to do here [*on returning from living in Spain*] and not wanting to go back. I think that unless we can move on, all of us in our own way, then we're trapped and belong in the past. That isn't good for the digestion or the complexion or anything. That means moving on in some way and re-evaluating or evaluating the past and saying, "OK, now is now."

Robin Ryde: I don't know if you have an answer to this question; it's clearer for some than others, but if you talk to some people, for example Penny Rimbaud, just as an example, he is very clear on his philosophical positions. So he might say, for example, I am an existentialist, or I am Zen Buddhist or that kind of thing. Do you have political or philosophical influences that you have used or inform how you think?

Vi Subversa: Well I never really studied any of these things. I did read some Zen stuff years and years ago, I had some early experiences with hippy stuff and drugs and that opened me up quite a lot and, of course, talking to people. But I was never a bookish person. I've never read Karl Marx for example or any of them directly. I know what they are all sort of about and the others, I look into them for ideas. But I'm not an intellectual, not really, not in the sense of studying properly [*laughs*]. I never seem to have the time and I never went to university and had to stop my education when I was 15, to help my mum and stuff. And I've had it up to here with 'isms'.

Robin Ryde: Prior to Poison Girls and prior to the mid-late 70s, were you part of the hippy scene, what were you doing in the 10 to 15 years before?

Vi Subversa: I certainly enjoyed the hippy music and I was very relieved to not to have to wear "winkle pickers" and give it up for sandals and loose clothing. I liked the Beatles and all that, yes. I was part of CND and the Committee of 100 [*British anti-war group set up by 100 public signatories*]. I supported direct action against nukes and sat down in demos. I was writing too; I was a woman; I was a part of the feminist movement and I was writing as a member of that in my own little way and contributing to the odd magazine, such as *Spare Rib* and a few friends were doing the *Red Rat*, that was a good one [*laughs*].

Then we moved to Brighton with my small children after a breakup of a relationship. I met people from Sussex University and got invited to join in a project to do a piece of theatre in Edinburgh for the Festival Fringe called *The Body Show*. I wrote some songs and did a bit of stuff in that. There I met Richard [*Famous, later of Poison Girls*] who said that he liked my voice. I wasn't actually singing in *The Body Show* but I was a part of the poetry of it in a way. I wrote lyrics. He just said that he liked my voice and he liked my words. So we started working together and that is how Poison Girls came to be. He'd come around with his guitar and off we went. So that is how it all fits together. We weren't "punks" really. We picked up a few other musicians including Lance [*d'Boyle*] and we went to a rehearsal place in the country in an old church.

Suddenly we wanted to play faster and some energy was coming through. Richard had had some contact with Richard Boon and Buzzcocks and he gave it a name. We started changing the way we were working and we came back from those rehearsals having transformed from a "hippy" band into a "punk" band and that was in '75 or something like that. It was like a wave of something that went through the land. I had never heard any punk but I did feel the buzz and the energy and the pace of it all and the urgency. That's what's missing now, isn't it, the sense of urgency.

Lisa Sofianos: It was a different type of permissiveness to the hippy permissiveness; for example you could be an angry girl, you didn't have to be a beautiful girl. You could be any girl you wanted to be and I wondered if the archetypes in the hippy scene were narrower?

Vi Subversa: Well that's true, but it's only partly true because I think we have never quite escaped from the desire to please men, which is the way we look. We try, and we dress for ourselves, I know, but it's still there and that is why I said I'm still a bit vain. It's partly for other women but it's not only.

Robin Ryde: We were talking about the way a lot of punk girls dressed at the time, which would often be very short skirts, perhaps stilettos or high heels of some sort, and then tights which could be torn and, in that way, it was sexualised. So in one way it was sexualising of women but it was also liberating because you could dress however you wanted to.

Lisa Sofianos: I always had a problem with it. You had a fantastic style of dress, for example, with Rubella Ballet that illustrated an extremely fantastic part of the liberating way in which one could dress. But on another side, a lot of girls dressed as if they had been the victims of sexual violence and I found that disturbing because it was still using the same language. It may have been turning it back but why not find a new language, like other bands would do?

Vi Subversa: I mean yes and what are they called, perforations and studs and things like that. I know they do it in primitive cultures, and why not. Who am I to say? But I don't know what it would feel like to live in that primitive culture. I don't know what they were dealing with when they perforated themselves and it doesn't for me answer the question to just say, well primitive peoples used to do it, so it's OK.

Charlie Waterhouse: How much of that sexualisation was taken from the other influences? How much can you put back to McLaren and Westwood? If you've got a very small scene of people in the Roxy or the 100 Club or whatever and they happen to be dressed in some way then there will be a fashion influence. Then all of a sudden that's what filters out to Swindon and Newcastle and so on.

Vi Subversa: I know it is part of the colonisation in a way that business takes it over. It's no longer a protest, it's conforming.

Robin Ryde: Going back to you, in terms of the things that you have done during your life, were you ever lured into working full-time day-in and day-out?

Vi Subversa: I never had a nine-to-five job that lasted more than a few months. I worked in market research as a part-timer and worked my way up to be an executive. Believe it or not! But my stomach was turned by what it was all about and my poor pay because they just exploited me. I never took work seriously since then, but I have been a potter for a while. I went to Israel and I worked in a ceramic factory. That was the best working situation I've ever been in actually. That lasted a couple of years. I have never been a serious worker with ambitions to get promotion or anything like that. No never, I've done lots of things and as well as I could… although I've always had to earn my own money. I joined two self-directed study courses at East and North East London Polytechnics; I was doing group dynamics and self-management in non-hierarchical organisations. I enjoyed all that and wrote weird dissertations.

Robin Ryde: Was there always a creative impulse in you to write, to create music?

Vi Subversa: Yes, I was writing poetry from a very early age. I was evacuated to Wales in the war when I was four, on my own without my family. I loved the country and I think that's where all my references to flowers and kittens come from because that was gorgeous. But of course I was also damaged: an outsider,

I was Jewish in a Welsh country chapel-going community and was never able to feel that I belonged anywhere. But the countryside was my parents. It was my family. I went back later and cried on the hillside where I could no longer see the wheel of the coal mine because they'd grounded it. The landscape had changed. I felt my parents had died; a real grief.

Yes, and I like writing and I think I was a poet before I was a musician and Richard supplied the musical joy of it. I was always writing words. And I painted and designed things and I've recently had a cataract operation. I'm waiting for the second one and I was delighted to see the colour come back. Because I didn't realise that with my bad eye everything was kind of dingy.

When I look through the one that has been done, it's all glowing again.

Rubbish

I will not speak of broken glass

Or fly infested kitchen waste

I speak of rubbish of the heart

The jaded soul — the fall from grace

The blinding dust that fills the air

The choking debris of despair

Step after step I stumble on

Towards a future looming dark

Hope — like a millstone round my neck

Hope — a warm treasure in my heart

Hope for some kinder sweeter air

World fit for children everywhere

Do we owe them a living? Yes, O yes — we do
We owe them fields and trees of green
A world that's filled with wildness free
And animals for company
Tigers lizards birds and bees
We owe them oceans yet unspoiled
By slicks of wasted dirty oil
Is it too late to pay the debt?
— Alas with shame and deep regret
I fear we have not started yet

Vi Subversa

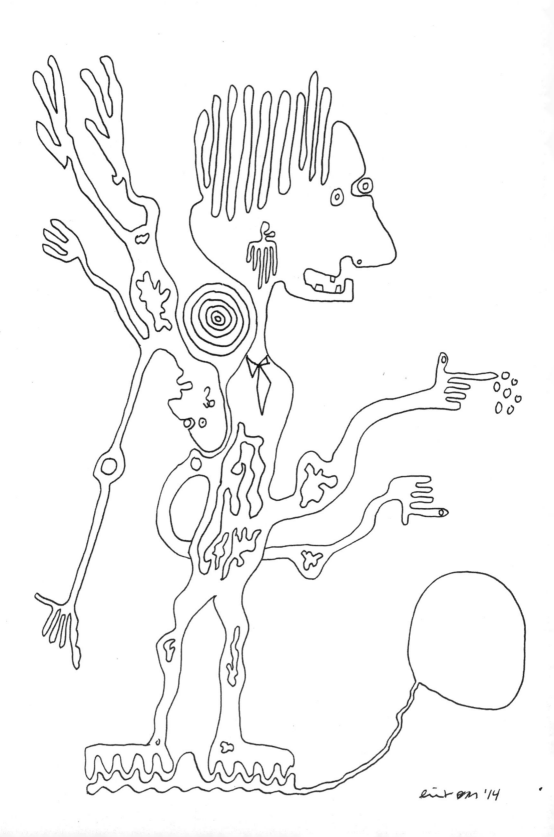

Thank you

In writing *The Truth of Revolution, Brother* we wanted to have the freedom to say what needed to be said – and not feel constrained by the requirements of a big publisher. We also wanted to make a direct connection to people who care about punk and its philosophies. We agreed early on we'd publish independently and when we were ready, get the money to print the book somehow – but not from a bank. So we'd like to extend a massive thanks to the people that supported us right from the start:

Abigail Bowen / AD Gallagher / Adam Throup / Adrian Lee / Alan Mountain / Alex Butler / Alexandra Kachkova / Alice, Fred & Rita / Allison Schnackenberg / Alvaro Bretel / Andrew C. Fox / Andrew Robie / Andy Diagram / Andy Ryde / Anne Hoebelmann / Anne Wind / Anthony Brown / ASH / Axel Guillemin / back2front zine / Barbara Waterhouse / bayleaf / Ben Dzidowski / Ben Gibb / Ben Jones / Bill Quarry / Bill Schaper / Billy Rhomboid / Birgitta Ronn / Bob / Bob Holle / Brian MacDonald / Carol Fuller / Ches / Chuck Dymer / Cow / Dafydd Lewis / Danny Mark Willis / Darian Weir / Darren J Beaney / Darren Vass / Dave "SPINACH" Malinsky / Dave Brownlow / Dave Clermont / Dave Fielding / Dave Roe / David Griggs / David Longbottom / David Meikle / David Sweeney and Bryn Hutchinson / Dean Rogers / Des at All the Madmen Records / Des Hoskins /Dinsdale von Kuttelfisch / Donna Watson / Donovan Valero / Doug Lawson / Douglas Axel / Edith Richbell /Einar Örn Benediktsson / Elliot Lord / Frances Cawthra / Frank Zenk / Freya Morton / Gary (Paz) Williams / Gary Thompson / Gavin Richards / Glenn Essom / Glenn Jones / Gordon Ewing / Graham / Graham Bowditch / Graham Burnett / Grimes Adhesif / Guðjón Jósef Baldursson / Guy Cubitt / Hanna Ahlstedt / Hannah Zoë Korb / Harry Hamer / Hetta Hardiment / Henrik Österdahl / Henry Broughton / HUMANWINE / Iñigo Ganzarain Fuente / Ian Edwards / Ian senior / Iain Seggie / Jacqui Curtis / James Purssell / Jason Atkins / Jay Roos / Jeff Lewis / Jeff Obermeyer / Jenny Proimos / Jo Brewis / Jo Hollowood / Joe Segreto / Johan Steunenberg / John C Dutchman III / Jon Stacey / Jonathan Raine / Jonathan Stafford / Jos Achterberg / Justin Varney / Kai Peters / Karl Poole / Kate Groves / Katherine Hough / Keith a Trego / Kevin Wragg / Koen Geurts / Kristian Gough / Kristof Van Den Bergh / Laura Vocat / Lauren Sadler / Leon Sofianos / Les & Stella Ryde / Liam Thomas / Linda Macpherson / Lisa Stuardi / Loz Jupp / Louise Metcalfe / Luc Waegeman *aka* Wagonman / Luca Occhini / Maciej Matysek / Marc Garrett / Marek Krolikowski / Margarat Nee / Maria Tirado / Mario Purps / Mark Chadderton / Mark Dempsey / Mark Harris / Mark Hodgkins / Mark Pickstone / Mark Seton / Mark Wilson / Mark Younger / Marlyn Tyler / Martin Duce / Martyn Higgins / Matt / Matt Ekins / Matt Guy / Matt Vecchio / Michael Scott / Mickey 'Penguin' / Mike & Belinda / Mike Thorpe / Mikey A Dredd / Min Stokes / Morten Haugdahl / Nathanael Wayne Nederman /Neil Barns / Neil Childs / Neil Williams / Niall John James MacDougall / Nick Shepherd / Nigel Ball / No Man / Paul 't Hart / Paul (foggy) Ingram / Paul Chapman / Paul Heron / Paul Lunt / Paul Martin / Paul Miller / Paul Spence / Paul Tiernan / Per Arne Flatberg / Peter De Roy / Peter Lilly / Peter Mihalik / Pete Webb / Phil Cook / Phil Greenhalgh / Priscila Lena Farias / Rachael Schirano / Rathy Srikanthan / René Wolf / Reza Shaikh / Rich Cross / Rick J Alexander / Richard Cannon / Richard Kilner / Richard Williams / Rob Cook / Rob Crossen / Rob Oubridge / Robert Chatwin / Robert Kolaczynski / Robert Rosendahl / Robert Smith / Robin Bell / Robin Harford / Roger Olofsson / Rosie Norgrove / Ryan Neeson / Sacha Tanyar / Sam Alarcón / Sam Krasp / Sarah Faulkner / Scotty Ramone / Sean Connor / Sebastian Cording / Shaun Pryszlak / Shaun R. Williams / Simon Nolan / Simon Rumley / Simone Page / Sophie Everett / Sophie Unterweger / Stef Cunningham / Stewart, Amy, Jake & Freddie Brown / Suzanne Popper / Taylor Doobay / Tero Viikari / Terry Anderson / Terry Lewis / Thomas "DerHul" Hulvershorn / Tim Hall / Tom York / Tiago Dias / Tim Dent / Tony Bacic / Tony Barber / Tony Young / Trevor / Vidar Ringstrøm / Vito Gargano / Wayne Skeggs

We'd also like to give special thanks to a small set of people in particular who've invested a lot of time and energy in this project. Whether making contact with contributors, editing, proofing, researching, offering wise counsel, financial assistance or just being there during occasional dark nights of the soul, we give special thanks to *Clive Russell, Susan Tomlinson, Nick Shepherd, Mark Nelson, Nick Grindell, Ali Hanan, Gee Vaucher, Penny Rimbaud, Mark Wilson* and *Tero Viikari.*

We love you all ×

About the Authors   [*Left to right*] Charlie, Lisa and Robin have been friends since their tender teenage years when they each DJ'd nights in Hull's glamorous Wellington Club.

Charlie's life was derailed when he heard the Fall's *Lay of the Land* on Peel, and has since stumbled perilously close to stalking Mark E. Smith, having seen the group 35 times (at the time of writing). Lisa's DJing career was almost strangled at birth by Steve Albini when she cued up her first record by Big Black at the wrong speed. *Kerosene* sounds even more sinister at 45 RPM. Robin cut his teeth on punk music at the age of 13 by sneaking into UK Subs and Stiff Little Fingers gigs. But his true awakening happened on first hearing of *Stations of the Crass* – after which nothing was the same again.

By day Charlie is a graphic designer, while Robin and Lisa attempt to shake up the way organisations work. Although none of them knew it, the *Truth of Revolution, Brother* was always going to be the result of their friendship.

Credits   Words by Lisa Sofianos & Robin Ryde, except where stated. Cover and interview illustrations by Clive Russell; Self-portrait p284 by Einar Örn Benediktsson; Front/End papers by Leigh Maclellan; Authors' photo by Jackson Ryde, all other black & white photography by Charlie Waterhouse.